I've known Christian for more than a decade, and his writing offers a refreshing and deeply insightful perspective, dismantling prevailing Western ideals in the most humble way. With real-life examples of serving our neighbors and living missionally, this book is a powerful call to actively live out our faith in a way that truly reflects the heart of God.

BIANCA JUAREZ, pastor, podcaster, and bestselling author of *Grit Don't Quit* and *Play with Fire*

Christian Mungai's *People Are the Wealth* is a powerful call to rethink missions through relationships, not just resources. Drawing from his journey from Kenya to America, he challenges Western churches to be catalysts, not controllers—listening before leading and serving alongside rather than from above. His "three-legged stool" approach—balancing proclamation, demonstration, and community—offers a much-needed shift from creating dependency to fostering sustainability. This book will transform how you view global engagement, moving from transactional charity to true partnership.

DOUG FIELDS, pastor, author, chairman of Milele International

From the first time my wife, Carol, and I met Christian Mungai, while he was a student in the US, we were struck by his charismatic energy and strength of conviction. As long as we've known him, Christian has carried a relentless passion for rethinking and reshaping the prevailing model of missions—moving beyond the traditional "from the West to the rest" approach toward one rooted in mutual respect, partnership, and dignity.

In *People Are the Wealth*, Christian teaches us that missions should not be about imposing solutions but about walking together with the people we serve, honoring the wisdom already present in the local community, and being open to learn from others as we serve together.

Christian's persistence in lovingly challenging outdated paradigms has resulted in a work that is both timely and necessary. This book is a must-read for anyone who believes that missions should not be about power, but about people.

> **MURIITHI WANJAU (PASTOR M),** senior pastor, Mavuno Church Movement and author of Mizizi (Rooted) curriculum

I learned many things from the evangelical theologian John Stott. I love what he wrote about missions and how we should relate to the world. And I'm a big believer in what he called the Third Way, where we are like Jesus when we go into the world and give ourselves in selfless service. We are to do the *work* of the gospel while sharing the *words* of the gospel—both showing God's love and telling about God's love. This is what we are sent into the world to do. The key to this is *relationship*, but for a long time I didn't understand what that really meant.

Through Christian Mungai I discovered I had a blindness. In thinking of missions as "from the West to the rest," I saw my role as going to show God's love, and I assumed I knew what loving was. I was surprised to learn that I had to listen and create real dialogue from a heart of humility, through conversations that honored mutuality and dignity and valued each church, people group, and country. It wasn't easy. In fact, it was one of the most challenging things I think I've ever done. But I couldn't have learned any other way, and I experienced the thrill of being part of the global church.

Christian Mungai is unique, and God has used—and is using—him in unique ways in America and around the world. I have experienced the truth of this book to be life-changing for me personally and the ministry of my church, and I believe it will do the same for you.

KENTON BESHORE, pastor emeritus, Mariners Church

People Are the Wealth is a transformative and much-needed reimagining of global missions. With deep wisdom, personal experience, and a passion for the gospel, Christian Mungai challenges us to move beyond outdated models of charity to embrace a missions strategy rooted in relationship, mutual respect, and the recognition of every person's God-given dignity. His insights, drawn from both his African heritage and his extensive ministry experience, offer a refreshing and compelling vision for the future of the church's global engagement.

Christian Mungai is a bridge builder, a storyteller, and a thought leader in the missional space. His ability to challenge and inspire, while remaining deeply grounded in biblical truth, makes this book a must-read for anyone seeking to engage in missions with wisdom, humility, and effectiveness. This book will not only change the way you think about missions, it will change the way you see people. Highly recommended!

REV. DR. SAMEH MAURICE, senior pastor, Kasr El Dobara Evangelical Church

In *People Are the Wealth*, Christian Mungai brings fresh and challenging insights into global missions through an African lens. He brings out biblical truths through great stories to move us from independence and dependence into an interdependent global body of Christ. As you read this book, I know you will be blessed, challenged, and inspired, just as I was.

JOSSY CHACKO, founder and president, Empart, Inc.

This is more than a book—it's a calling, a revelation, and a challenge to rethink global missions. My faith journey is blessed by knowing Christian Mungai, from our first meeting in Kenya in 2008 with Mariners Church leadership to sharing life and faith in a small group including him and his wife, Delta. For decades, I've watched Christian live out every word in this book, embodying the message he so powerfully shares. With inspiring stories, profound theological insights, and a compelling vision for the future of missions, Christian challenges us to move beyond "doing for" to instead embrace interdependence—listening, learning, and fostering reciprocal partnerships with the global church. Reading this book will stretch you, inspire you, and reframe your understanding of what it means to be the church in a globally connected world. This book is essential if you want to see missions through a biblical lens and engage in meaningful, sustainable, and transformative outreach.

INÉS S. FRANKLIN, teaching pastor at Mariners Church, founder of Trochia Ministries, and author of *Uncharted: Navigating Your Unique Journey of Faith* and *The Image of God*, a Deep Dive series study

AN AFRICAN VISION FOR A
PEOPLE-FOCUSED, MISSIONAL CHRISTIAN LIFE

PEOPLE ARE THE WEALTH

ANDŨ NĨ O ĨĨNDO

CHRISTIAN MUNGAI

TYNDALE
elevate®
ask. seek. find.

Visit Tyndale online at tyndale.com.

Tyndale, Tyndale's quill logo, and the Tyndale Elevate logo are registered trademarks of Tyndale House Ministries, registered in the United States of America. *Tyndale Elevate* is a trademark of Tyndale House Ministries. Tyndale Elevate is a nonfiction imprint of Tyndale House Publishers, Carol Stream, Illinois.

People Are the Wealth: An African Vision for a People-Focused, Missional Christian Life

Cover design by Eva M. Winters

Interior design by Laura Cruise

For information about special discounts for bulk purchases, please contact Tyndale House Publishers at csresponse@tyndale.com, or call 1-855-277-9400.

Library of Congress Cataloging-in-Publication Data

A catalog record for this book is available from the Library of Congress.

ISBN 979-8-4005-0808-0

Printed in the United States of America

31 30 29 28 27 26 25
7 6 5 4 3 2 1

Contents

FOREWORD by Eric Geiger *ix*
INTRODUCTION Shifting the Focus of Global Missions *1*

PART ONE **Theology 23**
1. Connection Before Content *25*
2. The Great Collaboration *53*
3. Justice and Compassion *69*

PART TWO **Philosophy 87**
4. Polycentric Missions *89*
5. Global Trends *103*
6. Indigenous Leadership *115*

PART THREE **Ethos 131**
7. Biblical Poverty *133*
8. Relationship-Based Ministry *149*
9. Servant Leadership *163*
10. Life Change *181*
11. Strategic Engagement *197*

PART FOUR **Practice 213**
12. Church Deployment *215*
13. Diaspora Engagement *231*
14. Global Movements *247*

APPENDIX Keys for Identifying a Ministry Partner *261*
Notes *265*
About the Author *275*

Foreword

God has used the book of Galatians in my life to remind me of his grace and to invite my restless heart to continually find rest in him. Within the book of Galatians there is a powerful verse that refreshes us with what Christ has done for us: "Christ redeemed us from the curse of the law by becoming a curse for us."[1] I am no longer cursed for my sin, because Christ was cursed in my place.

As I have traveled to meet with brothers and sisters in our global family—what we call our global partners at the church I pastor—I have learned to love this verse even more.

In Haiti, people fear someone pronouncing a curse on them; so to hear that Christ has removed the curse is such good news. In South Asia, there are some who are called "untouchables," the Dalits, so low in society that they are cursed to live outside the caste system. When they understand that Christ humbled himself for them, their joy is unspeakable. In the Middle East, many live in a climbing religion, always trying to earn their way to eternal life and never knowing if they have done enough. When they grasp that Christ offers what theologian John Stott called "a rescue religion,"[2] their commitment to Jesus because of his rescue is humbling. In Uganda, those with special needs are often viewed as if they are cursed. To serve alongside our partners and my daughters as we distributed wheelchairs and helped people who were left to crawl on the ground into a chair reminded me of God reaching down to pick us up.

Christian Mungai and I were together on all those trips (Haiti, South Asia, the Middle East, and Uganda). Our church enjoys being part of a global family. I enjoy being part of a global family. And God has chosen to use Christian, one of our pastors, to bring us all together. Christian's passion for the gospel rubs off on me and has helped me see the truth of verses like Galatians 3:13 through the lens of different cultures. The verse sits above every culture and is true in every setting, but seeing the verse at work in different cultures has stirred my awe for God's truth and grace.

Another verse that reveals the heart of God is Galatians 3:8: "Now the Scripture saw in advance that God would justify the Gentiles by faith and proclaimed the gospel ahead of time to Abraham, saying, All the nations will be blessed through you."[3] The apostle Paul is reminding us that God's intention has always been to rescue people from every nation through the gospel of Jesus. Genesis, the first book of the Bible, contains the promise, and Revelation, the last book of the Bible, gives us the final fulfillment—because Christ was "slaughtered and . . . purchased people for God by [his] blood from every tribe and language and people and nation."[4]

We live in the messy middle between the promise that God will bless all the nations and the reality of people from every nation in his presence. In the messy middle, we are commanded to join Jesus on his mission—to make disciples of people from every nation.[5]

The global family is setting the pace on making disciples from every nation. I have been in meetings where bold plans have been set in the Middle East to take the gospel to dangerous places. I have been on private Zoom calls with leaders in South Asia who are risking their lives to take the gospel to people groups who have not heard of Christ's finished work for them. God is using the global church right now to pursue people for himself.

The leaders I have met have blessed and inspired me, and their example has challenged me. The people are the wealth. I commend Christian's thinking and teaching to you. You will be reading the words of a very rare combination of missiologist/theologian/pastor, who before any of those titles is a faithful follower of Jesus and a great husband and dad. You will enjoy this book, and you will learn a lot.

ERIC GEIGER
Senior Pastor,
Mariners Church in Southern California

INTRODUCTION

SHIFTING THE FOCUS OF GLOBAL MISSIONS

Early in the twentieth century, a small group of people in a little Kenyan village would get up every morning and drop to their knees facing a nearby mountain. When they looked at the snow-capped peak, they felt a sense of awe and wonder. They surveyed the lush, green foothills and said, "This thing is so majestic, it must have some power behind it." So they would pray to Mwene Nyaga, "the owner of the mountain that has snow on it."†

When some missionaries from Scotland made their way to the village, they observed what these people were doing and tried to understand why they followed this daily ritual.

When the villagers replied, "Just look at that mountain. It is too majestic, too grand, too beautiful not to have some power behind it," the missionaries saw an opportunity to tell them about God.

† This reminds me of the apostle Paul's declaration in Romans 1:20: "Ever since the world was created, people have seen the earth and sky. Through everything God made, they can clearly see his invisible qualities—his eternal power and divine nature. So they have no excuse for not knowing God" (NLT).

"We actually know the story of the creator of that mountain," they said. "We know who Mwene Nyaga is."†

One of the villagers—my grandfather—said, "Please, tell us more. If you're right, then we want to know more about this creator of the mountain."

That's how my grandfather came to know these missionaries and began to travel with them. He ended up working as a chef in one of the schools they established—a school that still exists today. Over time, he heard more and more about the creator of the mountain and eventually decided to place his faith in him.

After my grandfather embraced Christianity, he raised his kids in the ways of God. My father also came to faith and ultimately became a Presbyterian minister. Not only did he serve faithfully in his own generation—in the National Council of Churches, in family life education, and at a university—but he also raised me to be a Christian.

When I was eighteen, my parents sent me to pursue a law degree in India. I had no desire to become a lawyer, but in Africa, you don't do things because you want to; instead, it's a family decision. For young Africans at the time, there was a holy trinity of careers to pursue at university: law, medicine, or architecture. If you didn't do one of those, you would disappoint your parents. People from individualist cultures make their own choices, but in a family-based culture such as we have in Kenya, you do what the family asks you to do. So, against my will, I went.

As an international student who didn't really want to be there, I found myself in a very difficult place. I felt isolated and way out of my comfort zone, but that's where my faith really began to take shape. God used those tough years to solidify, mature, and transform my relationship with Christ.

---

† Likewise, this evokes memories of Paul's approach to the philosophers on Mars Hill in Athens: "As I was walking along I saw your many shrines. And one of your altars had this inscription on it: 'To an Unknown God.' This God, whom you worship without knowing, is the one I'm telling you about" (Acts 17:23, NLT).

Instead of going on to sit for the bar examination when I graduated from law school with a bachelor's in social legislation, I handed my parents my diploma and asked for their blessing to let me go pursue what I wanted to pursue—namely, acting in Hollywood.

I reached out to a friend of my father's who lived in Pasadena, and he and his wife invited me to stay with them while I got situated in Southern California. But all my attempts to find an acting job fell flat because I didn't have the proper paperwork. I had come to America on a student visa and thus was unable to work legally. So even though I was called back on three separate auditions, no one would hire me. I quickly began to realize that I was not in a position to take care of myself, and after moving out of my host family's home, I ended up in a homeless shelter in Los Angeles.

Fortunately, I met a guy on the street early on who took one look at me and said, "You're not using."

"I don't do drugs," I said.

"Well, there's a church nearby that takes in people who are clean like you," he said.

And that's how I found the shelter where I stayed for the next seven months.

During my time there, I heard about a prayer breakfast in Pomona for Kenyan expats, and I decided to attend. When I showed up at the venue, lo and behold, I ran into three childhood buddies I had grown up with—Harry Mwaura Kiiru, Kaima Mwiti, and Kanjii Mbugua. These were guys I hadn't seen in more than ten years, when we were part of a Christian family fellowship in Kenya, where our parents were all Christian leaders.

I have come to see this unexpected reunion as a *divine reconnection*, because we could not have planned it in a million years. We were all in the United States at the same time and happened to show up at the same gathering. So we started hanging out together and talking and catching up.

Harry, Kaima, and Kanjii are all musically talented, and the Kenyan fellowship soon asked them to lead worship. When they said to me, "Hey, Christian, you should join us, because, you know, you can make noise," I laughed. But then they said, "You're an actor. You can *act* like a musician." So we started playing together at the fellowship, and that's how our Afro-fusion boy band called Milele (which means *forever* in Kiswahili) was formed.

At first, we had no aspirations of becoming a band. We were just some friends playing a few songs together. But then we met a group called Limit X from Uganda who told us, "You guys are pretty good. You should record an album."

When we told them we didn't know how to do that, they said, "Don't worry. We'll show you how." They generously paid our deposit at a studio in Northridge, and over the next three months we recorded our music.

When the album came out, it was sent to Kenya, and before we knew it we had the top four songs in the country. There we were, just four young friends who had put together an album, and all of a sudden there's a buzz in our home country about who we are.

In 2000, Milele was invited to spearhead a big Y2K concert at one of Kenya's largest stadiums. We ended up playing to 30,000 people at Nyayo National Stadium in Nairobi. It was about that time that it hit me: We had something precious in our hands. We were living in a sight-and-sound generation, and once people got to hear a group like ours, we could pretty much steer them in any direction we chose. It was very intoxicating to have such instant fame and celebrity, and I began to recognize that it would either make us or destroy us. I realized that we could use our fame for one of two things: either to draw attention to ourselves or to draw attention to something *greater* than ourselves.

All this time, I was dealing with feelings of inadequacy because I knew I wasn't a musician. I was the hype man and the spokesman for why we did what we did, but even with all our success—which the other guys deserved—I was suffering from impostor syndrome. So I told Harry, Kaima, and Kanjii, "We have to do something different. I can't keep acting like a celebrity musician when I'm not even a singer."

"What do you want to do?" they asked.

"I want to incorporate Milele as a nonprofit. and then we can use our music as a platform to draw people to something larger than ourselves—especially causes that are linked with changing Africa from the inside out."

This idea was based on conversations we had already been having about how Western missionaries in our experience had engaged with Africa—addressing *symptoms* rather than the underlying systemic issues. Having now been stateside for a few years, we had become disgruntled with the way American Christians portrayed Africa as a charity case. The prevailing mindset seemed to be, "Go to Africa—they need you," not recognizing that Africa has tremendous assets of its own that were going untapped. Instead of engaging with the African churches as equal partners and working to build reciprocal relationships, everyone approached missions from a "*we* are coming help *you*" perspective, which only perpetuated the stereotype that Africans needed Americans or Westerners to rescue them.

I was convinced that our music could help to reframe that story, so I said, "We need to rethink this." We incorporated Milele as a nonprofit organization with the idea of creating a platform to help change people's minds about how the American church approached Africa (and other parts of the world).

As we continued singing together, we found we were able to use our music as a gospel-driven Trojan horse to get us into churches, where we could then connect with their global missions programs and try to expand their understanding of "how to do missions" in twenty-first-century Africa. Once they had welcomed us in to perform, we would tell the people about an Africa many had never heard of.

"This is the Africa you may *think* you know," we said, referring to the common stereotypes of poor, undernourished kids with runny noses, "but there is an Africa you *don't* know." We would tell them about a vibrant generation of young Africans that we believed could solve the continent's problems—from the inside out, not from the outside in. Up to that point, we hadn't seen anyone coming in from the outside who seemed to recognize—much less be prepared to build upon—what God was *already* doing in Africa. This quickly became the focal point of our message.

The way you diagnose a problem determines how you will treat it. If your diagnosis is wrong, your treatment plan will also be wrong. So you can imagine how good, well-meaning Christians, who were used to being told, "Hey, these people are hungry, they need clean water, they need better schools, they need our help," were taken aback when they heard our message, which was more along the lines of, "Hey, stop doing what you're doing in Africa. Rethink your approach. What you're doing is actually not helping us. It's probably even hurting us."

Though the people always received us warmly and treated us well, most could not fully grasp what we were saying until we began inviting them to come to Kenya with us. We didn't know it yet, but Milele had created a unique niche. We were using the tools God had placed in our hands—playing vibrant African music while giving (primarily) American audiences a glimpse of African celebration. In return, the churches, schools, and other institutions would give us an honorarium and would buy our music, and we used these funds to invest in long-term solutions for Kenya.

At first, we were funding anybody back home who was doing a great job of addressing systemic issues. We were partnering with

Kenyans, in Kenya—not telling them what to do, but rather investing in what they were already doing. We did this until 2005 or 2006, when I felt a call in my heart that Milele should focus on changing how orphan care is done in Kenya by returning to traditional family integration versus the institutional model brought in by Westerners—a story I will tell in greater detail in chapter 12.

Eventually, Milele toured in more than forty US states for three consecutive summers. When we played for an outreach weekend at Mariners Church, in Irvine, California, it initiated a long-standing relationship that would take my life in a new direction—though I didn't know it at the time.

While things were running well with Milele, I met a Kenyan pastor who was assigned to a Methodist church in Santa Ana. He said, "You seem to understand young people. Would you help me start a youth group?"

"Absolutely yes," I replied.

So I started helping him at the church, with a youth group of five kids.

As a Kenyan, I am naturally very attuned to building community and engaging with people who are not like me. In my mind, a stranger is only a friend I haven't met yet. So for me it was simply a matter of getting to know the five kids in the group and asking them, "Where do you live? Can we go there?" Then we would go there, and I would say, "Who are your neighbors?" and they would tell me. And then, "Who do you hang out with?" Then I would go hang out with those kids and their neighbors and their friends.

As I modeled for them what it means to be a good neighbor and a good friend, these kids began to realize, *Hey, we're having a cool time with this guy from Africa*, and they started inviting others to join our youth group. Everybody wants to be invited to something. It's just that most people don't have the fortitude to do it. So when I encouraged these young people to invite their friends and said, "Hey, come on over, we're gonna have a good time," they would come and they would have tons of fun. The youth group grew from the original five to two hundred in about six months. We had kids from three demographics—Cambodians, Hispanics, and Vietnamese—with a few white kids as well.

I had been mentored as a younger guy, and now it was my turn to mentor others. Our pastor was teaching us how to do mentorship using movie clips. So I started doing the same thing with the guys who were coming to the group. I would show them a movie clip and then pull a biblical lesson from it, and they thought that was pretty cool. And when they found out I was a member of a band, they thought that was pretty cool as well.

The presiding Methodist bishop at the time, Bishop Swanson, heard about me, and he said to the pastor, "You have somebody who has grown your youth group. Maybe you should consider him for ministry."

So they asked me if I wanted to go to school. I said, "No, I'm not a minister. I like community development." But they said, "What if we helped you get into our seminary?"

I was completely unfamiliar with the Claremont School of Theology, and I wasn't all that interested in seminary or theology, but for a free education at a master's level, I said, "Okay, I'll go."

So I went to Claremont, and it was a struggle right from the start. The theology they taught there was very liberal compared to the conservative theology I had grown up with. In fact, in 2010, Claremont began to "add clerical training for Muslims and Jews to its curriculum" with the goal of becoming "the first truly multi-faith American seminary."[1] Today they describe themselves as "a progressive interreligious theological school."[2]

I think several of my professors at the seminary did not even believe in the existence of God, but what the environment there did was whet my appetite for apologetics. While I was at Claremont,

I started following people like J. P. Moreland, Greg Koukl, and others, and I prepared myself to rebut the teaching of my professors. It was very difficult, but I wouldn't trade that experience for anything because it really made me challenge my faith. Sometimes when you're challenged, it helps you check your own assumptions. I enjoyed that.

While I was in seminary, I was still part of the band and still involved in the Methodist youth group. I would oscillate between school, helping the church, and running the mission of Milele.

As a follow-up to our concerts in churches, I met with their global missions pastors to ask what they were doing in Africa. When they shared their thoughts and ideas, I would typically respond by calling their efforts ineffective and out of date—which, admittedly, was not an inviting, kind, or compelling approach. When I met with the pastors at Mariners Church in 2004, they heard me out but told me they saw no reason to change their approach to missions. As I told a reporter who interviewed me some years later, it's hard for Americans to learn from other people.[3]

In 2006, Mariners hired Matt Olthoff as their new global director. When I first met with him, I did my usual schtick, and as you might expect, it turned him off.

That evening, the Holy Spirit strongly convicted me that I had become the Ugly African—that is, "arrogant, self-absorbed, demeaning, thoughtless, ignorant, and ethnocentric."[4] I had become so frustrated by what I saw as "missions as usual" in the American church that I could hardly wait to tell them that their approach was all wrong and they should stop what they were doing. But now I realized I was going into these meetings with an *agenda*—just like an American would. Instead, like an African, I needed to lead from a place of *relationship*.

The next day, I called Matt Olthoff back and humbly asked for another meeting. I promised not to talk about Milele or Africa; I just wanted to get to know him as a person, to give him my *presence*, not any product or program, as the Holy Spirit had convicted me. Matt agreed to meet . . . but as it turned out, we didn't get together for another six months or so.

When we finally reconnected and spent some time just getting to know one another, that's when the change began to happen. Eventually, Matt asked me about Milele and our passion, and I was only too happy to explain it all to him.

Around that same time, he told me he was planning a trip to the Democratic Republic of the Congo. He asked if, while he was in Africa, he could stop by and see our home church, Mavuno, a fledgling but fast-growing congregation in Nairobi, Kenya. Our lead singer from Milele, Kanjii Mbugua, had recently moved back to Kenya and was serving as the worship pastor at Mavuno. By then, Milele and Mavuno Church were planning a joint tour of the US, dubbed TIA (This Is Africa)—taken from a line spoken by Leonardo DiCaprio's character in the movie *Blood Diamond*, where he declares that nothing in Africa works. We intended to use our music to debunk the lie.

Matt attended the launch of TIA in Nairobi and told me he had never seen such a vibrant group of change agents. Upon his return to the United States, he asked if we would play another concert at Mariners Church. I told him we could do our final performance of the tour there, which we did in November 2007. I didn't know it at the time, but that would be my first unofficial day on staff at Mariners. Matt asked me to help them plan the weekend, and once I was there I just never left. As I write this, Mariners has been my church home for eighteen years.

Also on that African tour, the leaders from Mariners Church met with Pastor Muriithi Wanjau (we call him Pastor M) from Mavuno Church. They wanted to hear his vision and plan for turning ordinary church members into fearless influencers of society. Pastor

M explained what Milele had always tried to communicate—that Africans, not well-meaning Westerners, must be the ones to provide solutions for Africa's challenges. And that meant we in the Western church needed to rethink our models of engaging in overseas missions.

Pastor M invited Mariners' then–lead pastor, Kenton Beshore, and his wife, Laurie, to travel to Kenya to see for themselves. He especially urged Kenton to meet with Bishop Oscar Muriu, Pastor M's own mentor, who leads a family of churches connected to Nairobi Chapel, which has planted more than three hundred churches around the world. The Beshores agreed to a visit, and in January 2008, at the height of some post-election turmoil in Kenya, a team of twenty-four Mariners leaders made their way to Africa for a visit that would result in a monumental shift for both Mavuno Church and Mariners.

The Dangerous African

Bishop Oscar is known for his willingness to speak directly to issues affecting the global church, and especially the church in Africa. Unfortunately, over the years, many from the West have not been willing to engage with him—even going so far as to label him "the dangerous African"—because of his hard-hitting approach. But what he has done for young African leaders in the church is to give us a voice. Under his mentorship we started feeling a sense of "Hey, we have some dignity. We have a sense of ability. We have something to offer the global church." So there's a whole generation of up-and-coming leaders who have been inspired by people like Bishop Oscar.

When Kenton, Laurie, and the rest of the team met with Bishop Oscar, he caught their attention and challenged them with these words: "There's a global party going on to which the American church is not invited. Your churches are dying, ours are growing, but you're still sending us missionaries. Shouldn't *we* be sending missionaries to *you*?"

Laurie Beshore later said, "We felt like we'd been slapped in the face with the truth."[5]

Though I can understand why some in the West might hear the bishop's words and think, *We're not invited? Fine. We'll just stay home or invest our time and money elsewhere*, such a reaction would be unfortunate. I believe Bishop Oscar was simply using semantic hyperbole, much like Jesus did when he said, "If you want to follow me, you must hate your father and mother," or "If your hand causes you to sin, cut it off," or "It's easier for a camel to go through the eye of a needle than for a rich man to enter heaven." In every case, Jesus was using arresting language to get people's attention and make an important point. Bishop Oscar is known for taking a similar approach. We have learned that the more we engage with these tough conversations, the more we grow. As the saying goes, no pain, no gain.

Bishop Oscar's comments also startled Kenton, but he wasn't put off by them. Instead, he wanted to know more. To his everlasting credit, he replied, "I've never heard anybody say anything like that before. I've always thought of missions as us going to the uttermost parts of the earth to *give* and to *help* and to *serve*. Tell me more about this global party."

I won't try to recapture their conversation in its entirety, but some of the topics they discussed included the tendency of the American church to bring a fix-it mentality to missions that is increasingly counterproductive and out of step with the types of issues faced by the global church. As I've heard Bishop Oscar say many times, "If there are two qualities that mark North Americans, it is your ability to solve problems and your *assertiveness*. You are quick to speak your mind. But your greatest blessing may be your greatest curse. Because when you come to Africa, you want to *fix* Africa. Well, you *can't* fix Africa. You must learn to come as *listeners* and as *learners*."[6]

He also addressed the idea that the global church must break free from the "culture of dependence" that is often created (perhaps inadvertently) by the classic Western approach to missions. The goal instead must be to "build bridges of healthy *inter*dependence" and "build *reciprocity* into the task of missions."[7] Indeed, *reciprocal partnership* is the emerging model (as we will discuss in a later chapter).

Bishop Oscar wanted the leaders from Mariners to understand that "the world has changed; the center of Christianity has moved to the Southern Hemisphere; our definition of what it means to be Christian is going to be increasingly defined from the two-thirds world; and our paradigm of missions must of necessity therefore change."[8] The Great Commission wasn't given from the lips of Jesus to the Western church. It was issued to his disciples and to *all* followers of Jesus who would come after them. Accordingly, indigenous churches around the world today have the *same* missional mandate to follow (which we will also discuss in greater detail in a later chapter).

Bishop Oscar has said,

> As we develop partnerships between the Western church and the two-thirds world church, such partnerships must work hard at developing and enabling reciprocity. Every time the West sends out a missionary to Asia, it should work just as hard to bring one back to the Americas. Mission organizations need to retool and re-strategize themselves—not just to send out missionaries, but to enable the budding missionary movement in the two-thirds world church, and to facilitate *reverse missions*,

> bringing in Africans and Asians and Latin Americans into Canada and Europe and North America . . . that they may come into *your* context, and they may enrich *your* faith. Do not allow missions to be one-sided. Build in reciprocity. For *this* is the nature of the body of Christ.[9]

For so long, the prevailing mindset in missions has been "from the West to the rest," essentially a one-way model of *us* going to *them*. But just as no part of the human body only receives and never gives anything back—that is, every part of the body depends on every other part of the body to make up a functioning whole person—so too in the body of Christ must every part learn to give and receive interdependently with the rest of the body.

"The African church *knows* it desperately needs the American church," Bishop Oscar has said. "But how does a church in North America *need* the African church? How does a church in Canada *need* the Asian church? I have spoken with pastors on this continent who cannot answer that question. They cannot imagine why the church in North America would ever need the African church. *What does Africa have to give? You are so poor, you have so little, you have no technology. What in the world could the African church ever give to the church in North America?*"[10] That is a question I hope to answer well in the pages to follow.

Because Kenton Beshore had the fortitude to engage with Bishop Oscar and grapple with these issues, the two became very good friends. Kenton would say to him, "We want to engage with you, but you're being too harsh." What would happen was that Bishop Oscar would be the one to slap, and I would be the one to soften the blow by telling the leaders at Mariners, "This is what he really means." You see, the bishop would do his thing and then go back to Kenya, but I was still at Mariners. So that's how the journey evolved. It's one thing to have a prophetic voice; it's another thing to carry a shepherd's staff.

I learned to shepherd our people by being involved with them, knowing who they were and caring about what they cared about. The more I did that, the more I was accepted, and the more they were willing to engage in some tough—even harsh—conversations. The key to it all is *relationships*. Speaking the truth in love, you can soften the blow through relationship. Even still, at one point Kenton had to say, "Hey, Oscar, we're listening. Stop slapping us."

Missions as Personal Formation

As we discussed the role of missions and evangelism in the church, Kenton said he had never thought of missions as a way for people to be fully formed in their faith or discipled from a global perspective. All he had ever heard was "Come help! Come help! Come help!" But now he could see how that type of appeal was doing *nothing* for the people at Mariners. Living in affluent Orange County, they were well-versed in sending money and going on short-term missions trips. They didn't need to be told to come help. But Kenton wanted to challenge them to embrace a new level of engagement. After spending time in Kenya and talking extensively with Pastor M and Bishop Oscar, Kenton realized that—now more than ever—the American church *needed* the people of the global church. Missions is not merely evangelism or doing good things to help people in need. Instead, it is an essential component of personal and spiritual formation through a global lens. As men and women and young people go out into the mission field, they must realize that, in the process, *they too* are going to be formed more closely to the image of God.

So now when we say, "Hey, let's go to Africa," it's not so that our people can *help*, but so they can gain a new perspective—on the world, on missions, and on themselves—a perspective they currently may not have.

When we first started taking groups from Mariners to visit Mavuno Church, people were surprised that we weren't taking along school supplies, food, money, or any of the other resources commonly associated with short-term missions. Furthermore, we didn't have plans to build a school, paint a church building, or do Vacation Bible School. Those things are all well and good, but we didn't want our people to focus on what they were going to *do* there; we wanted them looking for what God was *already* doing there and for what he was going to do *in them*. We want people thinking in terms of an ongoing *faith adventure*, not a short-term missions trip that would eventually fade in the rearview mirror.

For this to happen, we must become bridge builders. If we want people to change their mindset about missions, we must show them how to bridge the gap between where they are and where we want them to be.

For me, one bridge has been inviting people to go to Africa.

People ask me, "What are we going to *do* when we go to Africa?"

"Well, we're going to meet people who are doing XYZ, and we're going to get to know them."

"Yes, but what are we going to *do*?" The Western mindset that says, "I want to go *do* something, I want to *fix* something, I want to *accomplish* something, I want to *maximize my return on investment*," does not change easily. So I tell them, "What we're going to *do* is go *be human* with our brothers and sisters in this new place." It's getting to a place of actually seeing people as brothers and sisters, not just in lip service. We talk about our brothers and sisters in the Lord, but oftentimes it's just a manner of speaking—it's not a reality. But if we really see other people as our brothers and sisters, it starts to break down the impulse to try to *rescue* them or *fix* their circumstances.

This is where we get into the idea of *being* before *doing*. With your family, you don't try to *do* something to connect with them. You just live your life with them. So, what if our essence is simply *being* with people—meeting people where they are and engaging with them as they are? When you meet people as they are, you get to know them as fellow bearers of God's image. And that should make you curious. What do they care about? What do they know that I don't know? It becomes a different way of thinking. If we change our mindset from *doing* to *being*, it will move us away from the Western fix-it mentality or the African posture of begging. You see, for many Africans, what is ubiquitous is the idea of putting our hands out. It's like we always have our hands out because we're always looking for a Westerner to help us—not realizing that God has already deposited his image in us, and therefore we have a potency within ourselves. And what if we tapped into that potency?

So I tell people when we go, "Don't worry, there will be things to do, but they will be priorities established by the indigenous leadership, not some good intentions we're bringing in from the outside."

So, for example, Pastor Sam, an indigenous pastor in Haiti, has a desire to plant churches in Les Cayes. How can we serve as a catalyst for his efforts? We go down there and help them with the fifty-five orphans they're caring for. We spend time with the church leaders, the moms, the orphans—you know, playing games with the kids. Over the span of ten days, we experience the culture, see what is happening there, and have four training sessions—how missions is connected to the mandate of the church; spiritual warfare; cultural sensitivity; and how to talk about your story and how it connects to the larger story of life. We also incorporate team-building exercises into all four sessions because we have seen too many short-term missions teams that were dysfunctional.

We want people to understand that this is not just going to be about them *doing* something. It's more about who they're going to *become*. And as they become, they will start to realize the opportunities that God has for them, and that God is going do some incredible work in their hearts and their lives. What comes out of these trips is much more than what would have happened if we had simply gone to work on a project. We get to help advance what the indigenous churches are doing, and they have a chance to impart to us a sense of faith that we do not have, or perhaps insights on prayer and dependency on the Holy Spirit. Dependency on God and dependency on each other is something that is deeply embedded in African culture. There's an opportunity to serve together. but also to *grow* together as we learn to collaborate in reciprocal partnerships.

At the end of every day, we debrief. What did you see today? What is God telling you? How is your life going to be different? Who are you going to *be*? And only then, what are you going to do? During the reentry process at the end of the trip, we talk about how to integrate the experiences we've had into our day-to-day lives: Who is someone you're going to be in touch with? And we talk about rethinking ROI: What is the return on investment we're looking for in spiritual growth?

Let me tell you one more quick story to illustrate the power of a "being before doing" mindset.

In April 2024, I took a couple from our church with me to Uganda. They're both *doers*, so naturally they wanted to know the itinerary. I told them we were going to *observe* what Pastor Peter and the people in his church were doing. I said, "I want you just to sit and listen and be a part of it." And they did.

On our last night there, they said to me, "We've come to realize that what Pastor Peter and his church are doing we could never do. But we want to be a catalyst to help them reach their goals."

And they handed me checks totaling $340,000 for seven ministries they had seen in action. Now, they are generous people and people of means, but if I had simply asked them to give without first meeting the people and seeing where the opportunities were, they might have written a check for some amount and that would have been it. But being there and experiencing firsthand what God was already doing in Uganda opened their minds to unforeseen possibilities. And here's the thing: I didn't ask them for the money. That was their own decision. They told me they just wanted to have a stake in what Pastor Peter and the church were doing. They had been transformed by the renewing of their minds.[11]

It's hard for people to change direction. That's why we have to walk alongside them. And that's why my role is building bridges. Finding bridge builders is the key to changing people's minds—and the bridge builders don't have to be African, Asian, or Latin American. Anybody who learns the importance of mutual respect, healthy cultural engagement, reciprocal partnerships, and seeing the image of God in everyone can become a bridge builder. If more people would recognize this and do it, it would be a big win for the Kingdom of God.

Where Do We Go from Here?

In the remainder of this book, we will examine the theological underpinnings of missions and of a missional Christian life, and then reimagine the philosophy, the ethos, and the practices that will most effectively enable us, together, to pursue the Great Commission in the twenty-first century.

I believe that the most effective missional outreach and global engagement strategy in our age begins with understanding, acknowledging, and emphasizing that every person in the world is made in God's image. When we start with the realization that we possess the *exact* same nature as the people we're trying to reach (regardless of cultural differences), and that those individuals express the image of God to precisely the same degree that we do (no matter their station in life), we realign our theology of missions with the Word of God, which in turn changes our philosophy, ethos, and practice of missions.

The *content* of the gospel doesn't change, nor does the gospel *mission* change. But how we go about it—our methods, our means, and our mores—must inevitably change. As successful as world missions have been over the past 175 years or so, following a Western model, we are now in a new era due to advances in technology, political and economic factors, and the emergence of indigenous leaders around the world.

God still calls every one of us to go into all the world and preach the gospel, making disciples of all nations, baptizing them in the name of the Father and the Son and the Holy Spirit, and teaching them to obey everything that Jesus commanded us. That's true for both vocational missionaries and for every other Christian—those God has called into the business world, to the food service industry, to stay at home and raise kids, or to any other area of human endeavor. God promises a blessing to his children who feed the hungry, give drink to the thirsty, welcome strangers, clothe the naked, visit the sick, and minister to prisoners.[12]

How we do it is the subject of this book.

Agents of Change

In the pages that follow, I want to invite both individuals and congregations to reconsider what it means to become potent agents of change, to serve as compassionate ambassadors of the Christian faith by emphasizing the importance of cross-cultural sensitivity, mutually beneficial relationships, and strategic engagement. If we start where the Bible itself begins, in Genesis 1–2, with our creation in the image of God, our theological convictions about the inherent dignity of *every* human being will inevitably modify our philosophy of missions, which in turn will reshape our posture toward both the people who serve and the people we are serving, and will naturally and inevitably reform our practices. This does not mean that proclamation and demonstration of the gospel take a back seat. It just means there is an added third spoke to the wheel, which was intended from the beginning: the premise of *community*—and a diverse but united community at that.

People Are the Wealth provides a way for churches and everyone engaged in outreach to build bridges and foster understanding in today's interconnected world. We want to reengage ourselves and the local church with the global world and the global body of Christ, much as I've seen happen with my fellow believers at Mariners Church, where I continue to serve as the global movement pastor.

To make this happen, we must reimagine our strategies. And the sooner we start, the sooner we will find ourselves in alignment with what God is *already* doing around the world. God did not send us an argument for his existence; he sent us a living, breathing person who set aside his own divine power to become like us so we can become like him.

PART ONE

THEOLOGY

Let's begin by examining the key biblical concepts that undergird the entire book. This will provide the *why* behind the work. I emphasize theological underpinnings that deeply resonate with my African cultural experience—and yet theology always supersedes culture, transcending our ethnocentricities. God's Word never changes, even in a constantly changing world.

Jesus had an intensely people-centered ministry. He came to serve others, not himself. His style of ministry led to unity and cohesion of mission, which created a profound sense of conviction and authenticity. This, in turn, produced a deep effectiveness that continues to reverberate throughout time and rings true to eternity. Starting with the core idea of the image of God in all human beings presents a solid foundation for a people-centered approach to Christian missions. Finally, by no means am I calling for uniformity; rather, the centrality of God's Word in Christian missions calls us to unity in our diversity.

1 CONNECTION BEFORE CONTENT

My favorite theologian of all time is an unschooled, illiterate, barefoot villager from Kenya named Njoki. More often I call her Grandma, or Cũcũ in my native tongue.

Cũcũ Njoki grew up in a mission center called Thogoto—which is actually a Kikuyu word but is based on a phonetic rendition of *Scotland*. When Scottish missionaries arrived in the area where my grandma grew up, they said, "We are from Scotland."

And the people said, "What?"

And they said, "Scotland."

"What? Thogotoland?"

And so the place became known as Thogoto.

The missionaries built a center there and started passing along the gospel to the villages, and my grandma was one of the people who heard about Jesus that way.

Interestingly, my grandmother could neither read nor write, but because the gospel was shared orally, through stories, she got it. And as she became acquainted with God's Word, she started living it out—what she *heard*, she *did*. And she made theological observations the likes of which I haven't heard from far more learned theologians. Consider just a couple of examples.

Whenever we would insist on getting shoes for her, she would say, "Why do you want to give me the comforts of this earth that will never satisfy? I want to walk on the dust I was created from so I can be reminded daily that I am returning to dust."

One time, my mother asked if we could put running water in Cũcũ Njoki's house, but she vehemently rejected the offer. "I don't need that luxury," she declared. "I love to walk to the river, meet others who gather there to fetch water, tell them of the one who can quench their eternal thirst, and then take my pail of water and walk back to my house, ruminating on how Jesus carried a cross for my salvation."

I have attended seminary and read the works of many accomplished scholars, but I have never encountered such profound wisdom as I did from my illiterate, unschooled, barefoot village grandma, Cũcũ Njoki. And it all came from her hearing the Word of God, not reading it. "Faith comes by hearing, and hearing by the word of God."[1]

Even evangelism just became part of her daily life. She never used the word *evangelism*. She used to call it *ngwatanĩĩro* (*fellowship*). "I just want to go and fellowship with people and tell them about the way the Lord has been good to me every day."

My tribe has something we call *ũĩira*, which is *testimony*. Testimony is simply telling someone (often in a court of law) what you have seen, heard, or experienced. Likewise, Christian testimony is simply telling others what the Lord has done for you or how you came to faith. My grandma would meet people on the road and tell them, "Today, the Lord did this for me, and I'm grateful." Your testimony is simply what God has done for you today. That's how my grandma and the people in her village grew up. She also raised my mother and her siblings that way.

I used to go to my grandma and ask her to tell me what God had done in her life. And her stories were always amazing examples of faith in action. That's why I call her my favorite theologian. She would just tell me her stories, but I always heard deep truths in them.

One time when I was home in Kenya for a while, she asked me, "Are you in trouble with the law in America?"

"No, I'm not in trouble with the law, Grandma."

"Yeah," she said, "I saw you in a dream, being in trouble with the law. And I stood up and I told those people to leave you alone. You're a servant of God. Okay?"

This story didn't make sense to me until two weeks later, when I was returning home through LAX. As I was coming in, I was stopped by Immigration and Customs, and the immigration officer said, "Hey, you seem to have violated your status," which was true.

So for the next four hours—the longest four hours of my life—I sat there, expecting to be deported back to Africa, never to return.

While I was waiting, there was a shift change and another officer arrived to replace the one who had detained me. After a time, he came over to me and said, "I see that you have violated your status; but now you have a new status, and you have an opportunity to get it right."

I was dumbfounded.

"I see that you're doing ministry," he continued.

"Yes, I am."

"Go and serve the Lord," he said as he stamped my passport and released me.

My grandma had had a premonition of what was going to happen to me, and I had no idea. Unfortunately, she died soon after that, so I didn't get a chance to see her and tell her what had happened.

But that's the kind of faith that people like my grandma had—a faith I have never experienced from people who are well educated.

But if someone had gone to Africa and looked at my grandmother, they would have seen she was barefoot, and they would have said, "We need to get her shoes." They would have found that she was illiterate, and they would have said, "We have to give her education." All this without stopping to wonder, *What does this woman know? What does this woman think? What kind of faith does this woman have?* If they had done that, they might have realized, "Oh! This woman has a faith in God that we can learn from."

I tell these stories to illustrate how we can often miss out on profound wisdom, either by making assumptions or by moving too quickly to give people *content* before we establish a living connection with them. Too often, our Western models of global engagement and missions (whether for individuals or organizations) focus on disseminating information without first taking the time to get to know and understand the people we desire to reach—and perhaps discover what God is already doing in their midst.

I'm grateful that the missionaries who first encountered my grandfather didn't follow this typical pattern. Instead, they approached with wide-eyed curiosity, carefully observing what the villagers were doing, and seeking to understand their ways. They didn't immediately label these Africans as idol worshipers, but rather asked them why they felt compelled to worship the mountain. They sought *connection* with the people before giving them the content of the gospel, and that strategy made their message all the more powerful and captivating.

It has often been said that the way you diagnose a problem will determine how you treat it. Have we misdiagnosed the proper starting point for our outreach efforts? And if so, how do we reimagine them?

Different Marching Orders?

Most Christians who work vocationally in missions, or who as individuals have a great interest in global engagement, find their marching orders in the Great Commission, given by Jesus in Matthew 28. They fan out over neighborhoods, cities, regions, and the world to proclaim the gospel of Jesus Christ, teaching new disciples to obey everything the Lord commanded. That's nothing new. For centuries, people have written books about the necessity of fulfilling the Great Commission.

Others with a different focus on worldwide missions gravitate toward works of compassion and justice. They often cite passages such as Matthew 25:34-40, where Jesus commends his true disciples for feeding the hungry, giving drink to the thirsty, welcoming strangers, clothing the naked, tending the sick, and visiting prisoners in jail. Individuals committed to this expression of global missions often dig wells for communities that lack safe drinking water, build schools in areas with little access to good education, supply medical help to those with no health care, and so on. They, too, write books about the necessity of reaching out to impoverished and oppressed peoples, supplying them with the physical necessities of life in the name of Jesus.

Both of these approaches have their merits, and in my experience, most missions-minded people embrace one or the other. But rarely do they do both. In fact, these two groups have spent decades hotly debating which approach is the more biblical and the more loving. But if we have an integrated view of missions, the two parts are inextricably linked—acts of compassion, care, and justice are inseparable from proclamation of the gospel. To do one is really to do the other, and to neglect one or the other would be unjust.

Please don't misunderstand me. We must remain committed to *both* Matthew 28:18-20 and Matthew 25:35-40. We must proclaim the truth *and* demonstrate God's love; evangelize among the lost *and* alleviate pain among the hurting; share the gospel *and* show God's heart to the world.

But what if the question is not which *approach* is right, but where we should begin the discussion in the first place? What if we have started our missions journey at not quite the right location and thus have ended up at not quite the right destination?

Is the best starting point really in the Gospel of Matthew, three-fifths of the way through the Bible? What if, instead, we started in Genesis 1, where God himself began the human story, as our foundation for thinking about how to introduce Jesus to others? How might that change our approach to missions, whether in our neighborhoods or on the other side of the planet?

A Better Starting Place

In Genesis 1, we see God creating all things. He creates the sun and calls it good. He creates the earth and calls it good. He creates plants and animals, and day and night, and calls *everything* he makes good.

But note what happens when it comes to creating human beings. Suddenly, God starts referring to himself in the plural. He says, "Let *us* make man in *our* image."[2]

What would happen if we rooted our practice of missions, first and foremost, in the biblical doctrine of the Trinity? Scripture reveals God as a community of divine persons existing as a single deity, rather than as a solitary God, an individual God, or an isolated God. We understand God as Father, Son, and Holy Spirit—three distinct persons in one unified Godhead. What might change in our outreach models if we expanded our approach to include the unity in diversity we find in the Trinity?

God has *always* existed in community; his three-in-one essence predates Creation. And God made human beings *in his own image*, such that you and I and every other person on the planet bear the image of a God who reveals himself as a plurality, a community.

Not only that, but we all bear the image of God to precisely the same degree as every other person on earth—irrespective of race, ethnicity, class, or stature. We all possess the *exact same nature*. What if we were to make this reality the starting point for our bedrock theological convictions, especially regarding global missions and individual missional engagement? How would this foundational truth inform the nature of our convictions, bearing, and attitudes as we move out from our "Jerusalem, throughout Judea, in Samaria, and to the ends of the earth,"[3] in obedience to Jesus' command to make disciples?

What if we started looking at someone like my grandma as first and foremost a bearer of God's image, rather than as merely a barefoot, illiterate, elderly African woman? What if instead of trying to meet her perceived needs from the get-go, we first seek to know her and to call forth what God has innately placed in her? Making disciples of all nations should not start with asking, "What do these people need to learn?" but rather, "What does loving these fellow image bearers require of me?" Perhaps the greatest adjustment we must make to our thinking is to set aside all our answers, all our solutions, all our vaunted expertise, and approach the mission field as *listeners* and as *learners*, as Bishop Oscar has suggested.

It might take a change of mindset for people in the Western church to realize that people in Africa, in Asia, or in Latin America have something to offer us. But it starts with truly seeing people for who they are as created in the image of God.

Gregory Boyle, in his book *Barking to the Choir*, tells a great story about seeing through the facade to the image of God that lies beneath in every person.

> One Sunday, I was sitting with my friend and Jesuit brother, Al Naucke. Both of us had our coffee and were silently turning the pages of the paper when the doorbell started to ring repeatedly. Initially, Al and I hid behind our papers, waiting it out. The doorbell rarely rang, but when it did, it was almost always some homeless person. Finally, Al, the way better man, quietly put down the paper. There was no annoyed sighing (though who could blame him?).
>
> Some ten minutes later he returned, sat down, took a sip of coffee, and resumed his reading. After a few beats, I asked, without lowering the paper, "Well?"
>
> "Well what?" Al replied, not lowering his paper either.
>
> "Who was it?"
>
> From behind the sports section he said, "Jesus, in his least recognizable form."[4]

If we start by seeing every person as created in, and reflecting, the image of God—which is a picture of unity and community in diversity—it will enhance our Great Commission efforts, and it will enhance our compassion and justice.

That is the mindset change I'm talking about—that the impetus for everything we do is the image of God, the Imago Dei. On that foundation, we are being asked to build relationships, to build community and connectedness. In God we are all one. And in that connectedness, we'll realize that it's not okay for our brothers and sisters to go hungry; it's not okay for our brothers and sisters to go without knowing the gospel. People are the wealth because people are the only thing created in God's image. And if people are the wealth, it means that we recognize the image of God in every human being. Accordingly, this becomes the premise for everything we do in Christian missions.

Communal vs. Individual

Many of the most popular books on Christian missions were written by well-educated and well-intentioned scholars from the Western world. Though the majority world (or two-thirds world) is grateful for the positive impact these books have had, I believe too many of these works inevitably come up short because of a myopic perspective that leads to a gargantuan omission.

Western cultures tend to emphasize individualism rather than our communal identity as human beings born into societies and cultures. This might seem like a small thing to many Westerners, but it has an oversized impact on people from the majority world.

Consider the example of marriage. When two people from the West decide to get married, they do so on their own, as individuals. They might solicit input from trusted friends and family, but they alone determine that they are fit and ready to make that commitment. In the majority world, by contrast, most marriages result from a communal decision requiring several ceremonies before a couple is granted the blessing of marriage. In my own Kikuyu tribe, we have at least three (if not four) important ceremonies before the wedding nuptials.

Whether our perspective on Christian missions is individualistic or communal greatly affects the strategies we use. Though God certainly gives a *personal* call to missions, the much richer and deeper idea is that the Great Commission was given to *us* as the body of Christ, not merely to you or me as individual members of the body. This seemingly insignificant detail makes the key difference between a *people-focused* mission—communities that create countercultural cities on a hilltop that cannot be hidden[5]—and isolated individuals who do their best to share the gospel. Many of us have missed this reality and thus have suffered significant setbacks.

In this book, I'd like us to reexamine, rethink, and reconsider the idea of Imago Dei as it relates to a community and not only to individuals. As we do, we will align ourselves more closely with what we see in the Scriptures right from the beginning. Consider one salient example of what a people-focused and communal-centered mission can look like.

The Wisdom of Community

I got a big surprise one day as we were planning a short-term missions trip to Kenya. One of our African residents, Henry Wamai, who had recently come from Mavuno Church, which at the time was relocating to a new facility, said to me, "Do you know who we need to take on this trip?"

"Who?" I asked.

"Roman Garcia."

"Roman? Really?"

I must confess, I was dumbfounded. *Why would we take our head of facilities to Africa on a missions trip?*

Don't get me wrong, I love Roman. He has worked at Mariners Church for more than thirty years, and he is as proficient, dedicated, and experienced as they come. Roman knows every tree at Mariners, every light bulb, every nook and cranny. He's a joy to be around, and he takes his job *very* seriously. Roman and his team keep our facility in tip-top shape. They clean and care for and organize everything so that we always have a place to sit down and discuss our missions strategies. But it had never occurred to me—or to anyone else, apparently—to invite Roman to go on a missions trip. That's just not how we tended to think at the time. We had already assembled our team for this trip, with all the right people and all the right résumés for teaching, evangelizing, and bringing resources.

"We need to take Roman to Kenya," Henry insisted. "We're relocating to a new place that we will use to reach out to our cities and to the global world. We will need to thoroughly understand this new facility, this new place, and I've never seen anybody who is more capable than Roman at understanding a facility."

I accepted Henry's challenge to include Roman on our team, and everyone in the church was excited to hear the news. Team members usually raise support to go on a short-term mission, and Roman raised his money more quickly than anyone else on the team, because it seemed that *everyone* wanted him to be able to go.

When we arrived in Kenya, Roman met the head of facilities at Mavuno, an astute man named Peter Kabuki. Peter isn't your average facilities person either; he's something of an expert in logistics. He and Roman had a wonderful time, and Roman freely shared everything he knew.

Afterward, Peter approached me and said, "I have just realized that I'm not cut out to be head of facilities. If being head of facilities is being like Roman, then I'm nowhere near that level. That guy has more passion, more acumen, he's more astute about facilities than I'll ever be." Spending time with Roman helped Peter realize that he should not head up facilities at the new Mavuno campus. He told me, "I'll never care as much about that facility as Roman does."

Unless we are intentional about keeping the doctrine of Imago Dei front and center in our ministries, we will likely never consider an ordinary person like Roman to be a candidate for impact in the global world. Sure, he runs a well-oiled facilities crew in the States, but he's certainly not an evangelist . . . right? But Roman helped

Mavuno set up what would become a hub for launching ordinary people into their mission as infiltrators of the local culture.

Mavuno's mantra is "turning ordinary people into fearless influencers of society." So for them, anybody who comes into the church is an ordinary person, but they want them to become an *influencer* for the gospel in the sectors of society where they already are. Mavuno's mission is to reach young, upwardly mobile Africans who are detached from church and don't care about the gospel, but who are people in places of influence.

Pastor M told me that when people go to the mission field, they often look for people who are like my grandma—illiterate and out in the villages—or they find the people who are poor. What people don't go after are the well-to-do ones—because these people don't need us and they're not going to be easy to reach. But Pastor M said, "That's my demographic, because if I can get the people who are upwardly mobile in the upper echelons of society, then I will be able to shape them to influence our society in a different way than self-aggrandizement. They become potent agents for the gospel."

Mavuno does not have an outreach department; rather, they decided that *everyone* in the church is in outreach. Their people simply identify which sectors of society they are in, and that's where they seek to influence people with the gospel by showing and telling—sharing the gospel and living it out.

Roman and I roomed together in Kenya, and as we spent time talking, he told me how grateful he was to be invited on the trip, and how it had inspired others on our facilities team with the idea that they too might be invited to go on a global missions trip. They now saw themselves as an active part of the mission, and Roman said, "Not only are we able to give of our service, but we can actually give of our minds and our hearts as well."

Through our conversations, he also opened my eyes to see the image of God in other members of our facilities team back home.

"Let me tell you about Teresa," he said. "She has worked at Mariners for many years, and she's our 'mom.' She keeps us in line. She watches over us, and we all have great respect for her." I would later see Teresa at a wedding I officiated. Another staff member had gotten to know her well enough that he invited her to his wedding.

Roman also told me about Alberto, an older gentleman on our facilities staff who had eight grandchildren. Alberto was still working in his late seventies because he wanted to continue to provide for his kids—some of whom were not doing well—and he was helping his grandkids.

Roman, Teresa, and Alberto are people who are living with a certain sense of mission, but if we don't pay attention to understanding who they are, we may miss opportunities to contribute to their spiritual formation and to be formed *by* them.

Then there's Marco, who uses his vacation time to take clothes to his people in Guatemala. Marco's story will probably never be told in a missions conference—because he's "Marco from facilities," and many people are not aware of who he is. But he is living out his own identity as a Christ follower, and he's using his opportunities in America to support people in Guatemala.

During my time with Roman in Kenya, I learned more about the early days of Mariners Church, including how he'd had a unique friendship with Hudd Saffel, one of the church's founders, who went home to be with the Lord in 2019 at the age of ninety-seven. If I hadn't engaged with Roman and gotten to know him, I never would have heard those stories. He and I have since become good friends.

Since the time of that missions trip to Kenya, and with our ongoing emphasis on seeing the image of God in others, members of our congregation have become more aware of those who serve behind the scenes. Relationships have formed—even through language and cultural barriers—and we have learned to celebrate the inherent dignity of all people. These are not just people who serve at the church; they are people who are part and parcel of our community, and we are richer because of them.

When Roman's thirtieth anniversary at Mariners came around, he was probably the most celebrated person in the history of the church—even more than our former senior pastor and founder. People came out of the woodwork to join the celebration. People who had worked at Mariners or attended Mariners many years ago came back just to show their appreciation for Roman. It was inspiring.

I tell these stories to illustrate three important points:

1. We must learn to start *seeing* people before we can begin to appreciate the wealth they bring—of wisdom, experience, skills and abilities, understanding, and areas of expertise. Most people at Mariners know Roman as the janitor, but that is almost a total misunderstanding and undervaluing of his true role.

   We need to start seeing our *own* people through the lens of Imago Dei before we can ever hope to see people in other nations and cultures that way. Forget about going overseas; what about the people all around us right here at home? How can we begin to see the gifts that God has uniquely placed in each and every person we meet? Gifts he wants to develop and use. We at Mariners came to realize that we needed to be "transformed by the renewing of our minds"[6] in how we saw people and treated people *everywhere*. Honoring the "wealth" of people starts at home.

2. We must learn the importance of reciprocal ministry. As leaders, we can become so focused on our own agenda and what we are taking *with us* to the mission field that we don't stop long enough to consider what we want our people to get out of the trip in terms of their own spiritual formation.

3. We must recognize the importance of considering input from other perspectives. If I had not been willing to heed the advice of Henry Wamai, Roman might never have gone to Kenya, and we would have missed out on all the benefits that accrued from his participation on that trip. Moreover, Henry brought to our attention an important priority at Mavuno that we were completely unaware of—namely, the need to consult with a facilities expert like Roman. Again, we had our own agenda and plans, and we had not stopped to consider what our Kenyan brothers and sisters might actually *want* or *need* from us.

An Apostolic Philosophy of Mission

In 1 Corinthians 9:19-23, the apostle Paul lays out what amounts to his underlying philosophy of missions, though he doesn't call it that. Consider carefully what he says here:

> Though I am free from all, I have made myself a servant to all, that I might win more of them. To the Jews I became as a Jew, in order to win Jews. To those under the law I became as one under the law (though not being myself under the law) that I might win those under the law. To those outside the law I became as one outside the law (not being outside the law of God but under the law of Christ) that I might win those outside the law. To the weak I became weak, that I might win the weak. I have become all things to all people, that by all means I might save some. I do it all for the sake of the gospel, that I may share with them in its blessings.

The key Greek verb for "become," repeated multiple times in this passage, is *ginomai*. Paul says he *became* like a Jew so that he might win Jews to faith in Jesus. He *became* like someone living under the law—even though he wasn't, in fact, under the law—in order to win those under the law. He *became* like those outside the law, and *became* weak, and *became* all things to all people . . . why? He spent so much time and went to such great effort, he said, so that some of these people might place their faith in Jesus as their Savior. The apostle made himself a slave so that others might be made free.

It cost Paul a great deal to become "like a Jew," or "like a Gentile," or to become a "weak" individual, or to become "all things to all people." First, he had to learn a good deal about them. He had to investigate their lives, their customs, their likes and dislikes. He had to put himself on the same level with them. To gain the ability to become like someone else implies the exertion of significant effort. It suggests an earnest, energetic attempt to identify with other people, not just pop in to say a quick hello.

The apostle went to such lengths and worked so hard so that "by all means I might save some." He longed to see people in a right relationship with God. He focused on the people, caring for them so much that he willingly made himself a slave for their sakes. Paul did not put the *task* of proclaiming the gospel ahead of the *people* who needed the gospel.

Connected by Our Essence

Jesus' attitude toward the Sabbath may provide a good analogy to help us understand the proper relationship between the task of missions and the people whom missions is intended to bless.

By the time Jesus came to earth, the religious authorities in Israel had turned the Sabbath into a legalistic requirement, rather than treating it as a boon to the people created in God's image (as God had intended). Jesus therefore declared, "The Sabbath was made for man, not man for the Sabbath."[7] Humans came first, he insisted. The Sabbath was introduced only afterward, as a divine gift designed for our benefit.

Likewise with the gospel. Humans (created in God's image) came first, and the gospel appeared afterward as a divine gift designed to rescue men and women from their sin. That being true, what sense does it make to elevate the *task* of missions over the *individuals* whom Christ died to save? Yet, when we put *content* before *connection*, we can start treating people as merely the targets of our message, rather than as the treasure that prompted God to create the message in the first place. Both content and connection are indispensable; but biblically speaking, *connection* must come first.

As we read the Genesis account of God's creation of the world and everything in it, we encounter a repeated refrain: "God saw that it was good."[8] In fact, the only time God declares that anything in Creation is *not* good is in Genesis 2:18, when he says, "It is not good that the man should be alone." He then remedies the situation by creating Eve *out of* Adam, thereby creating both *relationship* and *community* on earth, patterned after his own nature, which is diverse and yet one. His nature preexisted time, space, and matter. Before we were, he always was, eternally existing in a devoted relationship of loving and being loved, enjoying and being enjoyed.

I find it interesting that after Adam and Eve were created on the sixth day, God took the next day to rest "from all his work that he had done."[9] Thus, Adam and Eve's first day after their creation was a Sabbath. They began their lives by resting in their *being*, in their belonging to God, and in their connection with God. As such, our "beingness" is inherent to our identity as humans created in the image of God.

God's identity is eternal—that is, he simply *is*. Yes, he also *does* things, but those things are expressions of who he already is. The same is true of *us*, as created in God's image. For that reason alone, we have value, even if we never do or say *anything*. Our *worth* is inherent in the Imago Dei.

Because we have eternal value, every one of us is vital to God's mission on earth. That's why Paul could say about the church, "The eye cannot say to the hand, 'I have no need of you,' nor again the head to the feet, 'I have no need of you.' On the contrary, the parts of the body that seem to be weaker are indispensable."[10] *All* Christians are connected in *one* body, Paul insists, and every part is equally important.

Bishop Oscar has paraphrased 1 Corinthians 12:14-27 to drive the message home. It's worth quoting in full:

> Now the body is not made up of one part but of many.
>
> If the American church should say, "Because I am not African, I do not belong to the body," it would not for that reason cease to be part of the body. And if the Canadian church should say, "Because I am not Asian, I do not belong to the body," it would not for that reason cease to be part of the body. If the whole body were European, where would the sense of joy be? And if the whole body were African, where would the sense of order be? But in fact God has arranged the parts in the body, every one of them, just as he wanted them to be. If they were all one part, where would the body be? As it is, there are many parts, but one body.
>
> The Canadian church cannot say to the Asian church, "I don't need you!" And the American church cannot say to the African church, "I don't need you!" On the contrary, the Asian parts that seem to be weaker are indispensable, and the African parts that we think are less honorable should be treated with special honor. And the Latin American parts that seem unpresentable are treated

> with special modesty, while the presentable parts like the big, wealthy American church need no special treatment. But God has combined the members of the body, and has given greater honor to the parts that lacked it, so that there should be no division in the body, but that its parts should have equal concern for each other. If one part suffers, every part suffers with it; if one part is honored, every part rejoices with it.
>
> Now you are the body of Christ, and each one of you is a part of it.[11]

That They Might Be One

In John 17, Jesus makes a remarkable request of his Father. He asks that every one of his disciples—there in the upper room, around the world, and throughout history—"may all be one, just as you, Father, are in me, and I in you, that they also may be in us, *so that the world may believe that you have sent me.*"[12] As if that isn't enough, he then prays that his disciples might "become perfectly one, *so that the world may know that you sent me and loved them even as you loved me.*"[13]

How's *that* for a key text about our global mission? Oneness—unity—in the body of Christ. Jesus says that people will see who God is by observing the countercultural, radical community among Jesus' disciples. This requires that we be *united* in our *diversity*. The more the world sees how united we are *in* our diversity (not despite our diversity), the more they will see who God is (in his triune presence as Father, Son, and Holy Spirit). By observing the diverse but unified body of Christ in action—the globally united, gospel-centered family of God—the citizens of earth will catch a glimpse of God's holy and loving nature.

I met my wife, Delta, at Mariners Church in 2009. She is a

blue-eyed blonde from South Dakota. I *never* thought I would marry an American, much less an American so completely different from me. But through God's grace in changing my heart, I came to the point where I fell in love with this beautiful young woman, and eventually we decided to get married.

Marrying someone from the very culture I had initially rejected made the journey toward embracing that culture all the more profound. Having a mixed-race daughter, Kabi, named after my mother, stretches us all even further as we navigate a ton of nuanced situations in American life. We are still learning and growing together.

In 2010, my groomsmen and I went to get measured for our wedding suits. In typical Kenyan fashion, the outfits were shiny, swanky, flashy—not the best look for my white brothers, but they looked great on the black guys. As the store employee took our measurements, he suddenly stopped and said, "I have a weird question. Please bear with me. But how do you guys know each other?"

He asked because our group consisted of three Kenyans, a Vietnamese guy, an Armenian, and a German. He could not help but notice our multicultural diversity.

"First of all," he said, "you guys all *look* different. But second, you're getting along so well. How do you know each other?"

His question opened the door for us to tell him we were all friends from the same church. "I'm a pastor working at the church," I said.

"I'd like to go to your church," he replied immediately. Imagine that: This man felt intrigued enough to visit our church, simply by seeing the unity and diversity among a group of friends. That day, we saw why Jesus identified *unity* as our primary gospel witness.

I can't end this section without briefly visiting Revelation 7:9-10, which pictures the staggering culmination of Jesus' prayer. There we see people from every nation, every tribe, and every language standing before God's throne and before Jesus, crying out in a loud, unified voice, "Salvation belongs to our God who sits on the throne, and to the Lamb!"[14]

The scene reverberates with such energy that even the angels around God's throne fall on their faces and worship God, shouting with great joy, "Amen! Blessing and glory and wisdom and thanksgiving and honor and power and might be to our God forever and ever! Amen."[15]

We must learn to engage globally in a way that reflects our creation in the image of a God who is a community, three persons in one. In that Trinitarian community, there exists both unity and diversity. The beautiful thing about this for us is that there is no one culture, or one person, or one context that can ever fully reflect the image of God. We need the entire world to fully reflect God's image.

Biblical, effective gospel work—whether by individuals or groups; on mission at home or on mission around the world—begins in Genesis and culminates in Revelation. All the way through Scripture, God highlights the inherent dignity and value of every human being. Recognizing the image of God in every human being leads to a robust, theologically orthodox, and effective commitment to global missions. I cannot think of a better way to view the practice of missions than through the lens of Christian unity.

How to Be Wealthy

My dad, the late Reverend David Kiarie Mungai, always told me, "Son, money will make you rich, but it will never make you wealthy. You're only as wealthy as the people you have around you." By that definition, we are *extremely* wealthy in the global church, because as a Kikuyu proverb says, *Andũ nĩ o ĩĩndo*, or "People are the wealth."

In order to equip individuals and local churches to engage the global community, and thereby create a lasting impact, we must think of people as the wealth. We must start by recognizing the inherent dignity and the image of God in everyone we meet. When we look at other people—regardless of their station in life—we are, in a very real sense, looking into the face of God.

My dad raised his children to be part of the church. He could have afforded to give us a home in a different part of Nairobi, but he had us live in Eastleigh, a poor area that many called "the ghetto." But we attended school where the wealthy people lived. He sacrificed a higher lifestyle to benefit our future, so that we could get an excellent education.

I went to one of the better primary schools in the country, but this created an unexpected tension within me. I wasn't "ghetto enough" for living in Eastleigh nor wealthy enough to acclimate with my classmates. I quickly found myself in no-man's-land.

In time, God used that tension to make me into a bridge builder. I understand what it means to be from a difficult, poverty-stricken area, but I also understand the wealthy and the well-to-do. I never quite fit in either one of those worlds, but I learned how to build bridges between them. In God's divine wisdom, and without my choosing, he predestined my life for connecting people.

There is an African philosophy known as *ubuntu*, a concept that originates from the Bantu languages of Southern Africa. It means, "I am because we are." These words emphasize the interconnectedness of all individuals within a community or society and underscore the importance of social relationships, collaboration, and cooperation. In that sense, it challenges the Western concept of individualism.

I see small examples of ubuntu whenever I lead group adventures to Uganda, Kenya, and Congo, and we pass out candy or anything edible to the children. They quickly go away and divide one piece into tiny amounts, so that everyone can have a little instead of one person having it all. In a sense they are saying, "How can I be happy if the others are sad?" The shocker is when we tell them we have one for each. They are left stunned with amazement.

Ubuntu encourages compassion, understanding, social harmony, and mutual respect. It also calls us to deviate from a common Western way of thinking. In the West, if you have five people and five fish, typically everyone will get one, because that's fair. But in ubuntu, one person might get two or three, depending on when they last ate. Others will give up their share to provide for those with the most need. Fair? No. Ubuntu? Yes!

I am where I am today because the people around me made me who I am. God has continually brought people into my life who could help me. Everyone in our lives brings something important, even if it seems small. That's how God works. He uses community to care for individuals.

As I prepared to graduate from high school, my parents thought that my very opinionated, vociferous, strong-willed personality might make me a good lawyer, but they couldn't really afford to send me to law school. On top of that, I lacked the grades to get into any of the major universities in Kenya, which would have been less expensive than a private university. So instead they sent me to India, which has some of the better, cheaper educational institutions, especially for a degree such as law.

My parents funded my Indian adventure by inviting a few church members and other friends to come together for a *harambee*, which means "pull together." *Harambee* is a concept that helped build Kenya as a nation, because we didn't have the money to build public schools, and *harambee* is how families in Africa can afford to send their kids to college. Every day, there's a fundraiser for a family somewhere. Everybody pitches in a little, and it doesn't even have to be for someone you know. The whole country does this. I never had to worry about setting aside money for my education—in part because I didn't have anything to set aside anyway, but also because I knew we'd all pull together to make it possible.

Harambee is also how Kenyans pay for funerals, because not many have life insurance. In a community-based society, your insurance is other people. When my dad died, people walking outside our door would see the wake and ask, "What happened?" Someone would answer, "Oh, the pastor died." And the person walking by would take out ten shillings, give it to us, and that ten shillings joined another ten shillings, and another, and in the end we had enough to pay for the burial.

But before that, when it came time for me to go to university, my parents raised enough money to pay for a one-way ticket to India and one term of tuition and fees.

"That's enough," they told me. "That's all you need. Go ahead. God will be with you."

When I arrived in India, I had the name of the university and nothing else. When I got off the plane and walked into the terminal, I saw a guy holding a sign that said, "Harrison," which is actually my first name.

Oh man, I thought, *God has sent somebody to me!*

"Are you Kenyan?" I asked the guy.

"Yes," he said.

"Are you waiting for *me*?"

"No, I'm waiting for Harrison."

"I'm Harrison," I said.

"No," he replied, "another Harrison."

It just so happened that another guy named Harrison had taken the same flight. When he showed up, they asked where I was staying.

"I have nowhere to go," I said.

"Come," they answered, "you can stay with us."

And so, Harrison and Harrison became roommates for a few weeks. Through God's providence and the kindness of strangers, I found a roommate. God was showing me that he would answer my parents' prayers, even using my name in his answer.

Further Divine Provision

Soon after that incident, God raised up a woman named Gladys Opperson, from Bakersfield, California, who had "just happened" to run into my dad ten years before in Chicago. While boarding a plane at O'Hare, she tripped and fell. My dad helped her up and they both boarded the plane. My father also helped her off the plane, for which she expressed profound gratitude.

"May I have your address?" she asked.

"I live in Kenya," my dad replied. "I'm here for just a very short time." But he gave her his post office box address anyway. She took it . . . and promptly forgot about it.

Ten years later, while cleaning up her home, she found an unfamiliar Kenyan address.

Who is this David? she wondered. And then she remembered: *Oh, he's the guy from Africa who helped me. I wonder if he still uses the same PO box?*

She wrote to my father, and he wrote back, saying, "Gladys, I'm well. We've actually just sent our son off to college, by faith, and we hope that God will provide for him."

"You know," she replied, "I've been wondering what to do with some money that I've set aside for something special. Maybe I could help your son?"

Gladys continued to pay my law school tuition until I finished. What an incredible person she was in my life. This story shows, once more, how *real* wealth is found in *relationships*. My dad once helped a woman who fell down trying to get on a plane, helping to preserve her dignity as an image bearer of God. Little did he know that she would be the person whom God would later use to bless his family. That's the true wealth we have in people. We don't go to the mission field with an agenda. We go to find out what is required to love these fellow image bearers of God. We recognize how much inherent dignity and worth resides in every individual.

If you want to find the heart of missions, then you must start in Genesis 1, where you see the heart of God and the crucial importance of human beings made in the image of God. And *that* becomes the impetus for everything else.

The Real Wealth of the World

The real wealth of the world lies in the divine image bearers that God created. Such wealth is inherently dignifying and powerful. And it is that God-given wealth that should motivate us to share the gospel, whether as individuals or as a part of a group.

Imagine what would happen if we engaged in missions work knowing that every person we meet is imaging God in some way. Picture how our interactions would change.

In his classic book *The Weight of Glory*, C. S. Lewis writes:

> The load, or weight, or burden of my neighbour's glory should be laid daily on my back, a load so heavy that only humility can carry it, and the backs of the proud will be broken. It is a serious thing to live in a society of possible gods and goddesses, to remember that the dullest and most uninteresting person you talk to may one day be a creature which, if you saw it now, you would be strongly tempted to worship. . . . There are no *ordinary* people. You have never

> talked to a mere mortal. . . . Next to the Blessed Sacrament itself, your neighbour is the holiest object presented to your senses. If he is your Christian neighbour, he is holy in almost the same way, for in him also Christ . . . the glorifier and the glorified . . . is truly hidden.[16]

If we fully embraced this idea and used it to reimagine our approach to missions, it could not help but change what we do. If we started with the idea that people are the real wealth, if we looked first at the inherent value of everybody we meet, I believe we would soon realize that we cannot engage globally without compassion and justice going hand in hand with our efforts to proclaim the gospel.

As an African, I call this a three-legged stool. According to my Kikuyu tribal tradition, a three-legged stool (known as *igũĩko*) symbolizes three main pillars of support: unity of the family; connection to the elders and ancestors; and economic self-reliance, which places major value on hard work. This three-legged stool suggests a holistic approach to life that balances spiritual, social, and economic aspects to create a flourishing community. As a Christian who also happens to be a Kikuyu, I use the image of the three-legged stool to showcase stability and balance.

We can only rightly expect God to honor and multiply our efforts in global missions when we combine a profound respect for the dignity and worth of every human being with a commitment to do our missions work with compassion and justice and with a passion to clearly declare the unchanging message of the gospel.

Don't we *all* want that?

2

THE GREAT COLLABORATION

When the Bible describes the followers of Jesus traveling throughout the world to preach the Good News and to be his hands and feet there, it typically uses "sending" and "the ones being sent." It does *not* refer to them as "ones on a mission."

In Galatians 2:8, for example, Paul uses the Greek word *apostolē*—which means "a sending away"—to describe the work of Peter. When the Bible was translated into Latin in the fourth century, the word chosen to translate *apostolē* was *apostolatus,* which means "the act of sending."

Where, then, did the idea of "missions" come from?

I suppose we don't know for sure, but one suggestion I've seen traces the concept to the mid-sixteenth century, when Ignatius of Loyola (a former soldier) and his Jesuit followers started going into some of the most difficult places in the world—wherever the pope saw fit to send them.[1] *Missio*, the Latin word for "sending," can be translated into English as "mission," which over the years picked up the connotation of "purposeful engagement" that undergirds the idea of being *sent* on a *mission*.

About a century after Ignatius, in the 1650s, a Lutheran nobleman named Baron Justinian von Welz gave up his privileged heritage to pursue missionary and social reform work. Some believe that Welz died in Suriname as a missionary. Many scholars believe he may have coined the term "the Great Commission," though it would be another two centuries before Hudson Taylor, the famed missionary to China, popularized the term.[2]

We rightly laud such heroes of faith, and yet in creating such a Jason Bourne type of missions identity, we may have robbed ourselves of the truth that *every* Jesus-following image bearer is invited into missions. *All* of us are "the sent ones."

In my view, the essence of Jesus' instruction in Matthew 28:18-20 is a great invitation to *collaboration*. What might happen if we started to think of his words as an *invitation* instead of a *commission*? An invitation is an honor. It's humbling. It's beautiful. An invitation says, "Choose this and you will receive a reward far out of proportion to whatever you do."

In this chapter, let's try to reimagine the purpose, potential, and power of what we've come to know as the Great Commission, but let's think of it in terms of the Great Collaboration.

The Purpose of the Great Collaboration

The New Testament tells us that Jesus, fully God as the second person of the Trinity, created all the intricacies and complexities of the universe.[3] He is the one who keeps the earth on its axis and holds everything together.[4] That's why he is able to say, "All authority in heaven and on earth has been given to me."[5] But have you ever stopped to think about what Jesus did with all his power and authority when he came to earth?

He set it aside. He laid it down.

> Have this mind among yourselves, which is yours in Christ Jesus, who, though he was in the form of God, did not count equality with God a thing to be grasped, but emptied himself, by taking the form of a servant, being born in the likeness of men. And being found in human form, he humbled himself by becoming obedient to the point of death, even death on a cross.[6]

What if we began to understand evangelism from that perspective? What if we learned how to lay down our power for the sake of the image of God in every human being, whether in declaring or displaying Jesus? What if we took as our starting point the attitude of Jesus—the one who held all power and knew all things and yet laid it all down in order to serve? What if we were to set aside the power, prestige, and authority that has accrued to us in the Western church and instead put on the mantle of humility for the benefit of those we want to help?

Too many people, I think, have gone into missions because they've told themselves, "If we don't, those people are going to hell." Think of how many missions appeals are based on the "human suffering index." We throw out numbers and say, "Here are all these people dying of hunger. We need to *go*. If we don't go, they'll die, both physically and spiritually."

But when we approach it this way, we make *ourselves* the heroes. We take our money and our power and our influence, and we head off to save the world. We may have all the best intentions—and the needs are certainly there—but our *posture* and our *mindset* need to change. Even though the gospel itself never changes, I've come to see that our strategies *must* change. When Jesus told us to "go into all the world and proclaim the gospel to the whole creation,"[7] he didn't give us specific instructions on *how* to do that. Why not? Because appropriate strategies will vary over time, adapting to changes in culture, technology, language, and a thousand other human-centered factors.

So, what *is* the role of the West in the emerging paradigm? How do we make the transition to a posture of humility when the way we've done missions up till now seems to work? How do we change our mindset to start fostering *cooperation*, *community*, and *reciprocal relationships* when our inclination is still to *initiate* and to go it alone into areas not yet reached?

Our new role is to learn how to participate in what God is *already* doing around the world. It isn't that we haven't been invited to the global party or that our participation isn't needed, but as Laurie Beshore has said, "We just have to realize that we aren't the ones planning the party or sending out the invitations. God is using the global church to influence other countries, including the United States. . . . He is also using the global church to teach us. This is about more than missions trips and evangelistic outreach. It's a humbling experience in which we learn to pray and worship, where we are discipled, and where we are even challenged in our culturally bound understanding of the gospel."[8]

From my perspective, it took tremendous humility for Kenton Beshore to say to Bishop Oscar, "Tell us more about this global party," and to say to Pastor M, "Please help us to understand more about what God is doing in your area," but Kenton seemed to understand that the more we engage with these tough conversations, the more we will grow. No pain, no gain, right?

I have yet to find a contemporary missions model that starts with, "We need to understand what God is *already* doing globally." Likewise, I had never seen a church that would be willing to take something from the Global South, bring it to the Global North, and actually use it as a missions tool, or as a tool for its own discipleship. But that's what set Kenton apart. Under his leadership, Mariners Church became interested in a powerful discipleship approach called Mizizi, which was pioneered at Mavuno Church. Having seen the fruit borne by this program, Kenton came home from Kenya saying, "America needs this."

What? I said to myself. *You need something from Africa?* I never thought I would hear such a thing from a successful American megachurch leader, but Kenton brought Mizizi to Mariners, a team adapted it for the American context, and that's how the discipleship program called Rooted came to be. Today, Rooted is being used successfully in some six thousand American churches. I was privileged to be a part of the adaptation process, which is what led me to start thinking more deeply about how we approach contemporary missions and how *every* person in the church is called to a missional Christian life.

A Yazidi Lesson

Years ago, with some Middle East partners, I visited an Iraqi village of the Yazidi people—one of the most persecuted groups in the world. About seventy genocides have been attempted against them.

We went to their village with a partner church from that region, as they were far more proximate than we were, coming from the US. We went to try to evangelize them.

"You guys don't have to worship everything," we told them. "There is one true God whom you can worship."

One of the Yazidi men told me, "The truth is that we worship whoever will leave us alone and give us the most peace, because we just want to farm our land."

Over the years, various factions have made multiple attempts to eliminate the Yazidis, deeming them demon worshipers for showing reverence to the devil. The Yazidis have tried to appease all sides, as they had no idea that God and Satan aren't opposite equals. They did not understand that God is above all, over all, and in all.

"What about the opportunity to develop your kids, your city, and your homes?" we asked.

"Why would we do that?" he replied.

"Well, so that you can advance, get an education, get good jobs."

"Why would we do that?" he said. He kept asking the "why" question.

Finally, after a few minutes of conversation, he held up his hand and said, "You know what we want to do? We want to farm our lands and be left with our kids, to enjoy them. You people do all those other things just so you can come back and enjoy your family. We just cut short the process. We go straight to the chase: We want to farm our lands and enjoy what they produce with our families. You feel driven to get an education, you have to develop this or that, you have to build buildings, you have to produce cars, you have to create roads, you have to do this, and this, and this. You do all of that just so you can return home and enjoy your family. Why would we not choose just to live simply and enjoy our families?"

That startling interaction taught me a lesson. My Yazidi friend had figured out a few things that I might need to consider. God used this image bearer in Iraq to challenge my Westernized thinking. He insisted that God had given him all the things he needed, and he was satisfied with that.

So, do the Yazidis have no need for God? Are they fine without Jesus? We know that no one without God is "fine." Augustine was right when he prayed, "You are great, O Lord, and greatly to be praised. . . . For you made us for yourself, and our hearts are restless until they rest in you."[9] No one can defeat the destructive power of the flesh on their own. The Yazidis need the grace and love and help and salvation of Jesus just as much as anyone.

But I needed to learn a lesson in humility. I needed to learn not to assume that I had all the answers; not to think that the Yazidi (or anyone) should listen to me simply because I was coming from the West—with plans, priorities, "time-tested wisdom," and bountiful resources. Laying down our authority means that we make *listening first* a priority.[10] We like to hit the ground running; but instead we must hit the ground *listening*. This means coming with a posture of humility, which is how Jesus entered the world. He came as an infant—weak, dependent, vulnerable. He didn't arrive with power and prestige. He didn't come with money, strength, or strategy. Instead, the ultimate power in the universe laid it all down.

The Great Collaboration calls us to lay down our power and authority for the benefit of those we wish to reach.

The Potential of the Great Collaboration

What could we accomplish together if we took seriously the potential of the Great Collaboration? A familiar story from Genesis 11 might give us an idea.

An ancient people once gathered to do something that God didn't want them to do—build a tower "with its top in the heavens,"[11] so they could all remain congregated in one place, rather than fanning out across the world as God intended. And God said, "If as one people speaking the same language they have begun to do this, then nothing they plan to do will be impossible for them."[12]

Because these people spoke a common language, their potential for collaboration was off the charts—even to do evil things. God therefore multiplied their languages so they could no longer understand each other. In effect, God was saying, "I created you to disperse throughout the world. I want the whole world to be filled with my glory. I want it to overflow with different cultures and languages and expressions of my image."

Though their unity showed the amazing things they could

accomplish by collaborating, their pride—wanting to make a name for themselves—caused them to leverage that unity for an evil purpose. God disrupted their ability to communicate, not because he disliked their unity, but because he didn't want their sin to corrupt their unity and allow it to be used for evil.

Thousands of years later, God reversed the curse of Genesis 11 when he sent his Holy Spirit upon the disciples, who were "all together in one place," and they "began to speak in other tongues as the Spirit gave them utterance."[13] Luke reports that "God-fearing Jews from every nation under heaven" were staying in Jerusalem.[14] It shocked these people to hear the disciples "telling in our own tongues the mighty works of God."[15]

These God-fearing Jews gathered in Jerusalem were a tremendously diverse bunch, but on that day they were united in the Spirit. As they dispersed once again into a world of many languages, the Holy Spirit gave them unity to speak boldly and clearly about the mighty works of God. On that day, the world saw unity in diversity. United by the Holy Spirit, the disciples reached out to non–Hebrew speaking men and women . . . and the church was born.

The irony of Babel was that the people were united in language and mission but missed the mark on *God's* mission and purpose for them. At Pentecost, the people were not united in language, but they came through with flying colors on their mission.

Acts 2 reminds us that God calls us to go into the world *collaboratively*. When Jesus commissions the disciples in Matthew 28:18-20, he is speaking to them as a group—that is, *you* in the plural. Folks in the South might say *y'all*. Therefore, we are not to go as lone rangers, but in cooperation with one another. Relationship is at the heart of our humanity. Because God is a relational God, and we are made for relationship, the collective "y'all go" makes sense. We go into all the world together as a united community.

When we look around today, however, too often we see a

lopsided collection of various missions groups, people running around "doing missions work" in their own way instead of pursuing it as a collaboration.

Do you see why we must rethink our understanding of the Great Commission? We must ask ourselves about its purpose and its authority. And we must ask why Jesus gave it to us in a plural context.

The group Missio Nexus says that "the Great Commission is too big for anyone to accomplish alone and too important not to try to do together."[16] I love that.

The Primacy of Unity

In order to work well together, first and foremost we must be united in purpose. That's why Jesus' prayer in the upper room—that *we* may be one, even as *he and the Father* are one—is so important.[17] *Being one* is a huge part of our gospel witness. That's why Paul could write to the Philippians, "Make my joy complete by being like-minded, having the same love, being one in spirit and of one mind."[18] Our unity can be the launchpad for fulfilling our collective mission.

While the idea of co-laboring is critically important, to co-labor effectively we must know each other, understand each other, and love each other. When people look at us, they should see our community as a city on a hill that cannot be hidden. The church is supposed to prompt observers to exclaim, "What a *beautiful* place!"

It saddens and frustrates me that we continue to deal with this issue today. The church is supposed to be united in displaying God's beauty to the world. We are meant to showcase God's love for everyone he created, the kind of love Jesus tells us about in John 3:16.

The Problem of Cultural Differences

Cultural differences can cause us to see things in different ways, which can divide us if we're not careful. For example, people in

Eastern cultures do not easily understand the idea of grace. "How can a powerful God tell someone who has messed up completely, 'You're free?'" They understand the *wrath* of God; that makes sense to them. But *grace* is a harder sell. It doesn't compute.

Westerners, by contrast, tend to see the wrath of God as incompatible with his love. But the Bible tells us that the *wrath* of God points us to the *love* of God. They are not mutually exclusive.

We all look at God, ourselves, and others through the lenses of our own culture. Thus we might observe the same phenomenon as someone from a different culture and yet perceive something very different. Our varied cultural lenses can become a hindrance to collaboration if we allow them to breed mistrust, division, and duplication—all of which diminish our ability to accomplish what God asks us to do.

Naturally, the enemy *wants* to see us isolated, divided, separated. If we are to co-labor and to engage together and thereby create the beautiful thing that God wants others to see—his image and glory on the earth—something must change.

To truly embrace the Great Collaboration, therefore, we must take time to understand the places we venture into and those with whom we go. We need to cultivate cultural sensitivity—developing a working knowledge and understanding of formal and informal cultures, direct and indirect cultures, levels of respect for authority, high territorial and low territorial perspectives, time-oriented and event-oriented cultures, cultures in which people work to live and others where people live to work. These are just a few of the things that divide us.

Whatever our culture holds as its primary *ethos* or *value system*, and whatever it does better than others—those are the matters that *really* divide us. We consider ourselves superior based on the things we do well. People living in task-oriented cultures feel good about themselves when they finish tasks, accomplish goals, increase their numbers—all very important things in those societies. People from relationship-oriented cultures feel good about themselves when they connect with others, share their joys, and celebrate together—when everyone is seen and honored. What divides us isn't necessarily our differences, but rather whatever we hold in high regard *over* others. Those things allow us to feel better about ourselves.

The Power of the Great Collaboration

I saw an excellent illustration of the power of collaboration in 2017, when Hurricane Harvey devastated the Houston area. When our church stepped in to do relief work there, we had two very different experiences. One took place on the east side of Houston, where the churches were not united. It seemed as if every church set out to do its own thing. They duplicated services and remained divided. We saw very little collaboration and very little effectiveness.

But in the small city of Katy, Texas, about thirty miles west of downtown Houston, we found something very different. The leaders of Katy had a unique thing going. The pastors there had been praying with each other for years. So when Harvey struck, they came together and said, "Okay, what if we divide our labor? Church A, you do food distribution. Church B, you hand out clothing." The entire city of Katy quickly became a functioning ecosystem where people knew that if they needed *x*, they went to *this* church; if they needed *y*, they went to *that* church. Instead of one church trying to do everything, each church focused on one thing, such that all the churches working in concert accomplished everything. Everyone grabbed their part of the rope, and they pulled together. It was beautiful to see.

The key, I believe, was that these churches had been praying together for a long time; their unity was based on their relationship.

Their collaboration didn't start with a common task; it started with communal prayer. It started with community.

Acts 1:8 says, "You [plural] will receive power . . . and you [plural] will be my witnesses in Jerusalem and in all Judea and Samaria, and to the ends of the earth." Notice that it's not one and done. Rather, it's a fourfold vision for reaching the world with the gospel. Another way to say it might be, "You will be my witnesses *wherever* y'all work, live, play, and go." Maybe your primary calling is to Jerusalem—your neighborhood, your workplace, your community. Maybe it's to Judea or Samaria—to the city, or the suburbs, or across the tracks, wherever people are unlike you and may not even *like* you. Or maybe it's to the ends of the earth—which for you might be Nairobi, Kenya; Bangkok, Thailand; São Paulo, Brazil; or Newport Beach, California (as it is for me). Nobody ever thinks of Orange County as the ends of the earth, because we think the ends of the earth are unreached people groups. But if you think about it, Orange County has some of the largest and richest people groups—people who believe they have no need for God. Just because they are physically healthy and wealthy doesn't mean they don't need a spiritual awakening.

When we go out into our Judeas, our Samarias, and to the ends of the earth, it's important to realize that those places are someone else's Jerusalem—and, as such, we should be prepared to work cooperatively with the leaders God has already placed there and who have been given the same Great Commission as we have. Likewise, because these indigenous leaders know their home environment and culture better than we ever could, our primary role should be as a catalyst for *their* God-given vision, priorities, and initiatives. I believe God intends for the Great Collaboration to start afresh and anew in every successive Jerusalem, and continue to spread into new Judeas, new Samarias, and further to the ends of the earth as these global Christians seek to fulfill their own purpose as designed and empowered by God. With that in mind, we must move from *starting* things to *catalyzing* what God is already doing. Our potential multiplies and blossoms as we work together, collaborating as equals, and on and on it goes in a series of new beginnings, greater expansions, and further reaches for the Kingdom of God.

Partnering together makes the extraordinary potential of the Great Collaboration real. It allows us to do much, *much* more than we could ever hope to accomplish on our own. We can do far more together than we can apart.

We in the West have a lot to learn from the global church, which makes such partnerships both critical and beautiful—especially now that two-thirds of the world's Christians live in the Global South.[19] What partnerships around the world are just waiting for you to join?

The Potency of God's Presence

The unlimited power of the Great Collaboration hinges on Jesus' promise of his personal presence. Though he laid down his power and authority at his incarnation, he took it up again at his resurrection. Though he was born in Bethlehem in weakness, he was raised at Calvary in power.[20] All power is his, and that power is available to us through his eternal presence with us through his Spirit.

If we were to gauge God's eternal presence by looking at many of our global missions efforts, it might seem as if God has left the building. How else are we to understand the strife, fatigue, and giving up that seem to beset our initiatives? Too often when we lose our sense of God's immediate presence, instead of repenting and seeking his guidance and wisdom, we simply start creating more things in our own strength.

"Draw near to God," James wrote to his fellow Christians, "and he will draw near to you."[21] Let's remember that when the potency fades away, it's not because God has departed. Rather, we have chosen to press ahead under our own power. We have taken a high view of ourselves and have lost our dependence on the Holy Spirit. If we see that God is no longer with us in our work, we must recognize that it's because we have said *no* in some way to his guidance.

While the power for the Great Collaboration truly hinges on the promise of God's presence, it also depends on our cooperation and obedience. Apart from God, we can do *nothing*.[22] But it's equally true that God works through *us*. We are his chosen instrument, the body of Christ on earth. While we desperately need the promise of his presence, he wants us involved as willing participants. He refuses to coerce us. For God to use us, we must say *yes*.

No Better Partner

Jesus tells us in Matthew 24:14 that once the gospel has been preached throughout the entire world to all nations, the end will come. In other words, after we in the church have fully engaged the Great Collaboration with its purpose, potential, and power, then the history of this fallen planet as we know it will come to a close.

This calls for us to think more deeply about the Great Collaboration, especially in regard to the distinct ethnic groups that populate our world. Every one of them—regardless of physical characteristics, languages, or customs—is God's image bearer. Our witness—and theirs—will be effective only as we joyfully partner together in the Great Collaboration that Jesus invited us into so long ago.

But let's be honest. If we move the needle with collaborative thinking, we must also recognize that things will move more slowly than we might like or than we're used to. It takes *time* to get to know people deeply. We may not have a great or a quick return on our investment. Unless we educate our people about the need to recalibrate, our efforts may not be well supported or well funded, because our key performance indicators and immediate return on investment will be hard to promote. We must be prepared to invest the necessary time, energy, and resources to build a solid relational foundation before our collaborative partnerships will begin to bear fruit.

Mariners Church connected with Gaba Community Church in Uganda in 2006, and I made my first trip there in 2008 with a team from Mariners. As the two churches developed a great relationship of mutuality and reciprocity, we made much progress together. Gaba Church and its affiliate, Africa Renewal Ministries, have a vision to be Christlike transformers of society, which they accomplish by embracing children, equipping leaders, and empowering communities. When I saw this work firsthand, I was in awe of how they served their community.

Paul Neff, one of the other members from Mariners on our trip, said to Gaba's leader, Pastor Peter Kasirivu, "It seems like you have done so much for the community. Is there anything you've wanted to do that you've never done?"

With his big smile and tender heart, Pastor Peter replied, "I have always wanted us to rescue abandoned babies and connect them to families who can raise them in a Christlike manner."

The pastor's statement hit Paul at a very visceral level, and none of us could have predicted what happened as a result.

As a baby, Paul had been adopted into a great Christian family, who brought him up "in the discipline and instruction of the Lord."[23] Paul went on to marry and raise his own incredible family, and God blessed him as a businessman as well. Paul and his wife, Kathy, started a private nonprofit organization called the Servant's Heart Foundation, in Newport Beach, California, that partners with missions groups to provide medical, dental, and surgical services to people in need.

Even though Paul and Kathy had been serving across the globe, when Pastor Peter told them about his desire to connect abandoned babies with loving families, the mission became intensely personal. Along with Pastor Peter, Gaba Church, and Africa Renewal Ministries, they started the Loving Hearts Babies Home, which to date has rescued and adopted out or reintegrated more than five hundred abandoned children. This ministry has also become near and dear to the hearts of Mariners members through Paul and Kathy's catalytic involvement in Pastor Peter's dream.

Co-laboring is both poignant and strategic. Without Pastor Peter, Paul might never have engaged with the ministry that has become a huge part of his life. Without Paul, Pastor Peter might still be dreaming of creating a children's home. But the two of them, working together, created a formidable initiative to advance the Kingdom of God by enabling his image bearers to flourish. Their partnership has fostered a connection to purpose for countless people around the globe.

I think of caretakers such as Miriam, who runs the home. When you meet her, you see her living out her purpose. The same can be said for the adopting families, the reintegrated families, and the corporate leaders in Uganda who get involved. The deep connection between two individuals has affected hundreds of God's image bearers, who together create a countercultural community.

Since the forging of this global ministry partnership, the members of the Neff family have become close friends of mine, even to the point of hosting my wedding rehearsal dinner (since I had no immediate family members in the US). They have embraced my family as well, and to this day we enjoy a rich relationship. The tentacles of collaboration reach far beyond the original individuals involved. To say it has created a ripple effect would be a vast understatement.

3

JUSTICE AND COMPASSION

Have you ever pondered how we are to live as Christ followers? Have you ever asked yourself, "Now that I'm a Christian, what am I supposed to do?"

If you're at all like me, you don't want to waste your life. You don't want to reach the end of your days only to discover that you missed the key thing. And because God doesn't want us guessing on such a fundamental issue, he explicitly answers the question in Micah 6:8:

> He has shown you, O mortal, what is good.
> And what does the Lord require of you?
> To act justly and to love mercy
> and to walk humbly with your God.[1]

Could the Lord be any clearer than that? He declares that he wants his followers to actively pursue three big priorities:

- act justly (pursue justice)
- love mercy (show compassion)
- walk in humility (be humble)

The Meaning of Justice

In the Bible, "acting justly" has two sides. The first is stopping wrongdoers by ensuring equal treatment under the law. The second is giving every image bearer their due by providing explicit special treatment for the poor. In his book *Generous Justice*, the late Tim Keller grapples with both sides. On the one hand, we must end the wrongdoing; but we must also render to people what is justly theirs. Biblical justice is holistic.

1. Equal treatment under the law for all

Leviticus 24:22 says, "You are to have the same law for the foreigner and the native-born. I am the LORD your God."[2] The word *foreigner* refers to a person of another race, another culture, or even another religion. In a society where family, race, tribe, and tradition were everything, it is both fascinating and strange for God to call his people to racial and social equality.

Why would he insist on such a thing?

I believe it goes back to the doctrine of Imago Dei. Everyone we meet, without exception, is created in the image of God. The foreigners among us are our brothers and sisters, made in God's image every bit as much as we are. So, God says, "Don't treat them differently."

God repeatedly challenged his people about how they dealt with individuals of various races and cultures. He forbade partiality and preferential treatment regarding legal, wage, and business practices,[3] which is why Peter declared that God plays no favorites.[4] Amos 8:5-6 attacks unjust scales—the practice of weighing out different quantities to different customers but charging the same price. God hates that. Malachi 3:5 and Jeremiah 22:13 address unfair wages, and Proverbs 11:26 criticizes those who drive up prices by hoarding resources. While some unfair practices may be legal in a society, God condemns them. We must do what is good for *all* of the community. Biblical justice means equal treatment under the law.

2. Explicit special treatment for the poor

This second aspect is even more challenging than the first. God calls his people to intentionally care for the poor.[5] We are to consider, think about, meditate on, and strategize how to lift them up.

Most Americans understand and agree with the idea of equal protection under the law, but they may balk at the call for explicit *special* treatment for the poor. But consider just a few Scripture passages on the topic.

Proverbs 31:8-9 declares, "Speak up for those who cannot speak for themselves, for the rights of all who are destitute. Speak up and judge fairly; defend the rights of the poor and needy."[6]

The rich typically don't need anyone to speak up for them, because people with means can hire the best lawyers. But those who lack means need others to speak up on their behalf; if we don't, we're not treating everyone fairly. We are to show special concern for the oppressed and the poor.

This is not merely charity, but also advocacy. Charity is something we do on *our* time, on *our* terms, and at *our* convenience. Advocacy is deeper and more engaged, as we stand on behalf of others who cannot speak for themselves.

Mishpat, a Hebrew word often translated as "justice," appears more than four hundred times in the Old Testament. At times it's translated as "righteousness" or "the upholding of a cause." According to philosopher and theologian Nicholas Wolterstorff, the word is often followed by references to "the quartet of the vulnerable low ones"—"widows, orphans, resident aliens, and the poor."[7]

The prophet Zechariah declares, "This is what the LORD Almighty said: 'Administer true justice [*mishpat*]; show mercy and compassion to one another. Do not oppress the widow or the fatherless, the foreigner or the poor. Do not plot evil against each other.'"[8] Did you notice the quartet of the vulnerable low ones?

Isaiah 58:6-8 is one of the most potent passages on justice. It gives us a list of how to treat the most vulnerable among us:

> Is not this the kind of fasting I have chosen:
> to loose the chains of injustice
>   and untie the cords of the yoke,
> to set the oppressed free
>   and break every yoke?
> Is it not to share your food with the hungry
>   and to provide the poor wanderer with shelter—
> when you see the naked, to clothe them,
>   and not to turn away from your own flesh and blood?
> Then your light will break forth like the dawn,
>   and your healing will quickly appear;
> then your righteousness will go before you,
>   and the glory of the LORD will be your rear guard.[9]

Isaiah 58 is startling because it addresses a very religious, ethical group. The Jews at that time fasted, tithed, humbled themselves, and were passionate about worshiping God. They faithfully observed many religious activities, and yet God tells Isaiah to "declare to my people their *rebellion*."[10] The kind of fasting that God desires is that which breaks the chains of injustice, sets the oppressed free, feeds the hungry, shelters the homeless, clothes the naked, and refuses to turn away from others who are created in the image of God.

What would it take for you to believe that the poor person with a Kenyan accent, the Ugandan friend, the boisterous Nigerian on the subway, your Indian doctor, a German engineer, a Mexican banker, are "your own flesh and blood," your cousins?

God declares that religious practices don't impress him nearly as much as caring for the less fortunate and destitute. He says, "If you pour yourself out for the hungry and satisfy the desire of the afflicted, then shall your light rise in the darkness and your gloom be as the noonday. And the LORD will guide you continually . . . and you shall be like a watered garden, like a spring of water, whose waters do not fail."[11]

It is a sin to treat our wealth as our own and not share it with the needy. If we say to God, "I earned it," he will reply, "No, I gave it to you."

Think about it: Did you choose the century into which you were born or the place where you came into the world? Did you pick your family, your life circumstances, your temperament, your intelligence, or the economic status of your parents? The majority of the inequitable distribution of wealth we see around the world exists from birth. For that reason, God calls us to give special treatment and show explicit concern for the poor—especially for the quartet of the vulnerable low ones, because they, too, reflect the face of God.

God told his people long ago, and he continues to tell us today, "You say you know me—but if you don't care about the poor, your relationship with me doesn't amount to much."[12] Does that stagger you as much as it does me?

The Parameters of Justice

According to the Bible, justice has a wide and extensive reach. Biblical justice includes three main stages—*relief*, *reinforcement*, and *reform*—each building on the one that comes before.

Relief means that when we see people who are hungry, thirsty, and naked, we work to meet their immediate needs. Christians are called to relief work; that's what we do in disaster response. But that's not enough. We must also move to the next stage.

Reinforcement entails coming alongside disadvantaged people to support their development and self-sustenance. We work to strengthen them and help them begin to stand on their own two feet. This reminds me of the story in Exodus when the Israelites fought the Amalekites, and Moses needed Aaron and Hur to hold up his hands to preserve the victory.[13] The two supported their partner, reinforcing his work. When Moses grew tired, Aaron and Hur together helped to hold up his hands. That's an image of reinforcement. We come alongside to hold up another person's hands. But as good as that is, it too is not enough. Scripture pushes us relentlessly to move to the final stage.

Reform means helping the poor so that they no longer need us. It means working to change unjust social structures that keep them poor and disadvantaged. As the old story goes, it is a good and noble thing to rescue people who have fallen into a rushing river; but at some point it might be wise to go upstream and find out who is throwing them into the river in the first place. That's when we start to create reform—dealing with root causes and restoring people's ability to flourish. Job spoke of this stage in defending himself against the false accusations of his friends when he said, "I was a father to the needy, and I searched out the cause of him whom I did not know. I broke the fangs of the unrighteous and made him drop his prey from his teeth."[14]

Biblical justice calls for us to engage holistically—which combines relief, reinforcement, and reform. We work with people to alleviate their critical needs, address their continuing needs, and help them solve their chronic needs. That's the progression and the ultimate goal.

When our singing group, Milele, first engaged with Mariners Church, I started following up with the church's global missions teams, asking, "What are you doing in Africa?"

When they told me, I would say, "Man, that doesn't seem right."

"Why not?"

"It feels like you're addressing a lot of our symptoms but not addressing any of our systemic issues."

The problem with a lot of social justice work is that too often we address only the symptoms. If we go to Africa and ask, "What's the problem here?" perhaps the first thing we'll see is abject poverty, lack of income, lack of education, lack of clothing, lack of health care. But what we don't see is what lies underneath, so the systemic issues go unaddressed.

When a Western missions agency shows up with people and other resources, few on the receiving end are going to encourage them to ask the right questions. And even the most well-intentioned Westerners won't stop long enough to say, "Wait a minute, Africa is the richest continent, in terms of natural resources. Why don't they have the income to match?"

This all-important question underscores the need for reform.

If you're at all familiar with the history of Africa, you know that the vestiges of colonialism are a big part of the problem. In 1884–1885, major European countries met in Berlin to parcel out pieces of Africa to each attending nation.[15] Then they came to the Africans and said, "You people are primitive. You need to be led." In effect, this meant, "Let's go conquer these guys so we can lead them." And that's what they did. As demeaning as it sounds, they were telling us, "This is who you are, and this is what you need."

In my opinion, the legacy of colonialism is still one of the greatest challenges in engaging with Africa. And if colonialism is the problem, then the solution cannot have a colonial face. We cannot solve a problem with the same mindset that created it. That's why we in Milele said, "Africa will never be changed from the outside in. It will only be changed from the inside out." The indigenous people must be the problem solvers.

Up until now, it seems the Western church has focused primarily on *relief* and *reinforcement*—albeit as outsiders coming in to try to help—because *reform* is beyond our reach as outsiders. But if change can only come from the inside out, what is the role of the Western church and Western nations in moving on to *reform* (in Africa and other places in the world where colonialism is part of their history)?

First, we must come to listen and learn, like Jesus did. He came quietly and humbly.

Second, we must notice the indigenous change agents who are *already* working to change their context from the inside out.

Third, we must engage with them—both to *learn* from them and to see what solutions they have already come up with—and we must find ways to *catalyze* their efforts, to speed up and enhance their results.

We must be careful not to ride in bringing our solutions from the West. In other words, don't give the indigenous leaders Saul's armor; it's too heavy. Instead, let them use the five smooth stones that fit their context.

Lastly, God has gifted the Western church with resources and capabilities that can be leveraged by indigenous leaders to create long-term reform.

It all begins with giving of ourselves by *living* among the people, *being* among the people, *understanding* the people, *seeing* them not as a project but as individuals who innately reflect the dignity, character, and nature of God. This means we must give them our biggest gift, which is our *presence*. This doesn't mean that Westerners who want to make a difference must move onto the mission field permanently. But we must start by establishing connections and building relationships, not simply by bringing our resources. We must lead with our presence, not our presents. That's what every human being needs. If we really want to care for people, we must give them ourselves.

Before Delta and I got married, my father told my soon-to-be father-in-law, "We're going to give you the best gift anyone has ever given. We're going to give you *ourselves*—our presence. We are yours. You are ours."

Do we seek after God because we will get the things that God can give us? Or do we seek after God because we get God? Presence is everything. That's why Jesus came the way he did in the Incarnation. He gave us his presence.

Other systemic problems endemic to Africa include issues of succession and certain tribal beliefs—things that can only be solved from the inside, not from the outside. It is vitally important for the Western church to understand this reality so we can rethink and reimagine how to engage.

We must also understand that tackling systemic problems is much harder, and will take much longer, than merely treating *symptoms*. It might take a generation or more to bring true and lasting change.

The poverty of Africa is not merely the poverty of money, food, and shelter. It is also the poverty of choice, political inclusion, safety, dignity, visibility, belonging, and being valued. Reform, the third stage in biblical justice, bears all of this in mind.

Our Motivation for Justice

From a biblical perspective, justice and compassion go hand in hand. Some people are completely justice-driven, while others are motivated by compassion; but Scripture insists on both. They're inextricable. Mercy and compassion are what motivate us to pursue justice—they are the *why* behind our actions.

Ultimately, we identify with the poor in compassion and mercy because God himself identifies with the poor:

> He is the Maker of heaven and earth,
> the sea, and everything in them—
> he remains faithful forever.
> He upholds the cause of the oppressed
> and gives food to the hungry.
> The LORD sets prisoners free,
> the LORD gives sight to the blind,
> the LORD lifts up those who are bowed down,
> the LORD loves the righteous.
> The LORD watches over the foreigner
> and sustains the fatherless and the widow,
> but he frustrates the ways of the wicked.[16]

> For the LORD your God is God of gods and Lord of lords, the great God, mighty and awesome, who shows no partiality and accepts no bribes. He defends the cause of the fatherless and the widow, and loves the foreigner residing among you, giving them food and clothing. And you are to love those who are foreigners, for you yourselves were foreigners in Egypt.[17]

God not only identifies with the poor, but Jesus became poor so that we who are spiritually poor may gain eternal riches.[18]

The cross is beautiful because there God became a victim of injustice on our behalf. He who deserved vindication was condemned so that we who deserved condemnation could be vindicated. God became poor and oppressed so we could be rich toward him. In his compassion and mercy, Jesus fulfilled justice on the cross.

At the beginning of his earthly ministry, Jesus chose to introduce himself to his hometown residents by quoting from Isaiah 61:1-2 in the Nazareth synagogue.

> The Spirit of the Lord is on me,
> because he has anointed me
> to proclaim good news to the poor.
> He has sent me to proclaim freedom for the prisoners
> and recovery of sight for the blind,
> to set the oppressed free,
> to proclaim the year of the Lord's favor.[19]

Luke tells us that Jesus then rolled up the scroll, handed it back to the attendant, and sat down (the typical position of someone about to teach). As everyone looked at him, he said, "Today this Scripture has been fulfilled in your hearing."[20]

God is serious in his desire that we become like his Son. He insists that Christ be formed in us.[21] He is transforming us so that we increasingly reflect his image.[22] He also instructs us to "put on" that image, to consciously choose to act in ways that reflect Christ's merciful and compassionate nature.[23] He has determined that we should eternally bear the image of his Son,[24] and even now his Spirit is continually working in our lives so that "we all . . . are being transformed" into the image of Jesus.[25]

One of the more obvious proofs of this process is in how we relate to others. In the Gospels, we often see Jesus acting out of compassion to meet the needs of people in distress. Matthew 9:36

gives us a potent description: "When he [Jesus] saw the crowds, he had compassion for them, because they were harassed and helpless, like sheep without a shepherd." Out of compassion, Jesus healed the sick.[26] Out of compassion, he fed the hungry.[27] Out of compassion, he raised a widow's son from the dead.[28] In response to a question about who qualifies as a neighbor, Jesus told the famous parable of the Good Samaritan, a foreigner who deserved the name "good" because he showed compassion to an injured man and took care of the man's needs even after the victim's countrymen had pointedly ignored him.[29]

Mercy and compassion are to become a way of life for us as followers of Jesus. Thus, the apostle Paul tells us to "put on . . . as God's chosen ones, holy and beloved, compassionate hearts, kindness, humility, meekness, and patience."[30]

When we see all human beings as individuals made in God's image, we will feel compassion for them and show them mercy. We don't just "do projects" with them; instead, we have a relationship. We visit them and spend time with them. We communicate with them. We become family with them. We are moved by grace, the unmerited, unearned, and undeserved gift of God. Our continual awareness of the common image we all bear allows us to engage in justice issues with a deep humility, fueled by a profound compassion for those we serve.

Pursuing Justice with Compassion

A good example of pursuing justice with compassion occurred in Haiti after the horrific earthquake of 2010. A group from Mariners Church traveled to Haiti, looking for partners we might work with who were already serving there. We soon found the Church of God by Faith, led by Pastor Joseph and his son, Pastor Sam. We came alongside to help with relief work, even assisting them as they looked for victims trapped in the rubble. At first, our team slept on the ground with the victims. Then we got them food and shelter.

For two years after the earthquake, all we did was relief work. We helped affected Haitians get shelter, clothing, and food. We worked to meet the immediate needs.

Then we asked Pastor Sam, "What's next?"

"Well," he replied, "we have fifty-five orphans we need to take care of. We've tried to place them in families, but no one has been able to take them. So we would like to go to the south coast of Haiti, which is beautiful, and buy a piece of land there where we can build six homes. It's pristine land with not much congestion. There's no crime. Then we can find some house moms to step in." House moms are women who have raised their own families and have sent their kids off into the world.

Again we partnered with them to help see their dream come true. But instead of doing traditional one-on-one child sponsorship, Mariners adopted the entire village.

I have to admit I'm not a fan of one-on-one sponsorships; in fact, I no longer recommend them. Though it's often a good marketing tool, I believe it works against the idea of seeing the image of God in everyone. I understand that people want to believe they are caring for a particular individual, but you can never really "own" someone or say, "This is *my* sponsored child." The problem is that when we focus on a specific child, it's easy not to care quite as much about the others.

My prescription for child sponsorship is no longer one-on-one, but village-to-village. Because we believe in the inherent value and dignity of every human being, we sponsor an entire group, as many as we can. Such an approach is not as easy to market, but it meets a broader need.

When we sponsor a group of children, I might say to interested individuals, "You're going to be part of a family, a village. Your church village is going to sponsor a village in Uganda [or Haiti or wherever]." Those who get involved may not give equally, but they give whatever they can according to their means. To sponsor a group of kids, however, costs a lot more than thirty dollars a month. If we're sponsoring a hundred kids, we don't need a hundred sponsors; more likely we need three or four hundred. Maybe someone can give fifty dollars, while somebody else can give a hundred, and someone else a thousand.

When you figure out the real costs of comprehensive care for one child for a month, the actual cost is somewhere between $150 and $200 a month. Hardly anyone does that individually. It takes *many* of us to take care of *one* of us.

When Mariners supported the village in Haiti, it cost $6,800 a month. Somebody in the church gave $1,800 each month; my young daughter gave $5. But we *all* gave to provide the necessary care for those fifty-five kids.

When we sponsored the village, we moved from *relief* to *reinforcement.* But what about *reform*? We started thinking about how we could help this community care for itself.

"What would it take for you to raise this money in-country?" we asked Pastor Sam.

"Well," he replied, "if we built a school, the school would not only educate the kids, but it could pay for their care. Education is so important in Haiti that people will pay whatever they can to get their kids a good education."

If they built and ran a school, Pastor Sam explained, they could get some paying clients. And once those paying clients came in, a portion of their school payments could be used to support the orphans.

"A school would raise enough money to not only take care of the orphans," Pastor Sam said, "but also to support the twenty-four church plants we have. But that would be a *really* big endeavor.

It would mean building a school for a thousand students, which would cost $1.8 million. But it would help to educate an entire region of the country, enabling students to dream of a new Haiti and to become change agents."

We thought about it, prayed about it, and decided to move ahead. A couple from Mariners who work as business design thinkers relocated their family to southern Haiti for six or seven weeks, spending their time doing research and writing a business plan with Pastor Sam's help. They visited other schools, did comps, researched the situation, and crunched the numbers to figure out, "Is this viable?"

The formidable business plan they developed was ultimately accepted, Mariners funded it, and the school got built. Pastor Sam and his people completed the facility in 2022. Mariners gave its final $6,800 stipend to the orphans project in 2023, and now all the money needed for both the orphans and the school comes from within Haiti itself.

By faith, Pastor Sam and the Church of God by Faith are where they are today. They don't need Mariners Church to support their work. Financially, they can take care of their own needs. They have a valuable and expensive asset. They have real estate, an excellent school a half mile from the beach. From the second-floor classrooms, you can look out over the blue Caribbean waters.

A few points I want to emphasize before we move on: Our involvement began as relief work in the aftermath of the 2010 earthquake. During the two years of humanitarian aid work we did there, we were also building a relationship with a local partner, the Church of God by Faith, with Pastor Joseph and Pastor Sam. When the time came to transition from relief to reinforcement, it was Pastor Sam who guided us toward caring for the fifty-five orphans, and in partnership with the local church, we figured out the most effective way for us to help meet the need. We had available resources, but the vision and the plan were agreed upon in collaboration with Pastor Sam. And again, when the time came to move from reinforcement to reform, it was Pastor Sam's big, bold vision for a self-sustaining school that took center stage. Mariners served as a catalyst to help bring that vision to fruition, but the plan from start to finish was to develop a work that was completely owned, operated, and sustained by the local church in Haiti.

Pursuing justice with compassion means not only stopping the wrong or the wrongdoer, but also giving people their due as God's image bearers. The holistic nature of justice and compassion requires a triad approach of relief, reinforcement, and reform. This template provides a new way to think about justice and compassion.

Jesus did not come just to stand *by* us. Nor did he come just to stand *with* us. Instead, he came and *stood in* for us, so that we never have to wonder where we stand with him. We respond not with charity but with passionate, radical, extravagant generosity, worship, and service, all wrapped up in a humble spirit.

The fact is, we need the quartet of the vulnerable low ones as much as they need us. When we engage with those who live on the margins of society, we learn about faith, resilience, tenacity, dependence, and joy in the face of difficult circumstances. I love the saying, "You never know that God is all you need until you realize that God is all you have." For that very reason, the apostle Peter tells us: "Clothe yourselves, all of you, with humility toward one another, for 'God opposes the proud but gives grace to the humble.'"[31]

Putting Justice into Practice

Acts 6 tells the story of a dispute between Hebraic Jews and Hellenistic Jews over the treatment of widows in the Jerusalem church. The apostles' solution was staggering: They chose seven Hellenistic Jews, who knew firsthand the widows' struggles, to lead the daily distribution of food. This was a cultural and racial issue that was dealt with in a very countercultural way. The most vulnerable were of utmost importance to the apostles, and the way the church dealt with them was so remarkable that "a great many of the [Jewish] priests became obedient to the faith."[32]

The work of justice is just as vital and important as the preaching of the gospel. And the motivation for justice is *mercy*, which is at the very heart of the gospel.

I have had the privilege of working with three remarkable women on my Outreach team: Nicole Muriu, Hailey Good-Man, and Natalie McLaughlin. These young leaders are passionate about the most vulnerable as they lead our church in various capacities. But how they live their lives is very compelling to me as well. They don't just talk the talk; they walk the walk in the very arduous job of reformation among the most vulnerable.

Nicole and her husband went on a grueling journey through the foster care system to adopt their son Levi. Hailey and C. J. Good-Man adopted two teenage brothers—the first teenagers to be fully adopted in Orange County in the past twenty years. Natalie and Colin McLaughlin have adopted three kids in less than three years—a story that only they themselves can recount properly due to its complexity. These families adopted *reform* as not just a good idea but as part of their identity, and they have all paid a price to embrace justice and compassion.

Kay Warren, cofounder of Saddleback Church in Lake Forest, California, once quipped that if one family out of every four churches in America were to adopt one child, the foster care system would no longer need to exist.[33] How about that as a call to action and real reform within the realm of justice and compassion?

PART TWO

PHILOSOPHY

What are the implications of a people-centered Christian mission? Let's explore three major trends that strongly urge us to reimagine how we approach global missions. The success of past Christian missions has paved the way for new strategies that call for deep partnerships with visionary indigenous leaders. We must grapple with important philosophical questions if we are to effectively pursue Christian missions that are truly people-centered, whether in our daily lives, in our local communities, or throughout the world.

4

POLYCENTRIC MISSIONS

The spectacular success of Christian missions over the past two centuries has established followers of Jesus in every part of the globe. The number of unreached or unengaged people groups—those who have yet to hear about Jesus or who have little opportunity to follow him—has drastically declined. In fact, the 10/40 Window, which used to be a major focus of Christian missions, has not only dwindled but has in many ways been dismantled by mass migration. Missions is no longer "from the West to the rest." It is now *from everyone to everywhere.*

The term *polycentric missions* captures this new reality.

The Maps Have Shifted

At the turn of the twentieth century, 82 percent of all Christians lived in the Northern Hemisphere. By 2010, the balance had nearly flipped. Today, almost 70 percent of Christians worldwide live in the Global South (or as I prefer to call it, the two-thirds majority world).[1] According to Philip Jenkins, author of *The Next Christendom*,

> Over the last century . . . the center of gravity in the Christian world has shifted inexorably away from Europe, southward, to Africa and Latin America, and eastward, toward Asia. Today, the largest Christian communities on the planet are to be found in those regions. If we want to visualize a "typical" contemporary Christian, we should think of a woman living in a village in Nigeria, or in a Brazilian *favela*. In parts of Asia too, churches are growing rapidly, in numbers and self-confidence. . . . Whatever Europeans or North Americans may believe, Christianity is doing very well indeed in the global South—not just surviving but expanding.[2]

Consider this: In 1900, Africa had about 10 million Christians; by 2010, that number was close to 500 million, and it is projected to be more than *one billion* by 2050.[3] The maps have shifted, and I see this as a great thing to celebrate. It means that Christian missionaries over the past two centuries have done excellent work. Their outreach efforts have enjoyed outstanding success. But clearly the world has changed, global Christianity has advanced tremendously, and our missions models must also change to adapt to the new reality—which many in the West have been slow to do. To continue to be effective in our outreach efforts, we must be prepared to change our mindset from one of *sending* missionaries to reach an unreached world to instead *coming alongside and empowering indigenous leaders*—the very fruit of our successful efforts in the past. The wisdom, resources, and experience of the

West are still needed—perhaps more than ever—in the burgeoning two-thirds majority world, but the role of the West has definitely changed.

Updating Our Strategies

In light of the new generation of Christians around the world who want to come alongside to work with us—not as inferiors or subordinates, but as equals and leaders in their own right—we must rethink our sending models and what it means to collaborate and form partnerships. We must contextualize our theology and think deeply about the reciprocal nature of missions. We must strive for mutuality and collective decision-making and increase our cross-cultural competency.

Part of this new approach involves understanding—and adapting to—differences in how Westerners typically communicate compared to how people in the rest of the world communicate. I believe that much of what I'm about to say is true of other majority-world cultures as well, but I will couch my observations in terms of my own experience as an African, and more specifically as a Kenyan who has lived most of his adult life in the United States.

Start with Relationships

Though I could write several chapters on the consequences of the shift to global Christianity, I will focus instead on what I consider to be the crux of successful Christian missions in today's world—namely, a relational or people-centered approach.

Viktor Frankl, in his book *Man's Search for Meaning*, introduced the idea that the primary driver for human beings is not *pleasure* (as Sigmund Freud suggested) or *power* (as Alfred Adler proposed) but the pursuit and practice of *meaning*. Meaning, Frankl said, is found chiefly through relationships, suffering, and practical life experiences.[4] Therefore, the church must orient itself toward *relationship* and *love* by satisfying the primary longings that every person has, regardless of culture: to be *fully known and fully loved*; to *belong*; and to be *valued*. And as we've said before, that value is rooted in our understanding that every person is created equally in the image of God.

During a visit to Egypt years ago, I learned that our church partners there never engage with people in their culture by starting with the head—that is, with facts and reason. Instead, they first extend a hand. They touch people in practical ways, which then moves the heart and eventually engages the head. From my observation, Westerners tend to think from *head* to *heart* to *hand*.

The church in Egypt taught me a different perspective: First draw near to people—even those with whom we don't see eye to eye—and once they realize that we have more commonalities than differences, their hearts will engage and eventually their minds may change.

People in the two-thirds majority world tend to be more relational and community-oriented than people in the West, where individualism and personal achievement are more highly valued. It's not that relationships aren't important in the West, but often they are transactional and take second place to "getting the job done." Westerners are task oriented, and spending the kind of extended time it takes to get to know people in a different culture can feel like something with very little return on investment. When we come home, we want to be able to report the goals we've met and what we've accomplished. When someone comes back from the mission field, we want to hear them say, "We have seen one hundred conversions in the last half year. We also baptized twelve people just last month." We do *not* want them to talk in terms of the relationships they are developing.

It's a fact of life in the West that showing *tangible results* is often what loosens the purse strings in the sending churches. So how do we change the mindset from "getting things done" to "getting to know people as image bearers," apart from some other practical reason for being there in the first place? We need to start seeing that establishing reciprocal relationships with indigenous leaders who are already cultural insiders and already at work fulfilling their God-given purpose *is* the mission, *is* the investment that—if we take the longer view—will produce profound results.

There's nothing wrong with tangible results, but people in the Global South first want to be known, to be valued, to belong. When you're working in the majority world, the people there first want to *know you.*

In the West, what you *do* tells me who you are; but for those in the Global South, your *family* and the *area that you come from* define who you are.

When we meet somebody in America, we usually ask, "What's your name? What do you do?"

In Kenya, when you meet somebody, you say, "Where are you from? Who's your family?" We want to know *location* and *connection.* If you tell me where you're from and who your family is, then I can know who you are. You don't have to say anything else.

If I say my name is Mungai, for example, and that I'm from the Kikuyu tribe, another Kenyan will ask, "What part? Where?"

When I reply, "Muranga," they will ask, "Who's your family?"

When I say, "Kiarie," they'll ask, "Like the senior chief or the missionary or the cook?"

"Yes."

"Yes, we know your people," they will say.

That's how we introduce each other in Kenya.

Africans also *disciple* by relationships more than through programs. In Kenya, discipleship happens through life experiences and facilitated conversations, not merely through classes and structured teaching.

What I'm saying is, let's not look at people as a project. Let's look at them first and foremost as precious souls created in the image of God. We can become so caught up in our global mission, in the Great Commission—which often feels like a task—that we lose sight of the humanity of the people we're trying to serve. We say, "Let's help people because they're hurting." But I'm saying, "Let's not start with compassion and justice. Let's go further back. Let's start with the idea of the image of God in every person."

If we start with the image of God, we're starting with an image of *community*, and acknowledging that God is seeking to restore the original state of *shalom* that existed in the Garden of Eden, a state of wholeness, peace, and unity. The image of God is unity in community—which existed from the beginning, before everything else was formed. What if what we are being asked to do is to build relationships and restore the essence of community and connectedness in the world? Then, in that connectedness, we realize that it's not okay for our brothers and sisters to go hungry, it's not okay for our brothers and sisters to go without hearing the gospel. But relationship and community are at the heart of it all.

From an African perspective, the image of God is embedded in our culture. People are the wealth, and relationships are the key to unleashing that wealth.

Understand Circular Communication

Part and parcel with the Western approach of task and achievement is the high value placed on direct communication. I'm not being critical here; it's simply an observation of styles. People from the West say, "We're here for a mission. We're here to do *x*, *y*, and *z*. Let's get started." But people from the Global South value indirect communication, and they tend to talk in circles.

Westerners want to take you on a point-by-point journey. "I'm going to tell you three things, and here they are: point 1, point 2, point 3." Again, not a problem. Linear thinking can be very, very good. It just doesn't always match up well with how people in other parts of the world communicate. Africans are circular thinkers. We have a roundabout way of approaching everything.

Here's a good example.

If an American is thirsty, he or she will say, "I'm thirsty; can I get some water?" But an African will say, "My throat is dry." If the other person has water, they may reply, "Oh, I have something to quench it," and they'll go get some water. If they don't have water, they may reply, "Mine, too," because they don't want to be shamed for having no water to offer. By being indirect in our inquiry, we are being sensitive to the other person.

When an American says, "I'm thirsty; I need water," they have a preconceived idea that the other person will have some water to give. But as an African, you never know whether the other person has water, so you find a way to ask without shaming.

Likewise, when you say to an African, "Hey, tell me about what's happening in your culture," they will likely say, "Ha! Let me tell you a story."

Circular thinkers talk in parables, they talk in stories, they circumvent the point. In America, we want to land the plane. "Get to the point, and give me the bottom line." But when dealing with Africans—and this is very important for engaging with people from many cultures in the two-thirds majority world—you must be prepared to sit down and listen to a story and try to decipher what the person is trying to tell you, because it may not be very direct.

That's the difference between circular thinking and linear thinking. And neither one is right or wrong; they're just different. Westerners are used to bullet-point presentations and getting to the bottom line. That's why sermons here are thirty-five minutes long. An African service can go two hours, because the pastor can dance around a single point, but say it in so many stories.

Embracing cross-cultural engagement means we have to be patient with the Africans in their circular thinking, and the Africans must be patient with the Western way of thinking.

I took my senior pastor to Uganda last April, and he preached for forty-five minutes to an hour. When he was finished, the people looked at him like, *Are you done? Do you not have anything else to say?* He later said to me, "I can't believe I was being shamed for speaking for an hour! People back home start getting antsy after thirty-five minutes."

It's important for Africans to understand that Americans make their points very quickly and very briefly, and they don't need to embellish the point. Americans and others from the West need to make room for circular thinking.

If you think about it, Jesus was more of a circular thinker. Someone would ask him a question and he would reply with a question of his own, or he would say, "A man was walking down from Jerusalem toward Jericho." He would speak in parables, in stories, in analogies.

When I started working at Mariners Church, they would tell me, "Hey, we're giving you three minutes to give announcements," and I would be thinking, *Three minutes is what I take to say hello.* So whenever I was onstage, they would tell me three minutes, but on the schedule for the morning they would budget *six* minutes, because they knew. They learned how to engage with me, and I also learned how to engage with them—and how to get to the bottom line more quickly!

Because I have these two worlds operating within me, I have learned the importance of understanding cultures and bridging cultures, of embracing each other's strengths and mitigating each other's weaknesses.

A 2020 book titled *Hide and Seek: The Sacred Art of Indirect Communication*, by Benson Fraser, offers some profound insights into how indirect communication works and why it often can be a more potent tool for understanding others than direct communication.[5] Dr. Fraser's book offers much great practical help for anyone planning to go on a mission to the two-thirds world, whether as a short-termer or for a longer period.

Recognize That God Is Already There

When we go elsewhere in the world on assignment with the Great Collaboration, we don't take God with us. He is already there. In fact, he's constantly busy, doing things all over the globe.

Henry Blackaby, author of the bestselling book *Experiencing God*, suggested that we should find out where God is working and then join him there.

> The church of which I was the pastor in Saskatoon sensed that God wanted us to start new churches across Western Canada. Since there were hundreds of communities that had no evangelical church, we first tried to find out what God was already doing in the towns and cities around us. We believed He would show us where He was at work, and that revelation would be our invitation to join Him. We began praying and watching how God would answer.[6]

Most places around the world no longer need pioneers. Today, we stand on the shoulders of those missionaries who did a great job of reaching the uttermost parts of the world. We honor them because so many left their homes and their culture to bring the gospel to people who had never heard the name of Jesus. From a human perspective, I owe my relationship with Jesus to the Scottish missionaries who led my grandfather to faith in Christ. Because of such faithful pioneers, we have people like my grandma, who possessed a strong faith in Christ, and a new generation of indigenous leaders who have come to maturity. The stage is now set for us to join these brothers and sisters in what God is already doing in their parts of the world.

As we go out to "do missions," we're like detectives dusting for God's fingerprints. Knowing that he is there among the people, and that he started working there *long* before we ever showed up, we look for signs of his activity.

And when God says, "Go and make disciples of all nations," it's not because he *needs* us; it's because he loves us. Even the idea that we are *the sent ones*—we are sent to be an extension of Christ's finished work on the cross. So it's not *our* effort; it's *his*. And we get to be a part of what Christ has invited us to do. *He's* the one doing the inviting.

Understanding the Great Commission this way can help us rethink and reframe *how* we are going. Maybe you've heard those missions appeals that go something like this: "If you don't go, people will die. If you don't go, people will never know about Jesus." It's almost like a threat. But God wants us to go out of *beauty*, not out of duty. He wants us to reflect his image to others created in his image, and thereby reflect the wholeness of his image in loving community.

So when we go, we are looking for how to build most effectively on what God has already done and to join in what he is currently doing. Instead of trying to import our short-term Western solutions, we go to find out what the indigenous leaders are doing or proposing as long-term, systemic solutions to the problems in their communities. With our resources and experience—and yes, our linear thinking—God has equipped many from the West to serve as *catalysts* for what he is doing in the two-thirds majority world. A catalyst speeds up a reaction without leaving a residue of itself. So an initiative that might have taken twenty years for the indigenous leaders to complete might take only ten years with help from the West. And we can advance what the local people are doing without having to build a name for ourselves.

Secondly, though equally important, by going in a posture of *learning*, we create an opportunity to be formed in our own faith, learning such things from the African church as resilience, tenacity, community, and a deep-rooted faith that is not based on mere head knowledge. There's a mutuality and a reciprocity in this approach, rather than everything flowing one way—from us to them.

If we are to engage in catalytic community with indigenous leaders and churches, we must grow in cultural intelligence. We must learn how to communicate cross-culturally, adapting our preferred style to fit the moment. This also means we must learn to be flexible and adaptable in our models and methods.

I know that when many Westerners hear this, they mistakenly think, *You're talking about compromising the gospel.* I assure you I'm not. Regardless of where we might live, the gospel laid out in Scripture remains the same forever—"once for all delivered to the saints."[7] But we must be willing to follow the *strategies* of Jesus as well as the *content* of his gospel.

Jesus took on the form of a servant. He asked many questions and carefully listened to people's answers. We can do the same with the indigenous Christians who live in closer proximity—both physical and cultural—to the people groups we want to reach. They can help us learn how best to engage with our Christian mission.

Our methods and modalities must change because of the sacrifice and success of many who devoted their lives to reach the unreached in previous generations. God gave them favor to such a degree that today there are millions of Christians where once there were none. In many places around the world, the situation has changed enormously because of the hard work and faithfulness of those Christians who have gone before us. And that's why we must embrace the hard work of contextualization, reconsider the place and form of partnerships, and give closer attention to mutual respect and cultural sensitivity.

The Necessity of Demonstrating the Gospel

Another implication of polycentric missions is the rediscovery of both proclaiming and demonstrating the gospel. The focus of most modern Christian missions, especially within the church, has been about evangelism and getting people into the Kingdom. In my view, the church has abdicated its Acts 2 identity, in which Christians met together, broke bread together, and prayed together, and no one lacked among them because they shared what they had with others. The unfortunate abdication in our day of the church meeting the needs of the needy led directly to the proliferation of nonprofit ministries and nongovernmental organizations (NGOs) to take up the slack. These groups saw a gap in the tangible demonstration of the gospel and therefore started delivering goods and services to the poor and neglected. In many places around the world, and even in the US, people are hungry, cold, and lonely. They need to see Jesus embodied through acts of compassion and mercy. As the church, we do this because *everyone* bears the image of God and therefore has supreme value and inherent dignity. When we look at other people, regardless of their station in life, we are looking at some aspect of God's image. Every image bearer deserves the dignity of enjoying food, clothing, and shelter, and every image bearer deserves to hear the gospel proclaimed.

We need both demonstration and proclamation in Christian missions. We need to show that we care and we need to share our resources. As we reengage with this aspect of the gospel, we start asking deeper questions about poverty. Questions like these:

- Why does the continent with the richest resources in the world—Africa—still struggle with food insecurity?
- Why are economies there failing?
- Why has so much money been spent or given away around the world, and yet we don't see much change in the lives of the people who need it most?

I'm asking these questions now to get you thinking, and I will address them in greater detail in parts 3 and 4. Still, in all our gospel outreach, we need to both *proclaim* and *demonstrate* the gospel.

When we go out, we're not going as superiors to those we serve. No, we're going to people whose inherent dignity resides in their identity as children of God. We therefore engage with them as equals, realizing that they have something to offer us as well.

Let us go with listening ears because we know that God has already been speaking. He has prepared the way for us. *Let's not miss our moment.*

5

GLOBAL TRENDS

Global trends powerfully affect how the gospel spreads throughout the world—and they always have. If we want to understand how best to carry out the Great Collaboration in our own era, we *must* get a handle on the global trends that most strongly shape our time.

Current Global Trends

The biggest trend, by far, that most powerfully shapes and affects our current efforts to engage with the Great Collaboration is *globalization*—a process of integration stemming from the ongoing interchanges of people, products, philosophies, and cultural elements. Globalization integrates differing traditions and cultures.

With major advances in technology, transportation, medicine, and communication, the world has become a much smaller place. Technological innovations have brought accessibility and enabled effective communication to help next-generation leaders around the world become global citizens. Whereas we once wrote letters that took weeks or months to arrive, modern telecommunications infrastructure means that we can now pick up the phone or go online and place a video call to somebody across the world in seconds.

Transportation has drastically changed as well. We can get anywhere in the world within twenty-four hours, something that was not possible even a hundred years ago. The internet has led to major shifts in communication and connection that have sparked new methods of Christian outreach. And we're just beginning to understand how artificial intelligence (AI) will impact the world, both positively and negatively.

With the rise of economic powers such as Brazil, Russia, India, China, and South Africa (commonly referred to as BRICS), single-state dominance has faded. In its place, we see a growing interdependence of economies. The US depends on China for manufacturing, for example, and China depends on America for food, oil, and parts. Not that long ago, manufacturing happened everywhere. Not today. We have become economically interdependent, thus accelerating global trade, with major markets opening in Africa, Asia, and South America.

The massive trend of globalization has opened new avenues for addressing systemic changes and is paving the way for creative solutions to problems that formerly depended heavily on Western funding and leadership. We must be diligent in our efforts to adapt how we share and demonstrate the gospel.

About 70 percent of the population in sub-Saharan Africa is under thirty years of age,[1] while negative population trends in Europe, the US, and other industrial countries (such as Japan) have led to aging populations. How can we rethink Christian missions with these facts in mind? How can we best invest our resources and energies in the years to come?

Migration as *the* Crucial Trend

The International Monetary Fund claims that globalization has four main aspects:

1. trade and transportation
2. capital investments
3. dissemination of knowledge
4. migration and the mass movement of people[2]

Of these four, migration is by far the biggest aspect of globalization. We are witnessing an unprecedented scattering of people groups from their original homelands as they relocate across the globe, forming new communities. Immigration has come to mean the movement of people *from* everywhere *to* everywhere. People from all over the world have made (and are making) their way to the West, while the two-thirds world is also rocked with mass migration of men, women, and children.

I live in California, along with thousands of other Kenyans. During my time here, I have seen churches send countless short-term missions teams to Kenya, seeming not to realize that large numbers of Kenyans are already here. That's the reality of globalization, and a huge opportunity for the American church. People from all over the world are coming to our doorstep—both legally and otherwise—and we should be finding ways to build bridges to these communities and reach these people for Christ.[†] That doesn't mean to the exclusion of going overseas, where we can still have a significant impact, but as missiologist J. D. Payne has said, "Something is missionally malignant whenever we are willing to make great sacrifices to travel the world to reach a people group but are not willing to walk across the street."[3]

† When we refer to dispersed people around the world, we have in mind immigrants, refugees, international students, and businesspeople operating biculturally.

Since 1990, more than 56 million people have immigrated to the United States. Of those, only about 400,000 are known to have joined a church. In fact, 20 percent of non-Christians in North America—almost 13.5 million people—say they "do not 'personally know' any Christians."[4] Moreover, more than one million international students attend college in the US every year.[5] Matthew Soerens of World Relief says, "The arrival of those of other faiths presents a missional opportunity . . . to 'make disciples of all nations' (Matthew 28:19) and to 'give an answer to everyone who asks' for the hope within us (1 Peter 3:15)."[6]

In Orange County, we have a Little Saigon, a Little Tokyo, and a Little China. Anaheim has a Little Kenya and a Little Nairobi. All these enclaves exist because of the scattering of people groups from their original homelands. That is the definition of *diaspora*, which is a fancy word for "dispersed people."

What are we doing to reach all these people? We must learn how to respond innovatively—and biblically—to this influx of new people who need to hear and *experience* the gospel.

Opening Our Doors

I had lived in America for ten years before I ever received an invitation to join someone for Thanksgiving. After I came to Mariners, a couple invited me to join them for the holiday . . . and I felt mortified. "Oh, no, I can't come," I replied. "These are family things."

They smiled and replied, "No, no, please come. Thanksgiving is a time for celebration."

Connecting with people from the diaspora can really be just as simple as that. Inviting someone to join you for Thanksgiving can change the trajectory of their life—but we rarely think of that as a possibility. Why not? Because we don't think of other people first and foremost as someone who bears God's image. We forget that everyone needs a warm meal, a place where others can get to know them and understand them.

When that family invited me into their home, I experienced real beauty. We became such good friends that eventually they gave me a key to their house.

"We know you have a long commute from where you live," they said. "Anytime you don't want to make the drive, just come here and use our spare bedroom to sleep." The husband, Doug, later went with me on a missions trip that transformed his life.

All it takes is the willingness to engage with another human being who might appear to be different from you.

Our Strategies Are Key

Once we grasp the reality of globalization, the question becomes, "How do we adapt our strategies, or create new ones, to better reach immigrants?" The following statistics, drawn from a variety of sources, can help to inform our refugee engagement.

- 86 percent of Protestant senior pastors affirmed that "Christians have a responsibility to care sacrificially for refugees and foreigners."[7]
- Only 8 percent of Protestant pastors said their church was involved in caring for refugees in their local community, compared to 19 percent overseas.[8]
- 44 percent of Protestant pastors said there was a sense of fear in their congregation about global refugees coming to the United States.[9]
- 50 percent of evangelical Christians say that the arrival of immigrants to their community "are a drain on economic

resources," while 40 percent say the influx of immigrants "presents an opportunity to introduce them to Jesus."[10]

- 44.8 percent of companies in the 2023 Fortune 500 were founded or cofounded by a refugee or other immigrant or their children.[11]
- Twenty years after arrival, the average refugee adult has contributed approximately $21,000 more in taxes than the benefits they have received in governmental assistance and services at all levels since they arrived.[12]
- Economists believe that the net economic impact of immigration on the US is positive, including 96 percent of economists surveyed by the *Wall Street Journal*.[13]
- Among people of non-Christian religious traditions in North America—most of them refugees, asylees, or other immigrants—60 percent say they do not personally know a Christian.[14]

We must learn to look at immigrants, refugees, international students, and businesspeople from other parts of the world as image bearers of God who are here to be seen, to belong, to be known, and to be valued. As we do this, we can quite literally change the world.

We might not even have to go overseas to do global missions. The global community has come right to our own backyard. Let's not miss them.

Do you and your organization have a strategy for reaching immigrants? Refugees have already been given legal status to be here; they are not trying to enter the country illegally. Too quickly we forget that the Savior we follow was once a refugee. Early in his life, he fled to Egypt with his parents and lived there a few years as a refugee. Had we lived back then and followed the same practices we often employ today, we likely would have missed Jesus.

Let's take care in how we engage.

What strategies do we have for engaging with the growing global diaspora? What strategies can we use to engage with international students, who represent a tremendous opportunity for sharing the gospel? For example, Saudi Arabia sends thousands of students to America every year. Right now, only about 6 percent of Saudi Arabia's population are Christians.[15] What if we reached out to those students? Most of them live in the upper echelons of their society and are the movers and shakers, the *crème de la crème*. At Mariners, we consider it a key strategy to engage with international students.

As an international student myself, I was rarely invited into American homes. I remember a great church where Milele used to play. We appreciated this church because they gave us a platform, but the only time we appeared onstage was during Black History Month. We never became a part of the church's culture or life.

I started leading a young men's group at the church, but they still thought of us as "those guys from Kenya we bring in during Black History Month." They never recognized us as potential leaders in reaching the local African community or other immigrants.

Sandy Lu, a young woman from China, came to Mariners while doing her PhD work at the University of California at Irvine, which is not far from our church's Irvine campus. At the time, we were finding it difficult to get into China, though we were trying hard to make it happen. Finally, we asked ourselves, "What if we engaged the Chinese community at UC Irvine instead?"

When we did, Sandy soon got involved with the Rooted discipleship process. She became a Christian, graduated from UC Irvine, and moved to Shanghai to work for a large multinational corporation. She's in a very prominent place, leading at the top levels of business in that huge and influential city. In essence, we "created" a missionary in our own backyard, and then she returned to her own people.

What opportunities are just waiting for you in your own backyard?

Opportunities in Little Arabia

As far back as 2013, Mariners has been engaging with refugees and international students from an area in West Anaheim known as Little Arabia, about twenty miles from our Irvine location. Many people of Muslim heritage live there, some of whom have become disgruntled with aspects of Islam and want to learn about religious freedom. How beautiful it's been to engage with these individuals. We've worked alongside fantastic groups such as Bridges International.

I recall doing a medical camp in conjunction with Christian Arabic Church of Anaheim. One of our volunteer couples, Carlos and Marilou Pena, connected with an Afghan family that had just arrived in the US. Not only did the Penas serve this family that day, but they forged a relationship with them that went on for many years.

About a year or so later, I ran into the Afghan family at a Mariners Thanksgiving dinner. When I asked how they were, they told me how they had come to faith and that they are deeply grateful to the Penas for both demonstrating and sharing the gospel.

How do we begin to engage more often and more constructively with the immigrants and foreign nationals who live right around the corner? First, I would say, "Check your assumptions." Reexamine what you think about immigrants or people from around the world who live in your country or even near your home.

Second, I would say, "Study God's Word for what it says about sojourners, refugees, and strangers." You might be surprised to discover how much you have in common with people you now see as far and distant.[16]

Third, if you want to engage in Christian missions from a people-centered perspective, delve into the arena of biblical hospitality.

Hospitality from a biblical perspective is about making friends out of strangers, as Jesus did with the woman at the well in Samaria.[17] In John 4:4-9, he squelches the idea of insiders and outsiders. What if we were to do the same? When the Samaritans, long-standing adversaries of the Jews, invited Jesus to stay with them, he accepted their invitation and stayed for two days.[18]

So hospitality is opening our hearts and our homes to strangers. And radical hospitality is accepting hospitality *from* strangers. This is something the Western church can learn from the global church—for example, learning how to graciously accept the "meager" gifts of people who have less than we do.

In 2009, a team from Mariners visited a partner church in Soroti under the leadership of Pastor Julius Eribu, a prolific church planter. Pastor Julius was so delighted to have our team there that he decided to take up an offering for us. His church was very modest, and the building wasn't even completed. So our team was embarrassed to receive a gift from them. I asked two of our members, Tyson and Ashley, to go forward to receive the gifts on behalf of our team. The people from the congregation began streaming down the aisle one by one, bringing whatever they had to offer. This included a few coins, several eggs, a handshake, and some chickens—the equivalent of a month's wages in this village. Ashley and Tyson stood in disbelief and in tears as they received the offerings. Never had we experienced such radical generosity. People gave whatever they had.

I suggest that you and your church begin to partner with Christian churches abroad to get a better glimpse of what God has uniquely given other believers in other places. If you want to see God's multifaceted aspects, look carefully at his people around the world.

A Spirit-Led Biblical Example

You probably know the unusual story from Acts 8 that tells how Philip, one of the church's original deacons, received an odd message one day from an angel: "Rise and go toward the south to the road that goes down from Jerusalem to Gaza."[19]

This instruction must have sounded strange to Philip, because the road down to Gaza was nothing but desert—and at the time, Philip was leading a great revival in Samaria. Thousands were coming to faith in Jesus. What sense would it make to leave at the height of the harvest? Philip could have thought, *Why should I go there? Here is where the action is.*

But he obeyed and went.

As he walked along the dusty road, he eventually saw a wealthy court official sitting in his chariot and reading a scroll. The Holy Spirit said to Philip, "Go over and join this chariot."[20] When Philip obeyed, he heard the man reading the words of Isaiah the prophet. In those days, people always read aloud, not silently to themselves.

He asked the man, who turned out to be from Ethiopia, "Do you understand what you are reading?"[21]

"How can I," the man replied, "unless someone guides me?"[22] The official invited Philip to join him in the chariot, and Philip began to explain that the prophet was talking about Jesus—in fact, that very passage describes what had just happened to Jesus in Jerusalem. Jesus was the long-awaited Messiah, who had come to save people from their sins.

The Ethiopian believed Philip's testimony and asked to be baptized. Philip found some water and baptized him. As Philip and the man came up from the water, "the Spirit of the Lord carried Philip away, and the eunuch saw him no more, and went on his way rejoicing. But Philip found himself at Azotus."[23] It's as if God used a *Star Trek* transporter to beam Philip from the desert to a small town sixty miles away. But Scripture doesn't dwell on the *oo-OO-ooh* part of the story. It simply reports that Philip was *here*, and all of a sudden he was *there*. "As you are going," Jesus said, "make disciples of all nations."[24]

The main point is that a man from a different land and a different culture heard the Good News because the Spirit sent Philip from a successful evangelism campaign in Samaria down to a desert road, just so a lone African man could hear about Jesus.

Do you suppose that man kept quiet about his experience after he returned home? Or do you think he might have told others? It may be a coincidence, but about 75 percent of the population of Ethiopia today is Christian.[25] Back in the fourth century, King Ezana of the powerful and ancient kingdom of Aksum adopted the faith as his own, and most of his nation followed suit. But Christianity had existed in the region *long* before King Ezana. Do you suppose that Philip, by engaging with an Ethiopian court official who just happened to be in Israel for a short time, might have played a key role?

We never know when a "chance encounter" we might have with a foreigner, or an immigrant, or an international student, or a visiting businessperson, might turn out to have eternal implications. But we don't really *need* to know, do we? Jesus invites us to make disciples "as we are going." Even if it's on a dusty desert road in the middle of nowhere when we might rather be somewhere else.

Where are *you* going today?

6

INDIGENOUS LEADERSHIP

Wherever I've gone in the world, I've found amazing indigenous Christian leaders. Many of them are true visionaries who take the Great Collaboration for all it's worth. They witness in their own Jerusalem—their neighborhoods, cities, counties, and districts. But they don't stop there. Because they take the Great Collaboration seriously, they also care about image bearers in their Judea, in the areas adjacent to theirs. It might be nearby cities or counties, but they've moved out of their immediate surroundings to plant churches and work with people in neighboring locales.

Many of these indigenous leaders also have a vision for their Samaria. Depending on their location, this might be a place where the people are not from the same tribe, ethnic group, or social class. These are more difficult places to reach, but they find a way.

I think of my dad, who was a Kikuyu but he went to the areas of Luoland, where tribal tension has always existed with Kikuyus. Because of that, many Kikuyus will not engage with Luos, nor will many Luos engage Kikuyus. But because of the doctrine of the image of God in every person, my dad said, "The Luos are our brothers and sisters," and he worked among them.

I have seen successful leaders who work among people who are very unlike themselves culturally, and among some who may not even *like* them. When my father died, a Luo man named Evans Arek sent him a tribute.

"The reason I got my education is because your dad helped me," he told me. "Please read this at your dad's memorial, because I want the world to know that this guy went past tribal lines. He did not look at me as a Luo, and I did not expect that from a Kikuyu, especially not from a Kikuyu leader."

We have leaders who have a concern and a vision for their own Samarias—places and ethnic groups that differ markedly from their own.

Maybe you're wondering how this can happen. It starts with seeing the image of God in whoever it is we're trying to reach. We must believe that the person with whom we have differences—whatever those differences might be—is not an enemy, is not above us or beneath us, and is not a lost cause. Instead, he or she is first and foremost a child of God, reflecting his image, every bit as much as we are. We don't go out of duty—"Jesus sent me, so I guess I have to go"—but because we believe that Jesus "has destroyed the barrier, the dividing wall of hostility."[1] Peace comes when we see ourselves as one people.[2] Therefore we go with the gospel to places unlike our own and to people unlike us, and who may not even like us.

My dad worked in Zambia, Uganda, and elsewhere, especially in the area of family life education. That was his vocation as a pastor and a leader in the National Council of Churches, where he headed the family life education department. We must see that

God has raised up such visionary indigenous leaders all around the world.

Angst About the Great Collaboration

Unfortunately, many times when people engage in global missions, they bypass the indigenous leaders because, in their understanding of the Great Commission, they believe that they themselves must go to these unreached people groups.

And so they head to Kenya, for example. They go to Nairobi, where they find believers. And they think, *The people in Nairobi already have churches, but there are no churches and very few believers in Turkana and Lodwar.* And so, what do they do? They go to Turkana and Lodwar, the arid and desert areas of Kenya, because unreached people groups such as the Pokots and Turkana live there. They say, "We're going to these unreached people groups because that's who needs the gospel."

And while that is a true statement, they seem to forget, or overlook, the many Christians *already in Kenya* who come from more proximate cultures and who live much closer to the Pokots and Turkana. Rather than going to Nairobi and building relationships with the established Christian leaders there, and perhaps hearing the vision that God has placed on *their* hearts for Turkana and Lodwar, and partnering together to serve the people there, they go it alone.

So even though mature Christians from local and proximate cultures are well positioned to reach beyond their Jerusalem into their Judea or Samaria (which for us might be the ends of the earth), we take the mandate of the Great Collaboration as primarily or exclusively our own and head out into the hinterlands, trying to evangelize unreached people groups. In doing so, we may miss out on what God is *already* doing there, or what he has planned to accomplish through the blessing of *collaboration*.

If we were willing to consider and engage with the indigenous leaders who are already on the ground there, I believe we would be far more effective.

A Partner Church in Egypt

One of Mariners' partners is the largest Christian church in the Middle East, with a presence in fifteen or twenty countries in the region.

I've been to Iraq, Lebanon, and Algeria with these brothers and sisters. We've worked together with people from Tunisia, where no American churches were working. We accompanied people from the Middle East as they traveled to proximate cultures—and even for them, it was difficult. Their cultures differ from one another and have many dissimilar nuances. Nevertheless, our Egyptian partners are *much* closer to these other cultures than we are.

When we work through indigenous leaders, we'll find that it takes longer up front, because we're not going directly. We'll have to manage our expectations, adapt to the rhythm and pace of cross-cultural collaboration, and accept slower initial results—in exchange for greater long-term potential and success because the results are being achieved by those on the ground, whom we are supporting.

Moving from Exporting to Collaborating

As we engage with indigenous leaders, we move from *exporting* to *collaborating*. We find out who God already has uniquely placed in those locations. Who are the visionary indigenous leaders? Who has a heart for their neighbors in proximate regions? Who wants to reach the tribes and the places where even *they* may not be welcome?

They're not necessarily the people we expect.

Many times, well-intentioned Westerners will find somebody in the hinterlands who wants to draw them in because of the promise of money. This is yet another reason why we must move from exporting to collaborating. If we go in with a local partner, one who has less of a cultural gap, the expectations on the receiving end will likely not be the same.

This principle applies not only to Westerners, but equally to leaders in the two-thirds majority world. Some will try to reach only the people within their own cities. I've seen this in my own country of Kenya. But I invite them to think beyond their Jerusalem, to realize that God has placed them in Kenya, not just for Nairobi but for those in other places as well—even to Turkana and other remote outposts.

Even then, instead of going out from Nairobi with their own plan in mind, they should find and work with the local leaders who are already there. I tell them, "If you go to Turkana, you'll find individuals who have come to faith in Jesus. What if you helped to raise them up? What if, instead of exporting the gospel to their people, you collaborate with them to plant their own indigenous churches?" That's a powerful and effective strategy.

More than fifteen years ago, I met a pastor in West Pokot named Emmanuel Longelech. Emmanuel is a remarkable image bearer who has a vision and a passion for church planting in the region of West Pokot. When we first visited, we saw a pastor in Pokot working where (to our eyes) the people still dress primitively. But for them, it makes sense. It's hot, it's arid, and you don't have to wear a lot of clothes.

Emmanuel has a passion to plant churches. When he plants churches in Pokot, he doesn't plant a Nairobi-style church. He doesn't build a brick-and-mortar facility. He builds grass-thatched church buildings because that's what most of the people there have.

A bishop from Uganda once came to Orange County to visit us at Mariners Church. As he drove around the area and saw the Fashion Island shopping mall and all the fifteen- to twenty-story buildings, he told us, "Your church makes sense. It looks like your environment. And if you come to my church, you'll see that it looks like my environment. It's grass thatched. I don't ask people to come and build a church with brick and mortar and stones. I tell them to bring whatever they use to build their own houses." So when people cut grass for their own homes, they cut some extra for their church building. They use indigenous materials.

As a practical matter, whatever you build must be commensurate with your own area. In missions, you have a much better chance of doing that wisely when you engage with indigenous leaders who already have a vision for that area. It's not imposing Western values and saying, "What you guys need in Turkana is a big building with air-conditioning." No, the gospel needs nothing besides the gospel. And so long as the people can meet where they are and engage in the rhythms that allow them to live out the works of the gospel, it's beautiful.

Moving from Initiator to Catalyst

I love the image of a catalyst. Simply because of its presence, a catalyst speeds up a reaction without infusing itself into the elements. Perhaps even more important, a catalyst leaves behind no residue of itself.

In today's Christian missions, let's move from being initiators to becoming catalysts to facilitate and speed up the process of accomplishing God's purpose in the world. When we partner with indigenous leaders, we don't have to initiate anything. If we really believe that the people with whom we engage on the mission field are God's image bearers for that place, who have been divinely called to reach their own context, then we don't have to start something new. Likewise, let's not impose Western models on the majority world, or, for that matter, impose models from any culture on another. Instead, let's go find out what God is already doing in a place, and then join him in the work.

What I'm suggesting is more of a mutual engagement rather than West vs. the rest. This is a posture that the African church is more familiar with. There's no need for exceptionalism or superiority. What's called for is simplicity and humility.

What if instead of bypassing the indigenous leaders and initiating something from the outside, we joined in partnership with them and helped to fan *their* flame? What if we came in as catalysts, speeding up the process while leaving no residue behind?

Could we start thinking about partnering with a pastor in Turkana, Kenya, or in the Sinjar Mountains in Iraq—someone who maybe has a vision to plant ten churches? What if because we came together and came alongside him, we served as a catalyst so that he could plant twenty churches instead of ten? He's the one who's there. He's the one who knows the people. He's the one who knows the local context. So how can we amplify his work and multiply what he's doing? We can come in to help, but eventually we're going to leave. Our role, then, is to help him figure out how we can energize what God is doing through him, and help him get started.

When we went to Iraq with our partners from Egypt, we didn't go to plant a Mini-Me Mariners Church. Neither did we want to plant a church in the image of our partner church from Egypt. We wanted an indigenous church, with its own identity, led by indigenous leaders who are there for the long haul. It's *their* calling. We were there to help them get up and running more easily and faster than they might have on their own.

The key is to have a very high view of the gospel and a very humble view of ourselves. A high view of the gospel transcends culture and country. A humble view of ourselves means we don't need to leave our name there.

I have known individuals from the global world who have gone elsewhere to build or plant churches and have left their names on a building. What ends up happening? The local people look at that structure and say, "That's *your* building, not ours. It has your name on it." Why would we leave our name there? Maybe we're trying to build a legacy for ourselves. Such a practice would reflect a high view of ourselves and a humble view of the gospel.

That's why we need to move from initiating to catalyzing, from doing it on our own to partnering with local indigenous leaders who have the vision and are already there.

Church Planting with Pastor D

In 2007, Mariners Church met Pastor Daniel Nuñez from Mexico. Pastor D (as he is affectionately known) was working for a US-based organization building houses in his hometown of Tijuana. At the same time, he was laboring to plant a church, which was his true passion.

He described to Mariners his dream of planting fifty churches in his lifetime—a scary, daunting, and unfathomable goal. As a church, we decided to come alongside him on his journey. We have engaged with him on multiple levels, including building houses, sponsoring kids, creating sustainable breakfast programs, and planting churches.

In 2021, we celebrated Pastor D's sixtieth birthday . . . and his fiftieth church plant. He accomplished his life goal by his sixtieth year. His son, Tury, and the younger pastors in the church felt so moved by this that they told him, "Your vision was too small. We will dare to plant five hundred more churches."

Their organization is almost decentralized. They have a main leader, but each member of the team has been given the autonomy to plant their own churches around Mexico.

This story celebrates the power and beauty of being a catalyst, but I must mention that Mariners was not the only catalyst here. Pastor D has other church partners as well, who have engaged with him, and *together* we helped him realize his goal.

Here is where reciprocal partnership can bear unexpected fruit. Even as we were helping Pastor D with his goal, he and his church catalyzed the discipleship of several Mariners members, as well as many individuals among his other partners. Our partnership has transformed the way many people in Orange County use their time, talent, and treasure. They now delight in pursuing a Kingdom agenda rather than a personal one.

One volunteer couple, Scott and Susan Griffiths, for example, crossed the border more than one hundred times in a year, serving faithfully alongside Pastor D as catalysts in this wonderful partnership. It's impossible to quantify that kind of life change.

From Independence and Dependence to Interdependence

Why should we partner with indigenous leaders? One reason is that the Global North and the Global South live by opposite views . . . and neither one is good.

On the one hand, we have the Global North view of *independence*: "I am my own person. I do things at my own pace. I do them in my own way." In the Global North, we teach our children to be independent. We raise them to stand on their own two feet, to be their own person, their own self. To be sure, this perspective has some healthy aspects, and I have no interest in denying that. But it also generates some unhealthy by-products because it encourages us to think we are self-made people. It pushes us to think that it's all about *us* and what *we* think. It's all about making our own decisions and controlling our own path. Ultimately, it's a lie. There is no such thing as a self-made person.

On the other hand, the Global South generally adopts a perspective of *dependence*: "I'm utterly and completely dependent on my community. I depend on others for everything." People in the Global South know there is no such thing as a self-made person, but that view also has a dark side. It can create a situation in which people always have their hand out, looking for the next gift.

I received my education because people in my church in Kenya raised funds to make it possible. They came together as a community to enable me to do something I couldn't do on my own. And that was good. But total dependence can also paralyze people. It can keep an individual, a community, or a nation from accomplishing what God has in mind for them.

The good news is that we can shift our perspective. We don't have to choose between unhealthy Global North independence, where we imagine we don't need others and we create models for other people, or unhealthy Global South dependence, where we just put out our hands to receive. We can instead choose and practice *interdependence*, where we engage each other's strengths and mitigate each other's weaknesses, realizing that we ourselves have both.

Who Is an Indigenous Leader?

Most indigenous leaders were born and raised in the country or location where they now live. But it's also possible to *become* indigenous in a sense by making a long-term commitment to live and assimilate in a new place. Instead of coming and going as outsiders, these "naturalized" indigenous leaders have invested their lives and lived among the people they serve, fully engaged within the culture, and have become part of the fabric of the local community.

One example of this transition from outsider to "naturalized indigenous" is a friend of mine named Juli McGowan Boit.

I first met Juli when she attended Azusa Pacific University in Southern California. After graduation, God called her to move to Kenya, and she relocated to a remote Kalenjin village with no electricity and no running water. She acculturated by living and working for years among the people, long before she started a venture of her own. She learned the local language and worked among the village leaders. She became so greatly loved by the people that they gave her a Kalenjin name. She married a Kenyan, and I would say that Juli today is more of a native Kenyan than I am.

Juli left America as a young woman, moved to Kenya, and married a Kenyan. She has lived there ever since and not only speaks the local language, but has also adopted the native culture. When I go back to Kenya to visit her village and work with her, I depend on her, even though it's my own country of origin. Does the fact that Juli was born and raised in America make her less "indigenous," just because she's a white woman living in Kenya? Hardly. By all measures, she's a *great* indigenous leader.

Over time, leaders like Juli, who show up and stay, become as indigenous, for all practical purposes, as the native born. As she says of her own journey, "I didn't come to *fix*; I came to be alongside, I came to realize that God was *already present* in the place."[3]

God called Juli to help change medical care in Kenya and beyond. Her noteworthy personal story is captured in two riveting books, *Brave Love* and *From Beyond the Skies*.[4] Her journey of engaging and embracing a community reflects Jesus' model of sharing God's love for humanity when he "became flesh and dwelt among us."[5]

I love the story of how God used Juli and the Kimbilio Hospice care center to change a friend's heart. Isaiah Henry is a community management professional who also sang in Mariners choir for many years with my wife, Delta. The two of them had become good friends even before Delta and I met. We often invite those who are deeply involved in our lives to go on a "faith adventure" in Kenya—what some would call a short-term missions trip. But when we invited Isaiah to go on one of these trips, he gave us the runaround for seven years. Ultimately, though, he gave in to our persistence and reluctantly came with me to Kenya in 2017.

Isaiah's life changed soon after he met Juli Boit. At Kimbilio Hospice, he saw what loving Jesus looked like in action. Isaiah felt so moved that he not only joined Juli's advisory board but has also now started an organization called the People Are the Wealth Foundation, which is geared to help people like Juli who are at the tip of the spear in caring for God's image bearers.

Because of committed leaders like Juli Boit—a girl from Redding, California, who assimilated into a Kenyan village and became part of the community—a successful businessman like Isaiah Henry not only began engaging in global missions but has now made it his personal mission to invest in people's lives to bring about real change. In 2022, Isaiah launched the People Are the Wealth Foundation as a way to keep furthering missions. He is also part of a select group of executives known as the Young Presidents Organization, so even people who are not involved in the church feel his influence. This is the beauty of engaging with those who show up and stay put.

A non-native who becomes an indigenous leader is someone who has lived among a people and has fully assimilated. Too often we see well-meaning missionaries who do not actually acculturate. When they go to the mission field, they create their own little enclaves. This has been a problem in global missions for decades, especially when we evaluate it from the perspective of the local leaders.

When you go to Kenya and ask, "What are the missionaries like?" you will probably get an answer that goes something like this: "They are wealthy. They go to different schools than we do. They live in the most beautiful places and drive the biggest cars. They hire a ton of people to help them." In America, we often have pity for overseas missionaries because they have sacrificed their lifestyle in the West in order to go to Africa. And from a Western perspective, that's true. But when they get to Africa or another majority world location, the people living there see them as rich, living in opulence, and sending their kids to all the best schools.

It has been interesting to see that, as more and more missionaries are being sent from majority world nations to other majority world nations, the expectations for their standard of living are quite different from those of missionaries going out from the West. When we do find missionaries—and missionary kids—who have acculturated, the impact they are able to have is remarkable. These missionaries seek to integrate their kids with the local kids. They live among the people. They treat the people who work for them very well. It's a much, *much* different experience.

When I first came to Mariners, we supported forty or fifty missionaries around the world. But many people in our congregation had no idea who these people were, where they were, or what they were doing. We were just sending money. We had no real engagement with them. As we began shifting our focus toward working more closely with indigenous leaders—a strategy that has proved to be much more effective and a lot less expensive—we contacted each one of the missionaries we were supporting. In many cases, we found they were duplicating things that were already being done—and oftentimes better—by local groups and leaders. We notified these missionaries that we were going to curtail our financial support, and for those who had relationships with people in our church, we came up with a rollout process, to either bring their missions work into alignment with our new vision or phase out our support over three, five, or seven years.

Today we ask our partners what they need, and most of the time they ask us to help them increase their capacity to hire people in their local context. Occasionally they ask for people from the West with very specific skills—such as special needs education, financial planning expertise, or counseling—to come work alongside them. And we continue to send people from Mariners on faith adventures, as part of our spiritual formation and discipleship programs. The old model of simply sending support money to missionaries is no longer compatible with our missions approach.

In the years since that course-changing decision, God has raised up some incredible indigenous leaders, and we have been able to partner and collaborate with them. When we find these leaders, we meet them in a posture of reciprocity, a position of mutuality, and a place of exchange. We don't go in thinking that we're going to do something on our own. Rather, we go in with the attitude that there's something for us to learn, something for us to give, and something for us to gain—in terms of spiritual formation for our people and fulfillment of our mandate to go into all the world.

Both Giving and Receiving

Paul wrote to the Philippians about the importance of both giving and receiving: "As you Philippians know, in the early days of your acquaintance with the gospel, when I set out from Macedonia, not one church shared with me in the matter of *giving* and *receiving,* except you only."[6]

Reciprocal partnership is a crucial aspect of working with indigenous leaders. It's not just giving, giving, giving. We also go with a posture of receiving—which is rooted in the Imago Dei; that is, in a partnership between fellow bearers of the image of God.

This is why I am convinced that we must have a high view of every person we meet, a high view of the gospel, and a very humble view of ourselves. Then reciprocal partnership in serving others and sharing the gospel is not just a mission; it's an invitation, a privilege, and an honor. We treat our mission with reverence and humility because we understand that God doesn't *need* us, but in grace he has chosen to use us.

Reciprocal relationships rooted in the Imago Dei change our motivation. When we go to the uttermost parts of the world, it's not because "If we don't go, they'll die," but rather because we get to be part of what God is doing around the world. That is a much better motivation for engaging in global missions, whether it's evangelism and proclamation or a demonstration of the gospel through works of compassion and justice. Whatever we go to do, we choose to go with a very humble attitude. We go, realizing that God has raised up capable, visionary, and equipped indigenous leaders who are there already.

Understanding the role of indigenous leaders is critical because it can move us from exporting to collaborating, from initiating to catalyzing, and from either independence or dependence to a beautiful picture of interdependence.

Yes, we really do need each other.

PART THREE

ETHOS

How do theology and philosophy form our values, which in turn direct our behavior? We'll find out by investigating a sound ethos for our work in global missions. How does our ethos help us form a distinctively Christian community, not only for individuals but also corporately? Here we consider our posture in doing missions work.

The Holy Spirit's formation of the church gives Christians a new identity that prompts us to take different actions, choose new behaviors, and make better decisions as we pursue a people-centered Christian mission. In this section we explore five perspectives that have been stabilizing pillars in my own missiology and church leadership. How distinct would our communities and personal lives be if we lived within the parameters of these five guiding principles?

7

BIBLICAL POVERTY

When most people think of poverty, they think of abject poverty—the destitute, the down-and-out, the disadvantaged. Many have gotten involved in justice and compassion work because they have a strong desire to vanquish extreme poverty. While we do need to respond to acute human deprivation, I believe we should ask ourselves another question first: Why does abject poverty even exist?

The biblical answer is that it happens because the image of God has been marred in every human being.

We Are All Poor

At the very beginning, when God created everything, he called it all *good*. In the first two chapters of Genesis, the word *good* is used almost a dozen times. But then comes chapter 3, and everything falls apart.

Sin enters the world and breaks the shalom—the wholeness, peace, and harmony—that God created. Biblical poverty arises from the brokenness of shalom. The tapestry is no longer intact; the fabric is torn. And everything unravels.

God created us to be a community in sync with him, in sync with ourselves, in sync with each other, and in sync with the earth, the environment. But because of what happens in Genesis 3, we have all been born wanting life on our own terms. We deny that God is our God. We want to be gods unto ourselves.

When our relationship with God unraveled, our relationship with ourselves also came apart. Physically, emotionally, and psychologically, we are broken people. "I don't know why I did that," we say when we commit some horrible offense; but the Bible explains that we are at war with ourselves. Our sin has fractured the shalom that God intended for us to experience, even within our own persons.

We're also broken relationally. Immediately after Adam and Eve sinned, they started blaming each other for what happened. Neither would admit that they had *chosen* to disobey God. And so, the shalom between them also shattered.

At the same time, the harmony and peace that had existed between them and the earth's environment also crumbled. Their environment turned against them, and they turned against it.

The result? A loss of shalom all around. Their sin had marred the image of God within them, resulting in the chaos we've seen down through human history and still see today.

The absence of shalom is the definition of biblical poverty. The wholeness and completeness that Adam and Eve at first experienced has been undone. Our world has disintegrated. True poverty, and the root of every other kind of poverty, derives from our broken relationship with God, with ourselves, with others, and with the earth.

So who among us is poor?

We're *all* poor.

When we finally grasp that indisputable truth, we are ready for redemption.

We're Born into It

What does it mean to say we are biblically impoverished? For starters, we can no longer say that people from Africa, and some parts of Asia and South America, are poor while we are not. According to the Bible, everyone in North America is also poor, because the fabric of shalom doesn't hold here anymore than it does anywhere else on the planet. The image of God has been marred in *every one* of us. Again, we're *all* poor.

Because Adam, the first human, sinned, we are all born into a lifestyle of sin. We come by it naturally, through birth. That's why David writes in Psalm 51, "In sin my mother conceived me."[1] He wasn't blaming his mom for some sexual sin; rather, he was admitting, "I was born a sinner. From conception, the old sin nature from Adam has been mine."

It takes the "second Adam," Jesus Christ, to restore what the first Adam lost in the Garden of Eden. You see, the Bible tells the story of *two* gardens. In the first garden, Adam messed everything up. But because of what Jesus did for us on the cross, he invites us into a second garden, restored and vastly improved—with the tree of life producing its fruit year-round and healing the nations with its leaves.[2] Jesus has the power to restore to us what the first Adam squandered away.

Because of what Adam did in the first garden, the image of God in all of us was marred. We all fell into biblical poverty. Because of our biblical poverty, we choose greed and self-aggrandizement. We want to amass *things*; materialism has become our normal posture. And when we amass things and refuse to share what we have, the result is abject poverty, along with wars and malice and bloody conflicts.

The Work of Restoring Shalom

To this day, our world suffers from the cataclysmic absence of shalom. However, immediately after the disaster recorded in Genesis 3, God began to unveil his plan to restore it. And he invites *us* into his work of restoring shalom.

Understanding what this means gives us a very different posture for engagement. Understanding and accepting that we ourselves are poor creates a proper sense of humility in us, along with a desire to see the Imago Dei fully restored in every human being. Without question, we want people to enjoy healthier, wealthier, more satisfying lives, but far more we want to see the image of God in them restored to what God intended from the beginning. And because we are all members of the human community, we can work with God to restore his image in others, and they can work with God to restore his image in us. There's a mutuality, a reciprocity.

When the world unraveled after our loss of shalom, very quickly there resulted an inequitable distribution of resources. As I've said, we did not choose the century into which we were born, the place where we came into the world, our family, our life circumstances, our temperament, our intelligence, or the economic status of our parents. Therefore, no one can say, "I pulled myself up by my bootstraps." No, we may do the best we can with what God has given us, but God is the one who has given us whatever we have.

So, what does it mean if worldwide inequities have existed since the Fall? It means we have a responsibility to our fellow human beings, our fellow image bearers. I believe that God set things up like this so that we would learn to share with others and not withhold good things from them.

I found it fun but not easy to grow up in Eastleigh, a suburb of Nairobi considered "across the tracks." I had a friend there named Adika, who was from a different tribe. He was as talented as they come—an incredible soccer player, academically gifted, charming and charismatic, and very good-looking. If we had voted back then for the kid most likely to succeed, Adika would have won hands down. But because he was born into difficult circumstances and had no safety net in the community, he fell on hard times and eventually disappeared. To this day, I wonder what happened to him.

By contrast, I had a village to support me, a community to wrap its arms around me. That's why I can share these stories with you. The main difference between Adika and me was not material wealth but the wealth of my community. Biblical poverty reminds us that, even when we have all the material things we need to succeed in life, things go awry when we lack a strong support system around us. Our duty as believers is to engage with the effects of biblical poverty by helping others regain a right relationship with God that leads to restoration in all facets of life.

Somebody once said that some people are so poor, all they have is money.[3] This statement gets at the truth that there's a much deeper poverty beyond the lack of money. And our money really isn't our own, anyway. Our material possessions, our intellect, our creativity—these are all resources and tools that God has given us to help restore the image of God in ourselves and in others. So how do we take responsibility for these things, as part of God's plan to restore our broken and hurting world?

Shalom with God

Genesis 3 tells us that after the Fall, Adam and Eve heard God walking in the garden in the cool of the day, a normal time of fellowship between them. But rather than seeking God for fellowship, they hid. Their sin had shattered their shalom with God.

As Adam's descendants, we are spiritually at odds with our Creator, which means our natural inclination is to hide from him. Obviously, that was not God's plan from the beginning.

Much to the contrary, God intends for us to have a significant part in the way this planet operates. At the very beginning, he said, "I am going to create humankind in my image and let them have rule and dominion over the earth I give them." Despite the Fall, God never revoked that charge. So if *we* have been given rule and dominion, then whatever is done here has to be done by you and me. God will not do what he has explicitly given us to do.

To make that possible, God himself came to earth as a man. Jesus arrived on our planet not only as our Savior, but also as our example. He wanted to show us how he wants us to live. Jesus is the perfect example of how to address abject poverty.

Again, God gave us rule and dominion over this planet. As part of that rule, he wants us to address the inequitable distribution of wealth that exists here. We have a responsibility to other human beings, not only to attack abject poverty, but to help them understand that they are created in the image of God. They must be given a gospel understanding, recognizing that they don't have to earn God's favor or work for it. Christ has already done everything necessary to restore shalom.

We evangelize because of the brokenness between us and God. Though God created us as *good*, we turned from him and were broken. But through faith in Jesus, he has brought us near to himself again. That's why we say we're *born again*. We belong to God *twice over*. He created us in his image, which made us his. After we marred that image through sin, he made us his again through the work of his Son, Jesus. We belong to him twice.

A musician friend of mine is named Born Twice. Why does he have that name? He realizes that the divine image in him was marred; but now through faith in Jesus, that image has been restored and he has been reconciled to God.

Shalom with Ourselves

The Fall described in Genesis 3 also shattered shalom with ourselves. We feel shame for our sinful behavior, even disdaining our core identity. How else can we explain all the self-destructive attitudes and behaviors in the world?

As believers in Christ engaged in missions, we serve others, trying to help them restore the image of God in *themselves.* As Paul told the Galatians, "I am . . . in the anguish of childbirth until Christ is formed in you!"[4] The image of God has been marred in all of us, which inevitably results in biblical poverty.

Very few people wake up in the morning, look at themselves in the mirror, and say, "You are such a great person. You're attractive and talented and accomplished."

No, we're more likely to say, "You are so dumb. You made the same mistake again. You weren't nice or kind to your family and friends. You're a terrible person."

We often tell ourselves demeaning or untrue things. Why do we do that? It's because of our biblical poverty. Our relationship with our true selves has been broken, marred. We often don't see *ourselves* as created in the image of God, much less anyone else, and it takes other human beings to help us restore it. That's why we must affirm other people.

We help others restore the image of God in themselves by helping them engage with who they are in Christ. That means we also engage with psychological issues and don't try to help people become healthier, wealthier, or holier without addressing the brokenness of shalom that has marred the image of God within them.

I've seen many well-meaning people take money into poverty-stricken areas, thinking that more funds will fix the problems there. They show up and give, give, give, hoping that giving money will change people's lives. But that isn't an effective way to help. If the image of God is broken in people, we have to start by working on how they *perceive* themselves.

That's why, whenever we go somewhere to serve the materially poor, we start by asking them what they *have* instead of what they *need*. By asking them what they have, we help to reorient their perspective. We're saying, in effect, "God has already given you something. What is it?"

If we ask people what they *need*, they'll tell us all the things they think will make their lives better. But if we ask, "What do you have?" they may say, "I have five loaves and two fish." And then we say, "Great! Can we take these five loaves and two fish, multiply them, use them, and maybe bring back twelve baskets full of leftovers?"

If, on the other hand, we go in and say, "Oh man, they're so poor, they have nothing, so let's give them *x*, *y*, and *z*," what happens? They use what they're given and put their hands out for more. We build a culture of dependence; they don't think about how to be good stewards of what they have. In the end, we never address the issue of real poverty, because the poverty we're seeing is not a poverty of money, but a poverty of mind, heart, and spirit. We must address the biblical poverty to help them understand who they are, who they belong to, and whose image is embedded in their humanity.

Every one of us has been created by a God who loves us. We have been given certain gifts, and we want to help others excavate their gifts, polish them up, and use them to improve their own lives and the lives of others. When they do that, they take ownership and responsibility.

Toilets to Make Us Proud

Through a Vacation Bible School, our children's department at Mariners helped build a church facility in Soroti, Uganda. The kids raised $25,000, and with the money the Ugandans built a church facility with a beautiful sanctuary that seats five hundred. It has a tin roof and tin walls, and it's really well done.

After we helped them build it, they called back and said, "Hey, could you help us build our toilets?"

"How much will the toilets cost?" I asked.

"Four thousand dollars."

"Okay," I said, but what I was thinking was, *This is a good opportunity to help them rewrite the image of God in themselves.* "How much of that four thousand is labor?"

"Probably $1,800 to $2,000," they said.

"Great. What would it take for *you* guys to provide the labor?"

"Maybe we could get one guy who knows what to do," they said. "He could direct us and we could do the main work."

"Then may I suggest that you do that?" I asked. "Why don't you invest your own labor, instead of paying someone else to come and do the work?"

"Okay, we can do that," they said. And they did. We kicked in $2,000 for materials, they found a local contractor to help them, he directed their labor, and they built the toilets.

Later, when we came back for a visit to the church, they didn't take us immediately to see the sanctuary. No, they took us to the toilets. They were *very* proud of those toilets because they had built them themselves.

Think of what happened there. We gave them half of what they asked for, but they enjoyed the result *far* more than if we had given them the full amount. And their pride and joy was the toilets, not the beautiful sanctuary building (though they were happy with that as well).

When we set out to restore the image bearer in every human being, we address poverty in a different way. There is a psychological benefit to helping people restore the image of God in themselves.

We help restore the image of God in people through evangelism, psychology, mindset shifts, and counseling. We dare not bypass the things that are critical to restoring the image of God in people. Counseling often becomes an integral part of our missions efforts. It's not just evangelism, or justice and compassion; we also use other tools that help us rewrite the broken neural pathways—which means investing a lot more time.

Shalom with Others

The Fall also shattered our shalom with others. Even today we continue to follow the lead of Adam and Eve, who immediately started blaming each other for their sin. The shame they felt prompted them to turn on each other. This brokenness with others also plays out in how we're always comparing ourselves to others so we can feel superior to them. As a deep result of shattered shalom with others, we have no joy in what we have; we only have joy in having more than someone else. The parable Jesus tells in Luke 18:10-14 is a great example of this as two people go to the Temple to pray—one a proud Pharisee, the other a humble tax collector. While the Pharisee prayed, "God, I thank you that I am not like other men," the tax collector kept his gaze low as he cried out, "God, be merciful to me, a sinner!"

As part of our Christian mission, we must seek to restore the image of God in our interactions with one another. This includes reconciliation and breaking down the dividing walls of hostility. We work to restore the broken shalom between people of different tribes, ethnicities, political parties, regions, and cultures. All these walls of hostility must be broken down.

People who do not have enough to eat not only feel hungry; they also feel neglected and rejected. Kenton Beshore, pastor emeritus at Mariners Church, used to tell us, "At some conference, John Stott would be given a plate of food and he would immediately divide it in half. 'You take half,' he would tell his hosts. 'I cannot justify having a full meal when others don't have half a meal.'"

Now, did the other half of the meal go to someone who needed it? No. But Stott meant it as a reminder: *Live simply so that others may simply live.* Enjoying three meals a day when someone else doesn't even get one is a mark of true rejection. This is part of understanding biblical poverty.

God is intent on restoring his shalom in the world . . . and he is equally intent on using *us* to do it. He uses you and me to restore shalom with each other. *He* does the work, but he does it through us.

Environmental Brokenness

Finally, we must help restore shalom with the earth. We seldom think about the environment as something we need to address as part of restoring God's shalom in the world. Whenever someone starts talking about the environmental aspects of this broken shalom, some in the church see that person as a heretic.

One of my favorite Kenyans, Wangari Maathai, is a woman we all thought was crazy. We used to call her a madwoman because she would do things that seemed so unorthodox.

Wangari started something called the Green Belt Movement to save trees in Kenya. She started planting trees here, there, and everywhere, and we thought, *What a crazy woman.*

One time, the government intended to destroy a beautiful park so it could put up some federal buildings. In response, Wangari decided to do something completely unorthodox. She recruited several elderly women, like herself, who went to the park and completely undressed. They got naked and dared the government to arrest them. In Africa, it's taboo to see an older woman naked, so they refused to arrest them. Uhuru Park is still there today, but it almost wasn't. Wangari saved the park by stripping down and standing up to defend it.

Wangari's story soon caught the attention of the world's news outlets, and before long she found herself as the recipient of a Nobel Peace Prize to honor her many years of fighting for the environment and against the government. We used to consider her a crazy lady in Kenya; but today, Wangari Maathai is a hero—not only to Kenyans, but to the world.

With her newfound fame and notoriety, Wangari began traveling extensively throughout the world to talk about saving the environment. She often told one of my favorite stories—a story about a hummingbird—that I have used over and over again.

One time, when a fire whipped through a forest, all the animals saw it coming and ran off as fast as they could. But a hummingbird looked at the fire and said, "I have to do something!" So the hummingbird flew to the river, picked up a drop of water with its beak, and flew back to the flames.

Now, you know the size of a hummingbird's beak. It's nothing. But it took a drop of water, flew back to the huge forest fire, and dropped the drop. And then, as fast as it could, it repeated the action: taking a drop of water from the river, flying back to the fire, dropping the water on the flames, and returning to the river.

As the animals watched the hummingbird's effort, they said, "What a ridiculous thing to do!" One of them shouted to the hummingbird, "You're crazy! Do you think you're going to put out that forest fire with *your* little beak?"

Without skipping a beat, the little hummingbird replied, "I'm doing all I can with all I have."

And then Wangari said, "Now, what if the elephant decided, 'I'm going to do all I can with all I have'? And what if the giraffe said, 'I have a long neck. I can do all I can with all I have'? And if the lion said, 'I'm going to do all I can with all I have,' maybe, just maybe, they could put out that forest fire."

I have a beautiful picture of a hummingbird at home. My closest friends all know I love hummingbirds. Anytime I see a hummingbird, I think of Wangari. My daughter also tells this story because she loves it too. Wangari was an image bearer whom God called to restore the environment.

Because our sin broke the shalom of God on this planet, the environment turned against us. But what if we did all we could with all we have? Whether it's recycling, keeping our cities clean, reducing pollutants, planting trees, or something else, we all have a duty to help restore the shalom that our sin shattered in Eden.

A Responsibility to Share

To understand abject poverty in the world, we must grasp the reality of biblical poverty, which is the absence of shalom. We all suffer from the lack of shalom; we are all poor. But if we understand that we're biblically poor, we can engage with others from a posture of humility. We will engage knowing that the things in our possession are not really ours. They've been given to us by God with a responsibility to share them with others.

God has called us to work with him to seek and to restore the shalom we lost in the Garden. Jesus set all of that in motion through the gospel. He came "to seek and to save that which was lost."[5] He made it possible through his sacrifice on the cross to restore our relationship with God and our relationship with ourselves. He also wants us to restore a right relationship with each other, and to restore a healthy relationship with our environment.

In this way, reconciliation becomes a big part of our missional journey.

One day, we shall all be glorified. We'll be present at the great consummation of all things. In the end, God will make all things right. There will be no more pain, no more sorrow, no more brokenness. When we work to restore shalom, however imperfectly, we foreshadow the events foretold in 1 Thessalonians 4:17, and Revelation 21:3-4 and 22:3-5, when we will be face-to-face with God in heaven. When we restore shalom, we catch a glimpse of what will be.

Our Predominant Posture

In this chapter, we've addressed not merely abject poverty, but poverty in its essence—that is, biblical poverty. Seen through the lens of biblical poverty, we are all just beggars asking other beggars where to find food. I learned this principle from Laurie Beshore.

What if this became our predominant posture?

Paul asks us in 1 Corinthians 4:7, "What do you have that you did not receive? If then you received it, why do you boast as if you did not receive it?" Jesus took on our poverty at the cross so that we might gain his heavenly riches.

At Calvary, Jesus took on everything: nakedness, pain, rejection, and humiliation. He cried out, "My God, my God, why have you forsaken me?"[6] In the Garden of Gethsemane, he pleaded with his Father to "remove this cup from me," referring to his crucifixion.[7] The very people he worked with denied him and abandoned him. The environment went crazy, going dark at three in the afternoon.

Every aspect of poverty began to be destroyed at the cross.

Because of the sin of the first Adam, we wound up where we are; but the action of the second Adam, Jesus, moved us toward restoration. What a joy and a privilege to move into the disposition of the second Adam, so that he can restore us. And because of him, ultimately *everything* will be restored.

8

RELATIONSHIP-BASED MINISTRY

A business executive named Doug Meece came with us on a faith adventure to Uganda in 2008. One day, he got pulled out of the adult church service to teach the kids in Sunday school. He agreed, reluctantly, though he had relished the idea of experiencing the exuberant, expressive worship at Gaba Church.

When he joined the kids, he asked them to open their Bibles to the story of the Good Samaritan. To his dismay, only one or two had Bibles—but it shocked him that most could recite the entire story almost verbatim. Doug's heart felt moved by the children's Bible proficiency, despite their lack of actual Bibles.

This incident reignited Doug's heart for God's Word. He knew he had enough Bibles in his house to go around his whole neighborhood. To serve the kids, he returned to the US and led a campaign, in conjunction with the American Bible Society, to provide Bibles to the entire school district in Uganda. The schools very much welcomed his efforts, but Doug also recognized that something was happening in his own heart. These kids had *blessed* him. He had enjoyed spending time with them, which reminded him how much he needed to do the same thing with his own son and daughter. His trip to Uganda had yielded a renewal in Doug and in Uganda—a memorable picture of mutuality and reciprocity rather than simply ministry *to* a bunch of kids.

Doug eventually sponsored a law student, Stanley, who now is a highly sought-after lawyer in Uganda. Stanley worked a high-profile trial in 2023, which was followed by many observers around the country. Rather than the accolades he received, Doug's legacy may very well be the change he first experienced and then embraced, along with the people he engaged and empowered.

Go as a Unified Community

Because God designed the church as a global community made in his own image, whenever we go on a mission, we need to go as a unified community. We're trying to rebuild a family, remake the community of God, knowing that every member is a valued image bearer.

Relationship-based ministry is rooted in the doctrine of Imago Dei, which means that *every* human being in *every* community is created in God's image and thus has inherent value. Therefore, ministry or missions are not something we do *to* or *for* people, but something we do *with* people. That's foundational. As image bearers, we're called to reflect and to represent God—who is inherently *relational.* How wonderful it would be if everybody chose to be someone who makes everyone else feel like somebody!

Because that image has been tainted and marred in us, however, too often we fail to treat others well. We miss the mark. We forget to treat other people as made in God's image. We try to find our significance through significant *things*, not significant *relationships.*

So as we go out into the mission field, the things we value most highly are often comfort, possessions, money, position, influence, power, and prestige. Too often we elevate the person who has the most biblical acumen, or who can convince others of something.

When we don't consider people *first*, we lose. We miss out on the best things. In forgetting that every person has supreme value and dignity, we forfeit both the truth and God's joy. We must come alongside people, work *with* them, and serve them, not "do missions" *for* them or *at* them. We must love *people* and use *things* rather than loving *things* and using *people*.

Two-Way Learning

More than a decade ago, I started an initiative now known as the Global Residency Program at Mariners Church. We brought people onto our staff from among our global partners, both to learn from them and so they could learn from us. A beautiful mutuality and exchange took place because everyone had something to *teach* and something to *learn*.

Tury and Nallely from Mexico were among our church's first Global Residents. They lived with a local family from Mariners. One day, while in a meeting in my office, Tury asked me a strange question: "Why is your grass always green?"

Everyone in the meeting looked at each other quizzically. Isn't grass *supposed* to be green? After a few moments of confusion, we asked Tury to clarify his question.

"In Mexico," he said, "if there is a green patch of grass, kids are playing soccer on it."

"Okay?" I said, still not tracking with him.

"Here, we have assets we don't even use. They're just for aesthetics. No one uses that lawn, and therefore we're wasting it. We're wasting an opportunity to use what we have."

When I passed along this observation to the leaders on the Mariners executive team, Tury's fresh perspective challenged us to start asking ourselves, "What else do we have that we don't use?"

A few weeks later, a local farmer's market group approached us after they lost their usual venue.

"Would you consider letting us use your parking lot?"

In times past, we probably would have said *no*. Too much liability. And who would make sure everything was cleaned up afterward? Using our facilities for something other than "church ministry" is just something we'd never thought about. We would not have seen our parking lot as an asset to be used to invite people who wouldn't otherwise step on a church campus to at least come and be there.

But I believe we heard Tury's voice ringing in our ears, and we really weren't using our parking lot except for church services—so we said *yes*. Now, every Saturday morning, that parking lot hosts more than 8,000 visitors—many of whom have ended up joining our church.

The "Why is your grass always green?" incident taught us the power of two-way learning. We all have much we can learn through fresh eyes and new perspectives, even as others learn new things from us, as well (some healthy and some not so healthy).

Why don't we see these things more quickly? It's partly because the image of God in us is just as marred and tainted as it is in everyone else. That's why we don't always treat others with respect. That's why we don't always see Jesus in his least recognizable forms. We fail to reflect the true character of God because we are unwilling to look for his reflection in others. The Lord wants to reflect who he is through *every* human being, including those we might otherwise disregard.

Doing missions *with* people requires that we look beyond outward appearances to see the image of God underneath. It requires that we not think more highly of ourselves than we ought to, and that in humility we value others above ourselves.[1] It requires that we foster mutuality and reciprocity.

Mutuality and Reciprocity

Though human beings are the *subject* of our missions efforts, they are not the *object*. Our work must be infused with *mutuality*, recognizing that every individual reflects some aspect of God's image that we need.

Because God has "chosen those who are poor in the world to be rich in faith,"[2] it behooves us to *listen* and *learn* as we go along. We have so much to learn from those who are rich in faith. They can teach us a lot about *perseverance* and *trust*.

People who are rich in faith can teach us *vibrancy* because they don't care too much about their own image. In the Western world, we tend to obsess about our image. We want to put our best foot forward, even if that "best foot" is a lie. That's why we love makeup, and filters on our phone cameras. We want to look better than we really are. We don't want to appear undignified, because looking undignified will make us feel "less than." But in the global world, people don't care about things like that. They might dance to the point where, like King David, their clothes fall off.[3] Who in the West *ever* feels that degree of exuberance?

We can learn much about *hope*, because in the middle of deep darkness, people who are poor in the world find that the smallest light shines even brighter. They find hope in little things. Somebody might describe the many catastrophes they have suffered—"I went through this, and then I went through that, and I went through this other thing"—but finally they'll add, "but I'm thanking God today that I still have breath." And they mean it.

Gennadiy Mokhnenko pastors the Church of Good Changes in Mariupol, Ukraine, while Anatoly Kaluzhny pastors New Life

Church in Kiev. They lead their respective congregations during a time of war—almost three years long at the time of this writing. We support these two churches with relief efforts as they support their countrymen during one of their nation's most desperate times.

A volunteer team at Mariners, led by a young couple named Ryan and Mila Birtcher, has tirelessly engaged with these churches for the past two years. Every week, without fail, they gather to pray with these two congregations from the other side of the world. Prayer has become our mainstay for supporting our brothers and sisters in Ukraine.

In America, we typically *do* things first, then we pray. But because of the Russia/Ukraine war, we are learning that *nothing* should be done without praying first. We have grown in prayer and dependence upon God as we have stood with these two churches in Ukraine.

We have seen the people's resilience in the face of much uncertainty and danger, their commitment to each other, the unity they have shown, and an embrace of suffering like nothing we've ever seen. In fact, their view of suffering has shaped our members at Mariners. As Anatoly observed, "God has not called his people to the role of robe wearing, but to towel bearing."[4] And Gennadiy said, "The fruit that suffers most produces the best wine. God is never more present than when he seems strangely absent—and a war zone will attune you to this fact. As C. S. Lewis said, 'God whispers to us in our pleasures . . . but shouts in our pain.' The war, as hard as it is, has led us to rely more fervently on God."

Camille and Esther Ntoto, our partners at Africa New Day and the Un Jour Nouveau School in Goma, Congo, work in what was once known as the rape capital of the world. They have dedicated their ministry and church to changing the narrative in what may be the world's richest country in terms of natural resources—one cause of the great unrest there. I once heard Esther say something often repeated by the church. As they focus on future leaders, they usually pray boldly, "God, we do not ask that you lighten our burdens, but rather that you give us stronger backs to stand against the challenges that confront us." Joy is truly *not* the absence of trouble but the presence of God.

We can all learn from that perspective, which comes from the least expected place. What an honor to know these men and women who teach us lessons we will never forget. As nineteenth-century theologian William S. Plumer said, "A calm which puts us to sleep may be more fatal than a storm which keeps us wide awake."[5] Tough times in the storm do not diminish the reality of God's presence. Oh, what we can learn from people across the world!

We in the West can become annoyed when the air-conditioning goes out, or it's cold outside and we feel uncomfortable. And then we hear these global disciples saying, "I had no food, my father died, my kids got sick, we lost our house, but God is holding me." They celebrate in their hope and take risks because of it.

They also prophesy. People in the global world are more apt to prophesy than those in the West because they don't think it's on them if the prophecy fails to come true. They say, "I am speaking God's words, and it is up to God whether that prophecy comes true." By contrast, we think, "What if what I prophesied doesn't happen?" We're so self-absorbed and self-conscious.[†]

The spirit of innovation in the majority world surprises us. Sometimes we think innovation comes from having something to work with, and it can. But it's also true that necessity is the mother of invention. That was true of my own childhood when we made our own toys. We'd take some sandals and the leftovers of a broom, put a stick through the sandal, and then take Coke bottles and put

† I know that some people use the word *prophecy* recklessly, speaking instead out of their own imagination. But I wonder how often we silence ourselves, not out of concern that a "word" pressing on our soul might not actually be from God, but because we don't see how it could possibly come true.

them at the end. *Voila!* The sandal became a car. We had no need to rely on Mattel or even on cardboard boxes.

Have you ever visited someplace in the global world and seen people making art or household implements out of discarded tin or old wood? They can mold those things into something amazing.

After the devastating Haiti earthquake in 2010, a friend of mine accompanied representatives from an NGO to the island to witness the human toll for himself. "The thing that impressed me the most," he told me later, "was the artists' alley they took me to in the capital. Very few tourists visit Port-au-Prince even in good times, but the alley was overflowing with amazingly beautiful pieces of art made of old oil drums and rubbish. It just staggered me."

As a little girl growing up in the Kaptembwa settlement on the outskirts of Nakuru, Kenya, Lorna Rutto would take metal bottle caps and melt plastic in them, giving the molded plastic a zigzag shape. Then she'd use her creations as earrings.

She grew up to be a banker. Eventually she became dissatisfied with consumerism and other issues in her position, so she decided, "I want to make a difference." Then she remembered how she used to make plastic jewelry.

"What if I took plastic waste and made fence posts out of it?" she asked herself. She founded a company called EcoPost, which exists to this day. She cleans up trash in the city using the labor of street boys, melts the plastic, and through a process she developed, makes the fence posts. She has created new jobs, cleaned up the environment, and saved acres of trees—all from an idea based on the bottle-cap earrings she made as a child. Now that's what I call innovation.

Properly Measuring Value

We must rethink how we measure people's value, even in ministry. Are we measuring value based on power, prestige, position, and possessions, or are we measuring value by the glory that is in each person due to their creation in God's image?

In Kenya, when you meet someone older than yourself, you don't just shake their hand. Instead, you take your left hand and hold your right forearm while you shake with your right hand. In this way, you're saying, "The gravitas of your glory requires me to receive you with all that I am."

Can you imagine doing that here in the US? We don't particularly care whether the person is an elder. Now, if he or she is a celebrity, a tech wizard, a bestselling author, or a professional athlete—you know, somebody "important" or famous—we might show some deference. But otherwise we don't seem to notice or care that they have the weight of divine glory on them, that they bear the gravitas of God's goodness.

What person in history had the most glory? If we're talking true glory, that would be Jesus. And aren't we supposed to reflect his glory to the world? As James writes, "Show no partiality as you hold the faith in our Lord Jesus Christ, the Lord of glory."[6] The *Lord of glory* equals "full of weight, full of gravitas."

In his celebrated Bible paraphrase, *The Message*, the late Eugene Peterson said that Jesus humbled himself, "became flesh and blood, and moved into the neighborhood."[7] And how exactly did he move into the neighborhood? As a carpenter. He defied all that we might have expected.

In ministry, missions, and day-to-day life, we cannot afford to forget this important truth: Something *amazing* resides in every human being. Because we are all made in God's image, we are relational beings who represent a relational God. We are all precious in his sight. We are all important in God's Kingdom. Every one of us is unique, with great worth and great potential. God therefore calls us to engage with every human being as someone of inestimable value. We need to look for that value, and recognize it when we see it.

Learning While Serving

When we come into this world—naked and gasping for air—the only thing we bring with us is the image of God. At the other end of our lives—again stripped naked—the only thing we take with us into eternity is the image of God. Everything else we've done and everything we've accumulated during our lives is left behind.

No one would seriously argue that point, but let me ask you a question: If we come in with nothing and go out with nothing, and all that really matters is what we've done with the image of God in us during those intervening years, shouldn't we start looking for and recognizing the image of God in ourselves and in everyone else around us? Why not, for example, sit at the feet of the poor and recognize what God has invested in them? With the proper lenses in place, we shouldn't have to look too hard to see how significant and beautiful it is. We have so much to learn from people we might be overlooking right now.

In week six of the *Rooted* discipleship curriculum, participants are asked to step outside their immediate community to serve others. As it says in that text, "foster kids, inner-city youth, undocumented children, pregnant and parenting teens, the elderly, the homeless, and others . . . are going to see the love of Christ through your service."[8]

When I led a *Rooted* group many years ago, during week six we decided to give meals to the homeless people who often congregated near the county courthouse. One of our team members, Sophia, was a former Muslim. She taught me about "the fifth Gospel," the life of a Christian.

"Most Muslims will never read Matthew, Mark, Luke, or John," she said, "but they're reading us." As the Bible says, we are living epistles, "a letter from Christ delivered by us, written not with ink but with the Spirit of the living God, not on tablets of stone but on tablets of human hearts."[9]

During our service experience, Sophia found a huge black guy who was living on the streets. "What's your name?" she asked him.

"My name is Mag," he replied.

"Mag, can I share a sandwich with you?"

I had told our group, "We're not going to *hand out* sandwiches; we're going to *share* them. We're going to sit down and listen to these people's stories. We're not there just to deliver food."

Sophia sat down with Mag, and they enjoyed their sandwiches together. As they ate, they had a conversation. Mag told Sophia his story. He was from Louisiana and had fallen on hard times.

At the end of their time together, Sophia asked, "Mag, how can I pray for you?"

Mag, this huge man with dreadlocks and a big voice, replied, "You're gonna pray for *me*? *You* are gonna pray for *me*? *Really*? How about I pray for *you*? And I know what I want to pray for you. *I* have the strength and the fortitude to be on the streets—but do *you* have the fortitude and the strength to come back here again? Can I pray for you to be able to come back again?"

"What?" Sophia replied.

"Yeah," Mag said.

She had thought she needed to pray for *him*, and he challenged her assumptions—and it rocked her world. She realized for the first time that the people we serve have as much to offer as we do—if not more.

As we sit down with people and dignify them with our presence, as we listen to them and get to know their stories, we should be on the alert for what God wants to teach us through these interactions. We should be looking for what these other image bearers of God have to offer us. People's stories are the currency of human contact.

In exchanging stories with someone, we discover how our own lives intersect with the gospel. We can share the gospel in the midst of exchanging our stories, but we can also help people see the image of God in themselves and how they can live out their full worth.

Sophia then described how some young women in her group had started trying to track down Mag's family. Eventually, they were able to put him on a bus to Louisiana so he could rejoin his family. All of that happened because of the challenge Mag had given to Sophia to not be a "one and done," but to have the strength and the fortitude to go back again and invest in the lives of the people down by the courthouse.

In a traditional missions approach, such an interaction would have looked quite different. Sophia would have given Mag a sandwich, maybe prayed for him, and then gone home and said, "Today I did a good thing. I served." But treating Mag as a fellow image bearer made all the difference—and it played a big role in the spiritual formation of everyone in our group. As a bonus, God made it possible for us to reconnect Mag with his family.

This is what I mean by ministry *with* rather than ministry *to*. There's a mutuality, a reciprocity, something new and important for us to learn. As we engage with individuals created in the image of God, we get to reflect and represent God to them, knowing that Jesus himself did the very same thing. We minister *with*, not *to*, and as we do, we find that other people also reflect and represent God in ways we never imagined. That's how we can resist showing favoritism, as James instructs us. We are all equal. We need to think more deeply about how we measure people's value.

Let's value people for who they are, not for what they have. Let's treat them with regard for their inherent dignity, as people with supreme value. They have as much to offer us as we have to offer them, and they too are full of God's glory. Our work is to figure out where that glory lies.

Eleven Commandments?

I once heard a story about a brilliant New Testament scholar from a previous generation who visited a small church. He went incognito and sat down without speaking to anyone. During the sermon, the preacher for some reason called on the scholar from the pulpit without knowing his identity.

"How many commandments are there, sir?"

"Eleven," the scholar replied.

The preacher scoffed and said, "Everyone knows there are ten. Why do you say there are eleven?"

"Because God gave ten commandments to Moses, and then Jesus told us, 'A new commandment I give you, that you love one another. Even as I have loved you, so should you love one another.'"

The whole place went silent.

I've heard people say, "Show me your friends and I'll show you who you are." We are largely a collection of our relationships. That means we have a corporate responsibility to love others.

Do you recall the story in Joshua 7 of Achan and the battle for Jericho? After the walls came down, Achan took some forbidden spoils and hid them under his tent. As a result, thirty-six Israelite soldiers died in a much smaller battle at a city called Ai. When Achan's sin was finally revealed, he and his whole family were executed.

"Hey, that's unfair," most Westerners might say. "Why kill the entire family?"

But God was declaring to his people that Achan could not have done what he did without his family's knowledge and complicity.

You and I are the sum total of the community around us, and God has declared that corporate responsibility is important to him. Do you remember how Daniel confessed the sins of his great-great-great-great-ancestors? He confessed their sin as his own.[10]

When we visited the Congo in 2014, we made a movie about Goma, the rape capital of the world. When one girl shared a gruesome story of her own rape, a young man who was part of the tribe that had raped her asked her for forgiveness. I've rarely seen anything more powerful. He sank to his knees and said, "On behalf of my people, I ask for forgiveness." The women who had been abused started crying and weeping.

Because we're made in the image of God and because we're a community, we bear a certain aspect of corporate responsibility.

My father frequently told me a story about an incident that happened in his boyhood days. He and some friends were throwing rocks into the river when one of the boys hit a woman. The woman took note, returned to her village, and reported, "That boy hit me with a rock." And of course the story traveled.

When my grandpa got wind that my dad had been with those boys, he gave him a beating. Now, my dad had not thrown the rock that hit the woman, but he was there. He got punished after my grandpa asked, "What were you doing with boys who were throwing rocks at women?"

That may sound unfair and unjust, but the truth is that it reflects corporate responsibility. We learned that if one of us hits a woman with a rock, then it's as if we all hit that woman with a rock. That's a very foreign concept to Western ears, but it's something we need to address.

There is a community aspect to our gospel work. When one person fails, we all fail. When one succeeds, we all succeed. We're part of a team, and teams win and lose *together*. If we really believe that people are the wealth, we wouldn't have it any other way.

9

SERVANT LEADERSHIP

Charles Schulz, creator of the *Peanuts* comic strip, once created a thought experiment to help people identify those who have significantly influenced their lives. Try it yourself:

- Name the five wealthiest people in the world.
- Name the last five Heisman Trophy winners.
- Name the last five World Cup winners.
- Name the last five Miss World winners.
- Name the last five Academy Award Best Actor winners.

None of these people are second-rate achievers. All are among the best of the best, the most famous in their fields—but for some reason, it's hard to recall them after even a few months. Schulz said this isn't hard to understand, because awards tarnish and we quickly forget achievements and accolades.

Now try a second exercise.

- Name five schoolteachers who had the greatest impact on you.
- Name five friends who helped you get through tough times.
- Name five people who have taught you something worthwhile.
- Name five people who appreciated you and made you feel special.
- Name five people with whom you enjoy spending time.

I'm confident that your second list is far easier for you to compile than the first. I'm equally confident that the people on your second list have affected your life more than those on the first. I don't mean that the rich and famous have no impact. But this exercise suggests that the people who make the biggest difference in our lives are those who care for us, serve us, and lead us well.

I recently saw a video featuring modern-day celebrities honoring their teachers. Such unsung heroes mold us into the people we are today. I recall how teachers in most of Africa are held in the highest regard, at times even higher than heads of state. This explains why a successful teacher in Tanzania could rise through the ranks to become president for many years. But throughout his years in office, Julius Kambarage Nyerere was known by the name Mwalimu, which means "teacher" in Kiswahili. He was known as "teacher" because in Tanzania that title is held in higher esteem than "president."

Great teachers are terrific servant leaders—and servant leadership is a key element of the ethos we need in Christian missions, both as individuals and as countercultural communities of faith. A *received* identity—who we are in Christ—is more important than an *achieved* identity. Jesus loved us and served us first, and therefore we serve and love others—not coerced by duty or a desire to achieve, but compelled by the beauty of Christ's example.

Concepts in Tension

The late Robert Greenleaf, who developed the concept of servant leadership, said that it embodies two distinct concepts that are often considered opposites. Servant leadership serves *first* and leads *second.* Though a tension exists between the two, serving others must come before concerns about productivity.

We usually think of leadership the other way around: *I'm a leader*; therefore *I serve*. But Greenleaf says, "*The great leader is seen as servant first*, and that simple fact is the key to his greatness."[1] True servant leadership means putting one's own self-interest *after* the needs of others. Servant leaders willingly give up the perks of their position and hierarchy to listen so they might learn and know.

Part of what it means to "hit the ground listening" aligns closely to what author Stephen Covey says in his classic book *The 7 Habits of Highly Effective People*: "Seek first to understand, then to be understood."[2] If we seek first to recognize and understand the image of God in other people, to start first with building *relationships*, we will meet people where they are but we will not leave them as they are. We will recognize their inherent value and dignity. We will see that God created them to enjoy an inner fullness that they can never experience apart from a living relationship with Jesus.[3]

How Did He Come?

How did Jesus come to this earth? Paul reminds us that Christ "emptied himself, by taking the form of a servant, being born in the likeness of men."[4]

When Jesus left heaven, he *emptied* himself of a vast portion of his divine prerogative. He emptied himself, not of his deity—that would be impossible—but of the infinite majesty that had eternally bathed heaven in brilliant light. No wonder he spoke of his full glory both in past and future tenses in his "high priestly prayer" in John 17. Toward the beginning of his prayer, Jesus asks his Father to "glorify me in your presence with the glory I had with you before the world began."[5] A schematic might look like this:

- Before Creation: full glory
- At the Incarnation: veiled glory
- After the Ascension: full glory

Except for a moment at the Transfiguration,[6] the disciples did not see Jesus in his full glory—and yet even what they saw left them speechless. John, one of the three disciples who were on the Mount of Transfiguration, later wrote, "We have seen his glory, the glory of the one and only Son, who came from the Father, full of grace and truth."[7] Peter, who was also there, said, "We were eyewitnesses of his majesty."[8] In 1 Corinthians 2:8, Paul refers to Jesus as "the Lord of glory." And the writer to the Hebrews says, "The Son is the radiance of God's glory and the exact representation of his being."[9]

Though Jesus veiled the full expression of his glory during his earthly ministry, he never ceased to be the Lord of glory. The popular Christmas carol "Hark! the Herald Angels Sing" wonderfully captures this truth:

Veiled in flesh the Godhead see;
Hail th' incarnate Deity,
Pleased as man with men to dwell,
Jesus, our Emmanuel.

I think it's important for us to see that Jesus accomplished his mission on earth while still full of glory, even though for a time that glory was purposely concealed.

It's highly significant that Paul begins his theological teaching on the "emptying" of Christ with some very practical words to the church in Philippi:

> If there is any encouragement in Christ, any comfort from love, any participation in the Spirit, any affection and sympathy, complete my joy by being of the same mind, having the same love, being in full accord and of one mind. Do nothing from selfish ambition or conceit, but in humility count others more significant than yourselves. Let each of you look not only to his own interests, but also to the interests of others.[10]

The word translated "conceit" is the Greek term *kenodoxia*, which comes from two terms, *kenos* ("empty") and *doxa* ("glory"). The term means "a state of pride without basis or justification," or "self-deluded conceit driven by personal delusions of grandeur," or "boasting where there is nothing to boast about." It is "based on nothing and comes to nothing." It's "glory empty."[11]

Paul says to his Philippian friends, "Don't be like that. Get rid of any personal delusions of grandeur. Don't be empty glory people; rather, follow the example of our Lord Jesus. Though he came to earth as the Lord of glory, he consciously emptied himself of many of his divine rights and privileges. He did this in his love and grace, so that he might become a servant to us all. Now follow his example."

Philippians 2 gives us the basis for the idea of servant leadership. If we look at the place where servant leadership is best embodied, if we look to find the best missions person, it's Jesus, hands down. God himself has the biggest mission: to save the world. But what did he do to accomplish it? He sent us Jesus, the most amazing servant leader in history.

He Came as Emmanuel

If our missions strategies and paradigms took seriously the reality that all human beings are made in God's image—though marred by sin—what would change in the way we do missions? What *should* change, if anything? The incarnation of Jesus Christ provides us with a beautiful picture of what global missions should involve.

The greatest missions effort in history began when God moved to restore the broken relationship between himself and the human beings he had created in his own image. Yet his strategy to accomplish this seems antithetical to nearly every contemporary strategy we observe. Let's remind ourselves of how Jesus went about his work.

He arrived weak and dependent

Jesus arrived on this earth in human form as a baby,[12] which doesn't seem like the most strategic way to start addressing the greatest mission. A baby is vulnerable, weak, and dependent, and can neither fend for itself nor defend itself. Jesus came in poverty and grew up in obscurity. He did not arrive on the scene as a full-grown, powerful adult. He came as an infant, fully dependent on the care of his parents.

The writer of Hebrews explains that "he [Jesus] had to be made like his brothers in every respect, so that he might become a merciful and faithful high priest . . . to make propitiation for the sins of the people."[13] He came to earth like us—weak and dependent—so that we can become like him.

He grew in wisdom and stature

Luke explains that, as Jesus came of age, he "grew in wisdom and stature."[14] He needed to mature in both his thinking and his body. Jesus grew physically and mentally, as all humans must. It startles me to realize that he did almost nothing that God chose to record in Scripture for the first three decades of his life. Why not? Why did Jesus wait until he was "about thirty years old" to begin his ministry?[15]

He could have preached at a younger age. Healed at a younger age. Taught at a younger age. Ministered and cast out demons and multiplied loaves and fish at a younger age. He could have died and risen again as a younger man. But he waited until he was thirty.

Why?

The choice wasn't efficient, by our standards. It wasn't quick. If heaven had required Jesus to send in missions reports in those early years, as we do, can you imagine what they would have looked like? We'd consider them scandalous:

"Today I built a table and hung a door."

"Today I walked to a field outside of Nazareth, where I prayed."

"Today I studied Torah."

The thirty-year approach would never fly in most of our contemporary missions models.

Why did Jesus wait so long before starting his public ministry? He was giving us an example. He was showing us what it means to be *present* before proclamation. *People* were at the heart of his mission. As Emmanuel, Jesus came to be *with* us, to *know* us, to be *like* us (except for our sin, of course), so that he can *change* us. Shouldn't his loving attitude and actions toward people frame our own theological convictions about missions, especially at the front end?

He learned how to relate to God and man

Jesus also "grew . . . in favor with God and man."[16] He grew spiritually. He studied Torah. He learned obedience. He suffered the indignities of human life. In order to relate to us, he came to earth as one of us. "Although he was a son," the writer of Hebrews tells us, "he learned obedience through what he suffered."[17]

To grow in favor with man means, at least in part, that Jesus needed to learn the customs of his people, their ways, their language, their habits, what they believed, how they lived, and what they liked and disliked. He started his mission by acculturating to his people. For thirty years, he participated as an active member of the community so he could understand his people. As Emmanuel, he could have arrived with that knowledge already in mind; he is God, after all. But he was willing to learn from the ground up so that he could accomplish his central mission of becoming our Savior and an example for us to follow.

He humbled himself even in his choice of work

Jesus was full of glory when he arrived on earth. He didn't come pretending to be something he wasn't. Yet his whole way of engaging involved humbling himself. What career did he take on? Craftsman or builder.[†] A noble profession, to be sure, but hardly something that shouts "glory" to us. He could have been anything, but he became a carpenter, or a stonemason.

He spent large chunks of time with his followers

Jesus chose to become part of the community before ever trying to reach or teach anyone. He said, "These are my people. I know them, and I love them." He began by being present, not by challenging people or trying to convince them to believe in him. Jesus' model of effective missions begins with an investment of *time*. For those who follow him, *presence* precedes *persuasion*.

[†] According to Palestinian scholar Daniel Munayer, who leads Musalaha, an organization that fosters reconciliation between Israeli and Palestinian youth, our Bible translations might erroneously peg Jesus as a carpenter. It's more likely, Daniel says, that Jesus would have been a stonemason. "Go and see in all of Israel, there are no wood buildings," he says. "Most of the work there is stone." Carpenters do more than build houses, of course; they also construct tables and chairs of wood and craft wooden utensils and tools and so on. But many scholars now suggest that the Greek word *tektōn*, usually translated as "carpenter," might more accurately be rendered as "craftsman" or "builder." Food for thought.

He looked for a diverse group of followers with potential

When Jesus began his public ministry, he started by aligning himself with a small group of no-name individuals. He went to the margins of society and looked for diversity. His disciples came from varied backgrounds: Zealots (whose mission was to kill others), tax collectors (whose job was to defraud others), fishermen (whose livelihood involved putting their lives in danger to catch fish). He came with a cultivation mindset, not an assimilation mindset. But despite all the diversity, he never lost himself.

As a servant leader, Jesus raised up amazing leaders. But who were they? He chose individuals in whom he saw potential, not those who already held positions of great power. What Jesus learned in his early years acculturating to Jewish society allowed him to identify the kind of individuals he wanted as disciples. He could say, "I've walked the streets and visited the markets. I know that the ones I need are not those who sit in seats of power. I need to get some fishermen—I see in them a tenacity, a faithfulness, a persistence, a work ethic. Yes, that's where I need to start. I'm going to take these no-names and mold them into men and women who will change the world."

He taught informally

How did Jesus teach as a servant leader? He didn't teach formal courses in a classroom; he taught by using life experiences and situations. As he walked in the fields, he said to his disciples, "Do you see these wheat and tares? Let them grow together."[18] He got into a boat on a lake and said to his men, "Let's cross to the other side," knowing the lessons that awaited them out on the water.[19] As he passed by the Temple in Jerusalem, he foretold its destruction and taught his followers about things to come.[20] He never told them, "Hey, sit down and take out your notebooks." He didn't overwhelm them with content. Instead, as he walked through life with them, he would sometimes stop and ask, "What do you see?" He drew out key ideas that he wanted them to remember and put into practice.

He helped his disciples learn how to work together

Jesus consistently put his disciples into tough situations where they had no choice but to learn how to work together. They had to live together, eat together, and travel together. They spent a lot of time together, and they didn't always get along.[21] But Jesus made it clear to them *how* they could learn to work together: "A new command I give you: Love one another. As I have loved you, so you must love one another. By this everyone will know that you are my disciples, if you love one another."[22]

He translated their gifts from one arena to another

Jesus took a diverse group of individuals, including several fishermen, and told them, "I will make you fishers of men."[23] He translated their gifts from one arena into another. Where they had been seeking after fish in the Sea of Galilee, he intended for them to seek and to save people who were in need of salvation. By acculturation, he would show them how to reach people from a posture of meekness and humility. It takes a strong person to be meek.

He prepared his followers for his absence

Jesus continually did something else that is a huge part of successful missions. He prepared his disciples for the time when he would no longer be with them.[24] He frequently reminded them, "I'm not always going to be here with you."[25]

What happened when Jesus ascended into heaven? Far more ministry took place on earth than ever before. No doubt that's what

Jesus meant when he said, "Whoever believes in me will also do the works that I do; and greater works than these will he do, because I am going to the Father."[26] Those "greater works" became possible because the Lord left his followers with the Holy Spirit to empower them and guide them. In his physical body, Jesus could be in only one place at a time. But once the Holy Spirit came at Pentecost, he brought the presence of Jesus everywhere his followers went.

Following Emmanuel's Example

Do we typically follow Jesus' pattern in the way we pursue Christian missions? Let's take another look at the characteristics of his ministry we just noted.

Do we go out to the mission field weak and dependent?

This feels so counterintuitive to people in the West that it's hard to even contemplate. But if we don't comprehend our limitations and our need to depend on God for everything, we will never accomplish God's purpose in the world. In practical terms, do we hit the ground *listening*, open to learning and coming alongside, or do we go in large and in charge?

Do we go humbly, open to growing in wisdom and stature?

Too often, we think we understand what is needed, and we take our problem-solving mindset into the field. Without investing the time needed to build reciprocal relationships and trust, and to discover what God is already doing there, we immediately start implementing our plans and proclaiming the gospel. We don't look for opportunities to learn from the locals, and therefore we bypass the hard work of gaining wisdom.

Are we learning how to relate to God and men?

Do we identify with the people who so desperately need the gospel? Or do we start with *content* rather than *connection*? Do we learn how to *pray first* and act later, or do we move ahead and then ask God to bless our efforts?

Do we go as servants?

Do we go with vulnerability, as servant leaders in the mold of Jesus, or do we succumb to a bias for action? Western leaders sometimes go into the global world not as servants but as sovereign leaders. Their money gains them leverage. Their easy access to cash puts them in a position to gain power. On the flip side, leaders in the two-thirds world sometimes use guilt to prompt Westerners to second-guess themselves and question whether they even need to engage globally. When we do these things, we all fail to humble ourselves, and nobody acts as a servant leader.

Do we spend large chunks of time with those to whom we minister?

Are we willing to invest the time it takes to really get to know other people? Even if it takes years, or even decades? Are we building reciprocal relationships based on trust? Are we committed to putting *presence* before *persuasion*?

Do we look for diverse disciples with leadership potential?

Just as I initially overlooked members of our facilities staff, like Roman Garcia, as potential participants on our global missions trips, most people would probably not see a poor fisherman as a future world changer. We wouldn't identify a Zealot as a future leader who could turn the world upside down (without using a dagger). We wouldn't peg a tax collector, a person loathed by his community and ostracized by his own people, as an influencer. But Jesus did. How should his approach to finding and developing leaders guide us as we seek to do the same? How should we choose the people we invite to come alongside us?

Do we teach informally?

In the West, we're accustomed to learning through seminars and workshops and reading books. But such an approach doesn't work quite as well in the majority world, where teaching is often more informal and relational. Informal teaching, the kind that Jesus did, requires *time* and an investment in *community*. There's no substitute for getting involved in people's day-to-day lives. That's how we learn what is important to them, and how we can best contextualize our teaching. How can we learn to do this better?

Do we help our partners learn how to work together?

Building strong, reciprocal relationships depends on learning how to work well together. And it all starts with humility. If we are willing to learn from others, they will be more open to learning from us. Working well together often means being a catalyst rather than an initiator. When we think more highly of others than we think of ourselves, when we look for the image of God in others and seek to draw out their gifts, we create an environment in which cooperation and collaboration can thrive. When the disciples "argued with one another about who was the greatest," Jesus sat them down and said, "If anyone would be first, he must be last of all and servant of all."[27] Are we coalescing our partners to work together? If so, how?

Do we help people translate their gifts from one arena to another?

Before we can help people translate their gifts from one arena to another, we must first be able to see what those gifts are. At the risk of sounding the same note yet again, it starts with seeing the image of God in them. Just as it took going to Kenya with Roman Garcia for me to see how his unique gifts were exactly what Mavuno Church needed for their move into a new facility, it takes spending time with people—and keeping our eyes open—to see how their gifts might translate. Humility, prayer, and paying attention are prerequisites for drawing out the best in other people.

Do we prepare others for our absence?

As servant leaders, we want the work to go on after we've left the scene. We don't want everything to stop once we're no longer around to keep it going. This is a vital component of the *relief, reinforcement*, and *reform* process we discussed in chapter 3. The whole point of the *reform* stage is helping the people we serve to stand on their own two feet so that they no longer need us. Whatever work the Lord does through our efforts does not have to live and die with us. In fact, Jesus has raised up an army of servant leaders in our day and age who can take on the mantle of previous leaders who have left and gone on to another task or died. Servant leadership is not hierarchical. It's not about power. It's about being in proximity with a leader who deposits in others what he or she knows, and who commissions those leaders to carry on the work in their own way.

Don't Quit

Many people lack the conviction of the first disciples, because when things go awry, they give up and throw in the towel. They say, "If it's this uncomfortable, I don't want to go," or "If I don't have money, I don't want to go," or "If I don't have perfect clarity from the start, I can't go."

But when I read the second half of Hebrews 11, the so-called Hall of Faith, I see godly people who were "tortured, refusing to accept release, so that they might rise again to a better life. Others suffered mocking and flogging, and even chains and imprisonment. They were stoned, they were sawn in two, they were killed with the sword. They went about in skins of sheep and goats, destitute, afflicted, mistreated—of whom the world was not worthy—wandering about in deserts and mountains, and in dens and caves of the earth."[28]

Near the end of Paul's life, he doesn't brag about the churches he planted, the young protégés he mentored, or all the letters he wrote (that now make up nearly half the New Testament). Instead, he speaks of "far greater labors, far more imprisonments, with countless beatings, and often [being] near death."[29] He continues:

> Five times I received at the hands of the Jews the forty lashes less one. Three times I was beaten with rods. Once I was stoned. Three times I was shipwrecked; a night and a day I was adrift at sea; on frequent journeys, in danger from rivers, danger from robbers, danger from my own people, danger from Gentiles, danger in the city, danger in the wilderness, danger at sea, danger from false brothers; in toil and hardship; through many a sleepless night, in hunger and thirst, often without food, in cold and exposure. . . . If I must boast, I will boast of the things that show my weakness.[30]

As his days on earth are winding down, he tells us that "all who are in Asia turned away from me."[31] He recalls the "persecutions and sufferings that happened to me at Antioch, at Iconium, and at Lystra—which persecutions I endured."[32] He declares, "I am already being poured out as a drink offering, and the time of my departure has come,"[33] and he begs Timothy, "Do your best to come to me soon. For Demas, in love with this present world, has deserted me and gone to Thessalonica. Crescens has gone to Galatia, Titus to Dalmatia. Luke alone is with me."[34] The apostle also reports that "Alexander the coppersmith did me great harm" and he warns Timothy, "Beware of him yourself, for he strongly opposed our message. At my first defense no one came to stand by me, but all deserted me."[35]

And yet, this great apostle, this amazing servant leader, even as he begins to hear the executioner's footsteps approaching, writes, "The Lord will rescue me from every evil deed and bring me safely into his heavenly kingdom. To him be the glory forever and ever. Amen."[36]

So He Sends Us

Jesus came to earth as a servant leader. And just as God sent Jesus into the world, so he sends *us*. We leave our places of comfortable familiarity and go into the global world as Christ did, with humility, with empathy, with hearts full of love and respect for all those we meet.

Like Jesus, we go "full of glory," because the Holy Spirit fills us. We can therefore empty ourselves; we can be meek; we can be vulnerable, dependent, and weak as babies. We can come in obscurity and in poverty, and we can spend time with the people God has called us to serve—maybe investing even thirty years learning and getting to know them. We have the opportunity to see the true potential of people we might never have chosen on our own.

God isn't looking for rock stars, but for people who want their lives to bless others. Because they have seen Jesus and walked with him, they are willing to give their entire lives to him.

When Jesus prays in John 17, he isn't praying only for the disciples who were with him in the upper room; he's praying for *all* his disciples down through the ages. As he prayed that night, he was praying for you and me as well. That's a servant leader. And that's who we want to be like.

The late Pastor John Bisagno of First Baptist Church in Houston once said, "We give our life to Christ not because He demands it but because He deserves it."[37] As servant leaders, we get to create a community that will last beyond our time. We do so by remembering that it takes all of us to care for each one of us. Servant leaders put character above function, motive above action, humility above promotion, faithfulness above success, and others above self. Humbling ourselves like the timeless one, Jesus, we pursue the Great Collaboration. Jesus had it all, but he laid it all down so that we might be reconciled to him.

Let's not be so busy with platforms, publicity, profits, and platitudes that we forget that Christ's finished work on the cross is sufficient for us to go out in joyful servitude. Leadership isn't just about being in charge, it's about caring for those in your charge. It means not serving yourself but serving others—and no one models this truth like Jesus does. Will we be courageous enough to follow his example?

10

LIFE CHANGE

Our lives should naturally change as we go into missions. Working with and serving others is just as formational for us as it is for those to whom we minister. We're not just "doing a mission" or accomplishing something; we are being formed into the likeness of Christ. If we are on mission, we should expect to be transformed.

In America, I learned an easy way to tell whether life change is happening in a person's life. Simply answer these three questions:

1. How do they spend their time?
2. How do they spend their talent?
3. How do they spend their treasure?

Let's look at all three areas and see how much life change we ourselves are experiencing.

Rethinking Our Time

How does missions change how we spend our time? We were spending time doing one thing, and now we're taking that precious time to do something else.

I've observed that one of the most expensive possessions for my Western brothers and sisters is *time*. Many would rather give their money than their time, because they consider time their most precious commodity.

But what if we started thinking about missions in terms of investing our *time* rather than our money? We spend time with people because we value them—we believe they have enough worth and dignity to warrant the investment.

Do you want to know if your life is being changed? First consider how you spend your time.

If you're involved with justice and compassion, do you avoid offering quick solutions? Do you dig deep to find out what's *really* happening on the ground?

If you're involved in evangelism, do you just give people the gospel message, or do you work to *embody* the gospel message? How do you *show* people what the gospel looks like in real life? Remember, we're not just trying to save souls; we're working to restore image bearers. We want every image bearer to find the Lord's path back to their full glory, as originally intended by God himself.

None of this happens without spending time with people. How are you spending your time?

There's a saying I've heard in the majority world: Americans have their timepieces, but we have the time. In most of the world, an event starts when it starts and it ends when it ends. It doesn't depend on a clock. We live more in tune with the rhythm of the world, so we're free to spend as much time as necessary. We're not watching the clock and counting the cost.

Can we in the West rethink and reimagine what time means? Do we dare to invest our most expensive commodity, our most valuable asset, in missions? Often, it seems, the answer is *no*. Whether it's evangelism or justice and compassion work, we want quick answers, we want an efficient experience, we want a tidy return on our investment.

But here's the thing: Giving *time* allows excellent things to happen. Giving time can change people's lives. The amount of time we give affects the quality of our disciple-making because discipleship takes time. Discipleship is not an event; it's an ongoing narrative. It takes a good chunk of time because we often don't know when life change is happening.

Do you remember the brief story of Enoch in the book of Genesis? "Enoch walked faithfully with God; then he was no more, because God took him away."[1] God and Enoch walked together on earth for hundreds of years, and through their walking together, Enoch was being transformed. Then one day he found himself in heaven. I can just imagine the scenario.

"What are you doing here?" an angel asked.

"I was just keeping in step with God," Enoch replied, "and I wound up here."

That's how Enoch got to heaven. He never died.

The Bible says, "Thus all the days of Enoch were 365 years."[2] Enoch and God spent bunches of time together, and as they did, Enoch was being restored to the image of God.

We must rethink our perspectives on time. We must take the long view. We must move away from our devotion to the clock and start spending real, unhurried time with people.

Think about the typical discipleship process, especially for missions. We need to understand that our *programs* don't disciple people; *people* disciple people. Though our Rooted program has proved to be a great tool for discipleship, it's still only a tool—and a tool is only as good as the way it is used. One of the key features of Rooted is that it takes time to do it well. Rooted is not a class; it's a life experience.

Rooted is not primarily *teaching*. Teaching is quick, contained, efficient. Rooted is all about facilitating action, which is difficult because you never know what's about to happen. A facilitator must be equipped and ready to spend extra time—because if somebody says something earth-shattering, it will likely take some time to unpack. The facilitator simply doesn't know how others will react. An investment of time is required, sufficient to the needs of the day.

What does it mean for us to go into missions—not as teachers, but as facilitators? I think of the men and women who left Scotland and journeyed to Kenya. They could have come and preached at my grandfather and his people, saying, "Hey, don't worship mountains or idols! Let us tell you about the real God, who wants your worship. You don't have to worship dead idols." But they didn't do that. They took time to observe and understand what the villagers were doing. They did not immediately teach; they facilitated, and eventually they were able to make a connection that opened the gospel to an entire tribe.

Rooted is built around an expansive need for time. Week 3 is devoted to prayer, but most people don't even know how to pray. So how do we help people learn how to pray? One thing I usually do—and this is extremely pertinent for going into the global world in missions—is to take some time. If people don't understand how to pray, I'll stop and ask them, "How many of you have ever prayed out loud?"

"I've never prayed out loud," many typically will answer.

"Great!" I say, "Today we're going to learn about prayer."

Then I'll look around at the group and maybe say, "Ari, if you were going to pray, what would you pray for?"

Ari might reply, "I'd pray for my daughter and her situation at school, I'd pray for my wife and her sore back."

Then I move to the next person and ask the same thing. I might spend an hour, asking each person in the group what they would pray for. And at the end of that hour, I say, "In Jesus' name, amen."

Until that moment, many of the group members hadn't realized that they were *praying* during that whole hour. They didn't have to close their eyes. They didn't have to bow their heads and say, "Father in heaven." All I did was ask them what they would pray for. And in those moments, they were quite literally talking to God.

"All of you, just now," I tell them, "have prayed out loud."

That's what prayer is: It's talking to God. It's casual, but it takes time.

My wife used to work in the automotive industry. She often came home tired and annoyed, and I could hear the exasperation in her voice.

One day I said to her, "Why can't you just be happy?"

That was the wrong thing to say!

"I wish *you* spent time with people who do not know God, so that you would feel the weight of all that I feel—the things people say and do all around me," she replied. "I actually do more ministry than *you* do. You're always around the truth at church, always with people who are praying and loving Jesus. You're a pastor, but I'm out there with people who are cursing at me the whole time. You don't even know anybody who isn't a Christian."

"Wow, that's true," I had to admit. "I live in a bubble."

So I started hanging out once a week at a local wine bar. As I started getting to know the people and their stories, I had the opportunity to tell my own story. At one point, some of the people grew so curious about my story that they said, "Interesting. Tell us more."

Can you guess what I did? I told them, "Come every week and we're gonna talk about some topics that I address in my own life—issues like 'Where is God when you're suffering?' 'What do you believe about God?'" In essence, I started a six-week Rooted group without using the book.

At one point, one of the men, a guy named Sam, heard me say I was going to Taiwan.

"I'm from Taiwan," he said. "Do you need money?"

"Well, we do raise money for our trips," I replied.

Right there and then, he wrote me a check for two thousand dollars. I could not have anticipated that. And I wasn't asking anyone there for money for my trip. But he gave it to me anyway.

"You know . . . just because," he said.

I attribute all this to the fact that I took time to get to know him, I engaged with him in his own environment, and I sought to understand him for who he is.

Life change happens when we change how we value and use our time.

Rethinking Our Talent

Life change also happens when we invest our talent more effectively. Our abilities are a gift we have received from God. As the apostle Paul said in writing to the church in Corinth, "What do you have that God hasn't given you? And if everything you have is from God, why boast as though it were not a gift?"[3]

Unfortunately, too often we go into missions asking people what they *need* rather than what they *have*. But what if we turned that same question back on ourselves?

"What do *I* have?"

The gifts and abilities that God has given each one of us can be put to good use serving others, both at home and abroad. All it takes is recognizing what we already have, rather than focusing on needs and shortcomings.

One time I was looking at a list of people who had gone to Uganda with us, and two names in particular—Doug and Eric—stood out to me. Both are accomplished businessmen, and they had gone to Uganda to give out wheelchairs so that some of God's image bearers with disabilities would no longer have to crawl in the dust.

Now, it's great to give out wheelchairs. People with disabilities around the world need them. But it had never occurred to me that these two tremendous businessmen from America might also be able to sit down with some Ugandan businesspeople to help them improve their understanding of sound business principles. And they could still hand out their wheelchairs.

I'm not a businessman, but I can imagine some of the topics that might be covered: How to diversify. How to raise capital. How to reinvest profits. How to roll out distribution. Just by having those kinds of conversations, some people might find a new purpose within themselves, a new and enhanced use for their own talent. Some people might have promising enterprises that they want to develop and build, but they lack wisdom, experience, and knowledge, and they need seasoned counsel.

From this flash of insight, I learned an important lesson: *Don't get tunnel vision.* Look for every opportunity to connect the gifts and abilities of your people with corresponding people in the places you are going. Go in with an attitude of reciprocal learning—everyone learning from everyone else—and see what God will do.

When we fail to consider the full range of talent, wisdom, experience, and skills of the people on our missions teams, we miss out on opportunities to help others become better, more effective image bearers. And that's applicable on both sides of the equation—with those who are able to use their gifts, and those who benefit from those gifts. So how do we change? How do we rethink our talent, skills, and experience?

I've always wanted to take an offering of *talent*, rather than money (and someday I hope to do it). What if instead of asking people to reach for their wallets, we asked them to give an offering of their talents?

Maybe Daria works as a writer. What if we found a person where we're going who is trying to contextualize a curriculum, or adapt some text from another culture or language, and needs help? Could Daria help that person? I would ask her to come with us so we could use the gifting God has given her.

I would also try to find individuals in the places where we're going who have gifts that they could share with us. In that way, we can experience a beautiful, mutual exchange of gifts, insights, and abilities.

I think we've been missing the boat here. We haven't been tapping into the talents and gifts of our people, and of others, because we haven't looked, we haven't asked. But when life transformation occurs, it alters the way we invest our gifts and talents. I've seen it happen.

I once took a young woman named Betsy to Kenya. When she returned, she said, "The people in Kenya are so passionate. They're so good. I don't have that kind of passion. I just don't."

"Betsy," I replied, "what do you do for a living?"

"I work for an accounting software company."

"So, Betsy," I said, "does that mean you like spreadsheets?"

Her eyes lit up, and she said, "I *love* spreadsheets."

"The people in Kenya may need somebody to help them with their spreadsheets," I said.

"Really?"

We connected Betsy with Regina, who was working for a Kenyan school. Regina asked Betsy to help her balance the books, and I don't think I've ever seen anyone as unleashed for missions as Betsy was. She became *crazy* about this—in a good way. She became a huge advocate for Regina, and from that point on, Regina never had to worry about financing and funding. Betsy is a great example of using her talents and gifts for missions.

Another young woman, Christy, also went with us to Kenya, and she said a very similar thing: "The Kenyans are so passionate about their cities, but I'm not passionate about the city where I live. What if I became passionate about my city?"

At the time, she was attending UC Irvine. So she changed her major to urban planning, and today she works for the city of Anaheim as an urban planner, helping marginalized communities save money through better housing and equipment. Whatever the program participants save, they put toward a college fund. Christy is using her gifts to help people in Anaheim because she went to Kenya and ignited a new passion. The talent was already there, but she needed *vision*. Now she is taking her talents to a different level.

The late evangelist Luis Palau used to travel the world, holding evangelistic festivals. He would bring along famous sports people—maybe a young athlete who was a world-class martial artist or a BMX rider or a professional skateboarder—to draw people in. Their talents and notoriety could be used to attract the attention and interest of people who didn't yet know Jesus, and they would pass along the gospel message.

Nobody can give themselves a talent or a skill. Everything we have comes from God. The athletes who partnered with Luis were saying, "My talent is not mine. It's my Savior's. I'm just going to lay it down."

Do you remember the parable of the talents in Matthew 25:14-30? God gives us talents to multiply for him. In the process, disciples are multiplied around the world.

A man named Ken Mwalabu went to work in the informal settlements around Nairobi. He was concerned about the number of young girls who were becoming pregnant.

"They get pregnant because boys are idle," he said. "They sleep with girls as a form of recreation. So we've created soccer teams—U12, U14, U16. If we give these boys something to do that uses their gifts and talents, they won't be out there sleeping around with girls."

Can you imagine? As Ken assessed the situation, he realized, "The problem is with the boys, and the solution is recreation. These boys are looking for something useful to do, to keep them busy. So let's start some soccer teams."

Milele helped Ken and his team start a soccer ministry in the settlements, and they have had amazing success. Soccer has kept a lot of boys away from promiscuity, which has saved a lot of girls from early pregnancies.

Do you see how this works? It's just a different approach. It's tapping into the things that people already have. Everybody has *something*, even when they think they don't.

There's an interesting story in the book of 2 Kings, during a dark time in Israel's history:

> The wife of a man from the company of the prophets cried out to Elisha, "Your servant my husband is dead, and you know that he revered the LORD. But now his creditor is coming to take my two boys as his slaves."
>
> Elisha replied to her, "How can I help you? Tell me, what do you have in your house?"
>
> "Your servant has nothing there at all," she said, "except a small jar of olive oil."
>
> Elisha said, "Go around and ask all your neighbors for empty jars. Don't ask for just a few. Then go inside and

> shut the door behind you and your sons. Pour oil into all the jars, and as each is filled, put it to one side."
>
> She left him and shut the door behind her and her sons. They brought the jars to her and she kept pouring. When all the jars were full, she said to her son, "Bring me another one."
>
> But he replied, "There is not a jar left." Then the oil stopped flowing.
>
> She went and told the man of God, and he said, "Go, sell the oil and pay your debts. You and your sons can live on what is left."[4]

When Elisha asked the woman what she had to give, in her deep grief she saw herself as destitute, empty, a total vacuum. But then, almost as an afterthought, she added, "Except I have a small jar of oil." God took that woman's "nothing at all" and multiplied it into enough oil to not only pay off her husband's creditor but to also give her something to live on.

God delights in taking a little and turning it into more than we can imagine. We simply have to rethink our talents, our assets, and our experience and offer them to him.

Rethinking Our Money

In the West, when we consider global missions we usually think of money. But the money we give to missions is almost always *extra* that we know we can spare.

But when our lives are changed, it ultimately changes how we spend our money. We will be less inclined to hold on to treasure for ourselves, because our priorities will have changed. We will no longer use that money primarily on ourselves, but for others.

Life change *always* changes the way we spend our money.

Before the transformation, we would say, "This is my money, to spend however I choose." After life change, we start saying, "The money I spend on myself is money that's not available to spend on others." We change our mindset. Now we want to use that money for a short-term missions trip or to support a ministry partner somewhere in the world.

Life change is massively important, because when the love of Jesus transforms our lives, our perspective on the money God has entrusted to us changes along with it. Eventually we start looking at money as God's, not our own.

What would it take for you to start looking at money as God's money, rather than as your money? I'm talking about more than financial generosity given out of abundance. As we start visiting places around the planet, we start seeing that people in the global world have a lot to offer financially, even if they don't have much money (by our standards).

The apostle Paul says no one is too poor to give. We can all give something. The church in ancient Philippi was monetarily poor, and yet Paul was able to write to its members, "In the early days of your acquaintance with the gospel, when I set out from Macedonia, not one church shared with me in the matter of giving and receiving, except you only; for even when I was in Thessalonica, you sent me aid more than once when I was in need."[5] No one is too poor to give; everyone can give *something*.

I read a story recently about a Christian church in one of the poorest parts of India that not only supports itself financially but also sends out hundreds of missionaries. Their secret is found in "a handful of rice." Every time the church members fix a meal, they set aside a handful of rice to donate to the church. The church then sells the rice to raise money for their work. No one is too poor to give; everyone can give something. As the pastor of the church says, "It is not our richness or our poverty that make us serve the

Lord, but our willingness. . . . As long as we have something to eat every day, we have something to give to God every day."[6]

This story reminds me of the time when the apostle Peter told a man who had been disabled his entire life, "I have no silver and gold, but what I do have I give to you. In the name of Jesus Christ of Nazareth, rise up and walk!"[7]

And I love what the very next verse says. Peter didn't just tell the man to get up and walk and then leave him. Instead, "taking him by the right hand, *he helped him up*, and instantly the man's feet and ankles became strong."[8] That's powerful.

I think of the early church, who gave out of their poverty, and yet none of those new disciples lacked anything.[9] When *everybody* gives because *no one* is too poor to give, it changes the way we give.

It frankly bothers me when I hear of people described as having "the gift of generosity." More often than not, we have in mind people with a high net worth. But generosity isn't determined by how much someone gives. It has far more to do with the attitude of their heart. Would you like to evaluate your own generosity? Then don't look at what you're giving. Look instead at what's left *after* you give. That will help you understand your true level of generosity. We need to dispel the myth that generosity is determined by cash flow and that it is spontaneous. Instead we should see it as a lifestyle and a journey. We may not *feel* rich, but we really are by any objective standard; and we may *feel* generous, but we really aren't—again, by any objective standard. With very few exceptions, we have a lot of room to grow.

Shortly before Jesus gave himself for us on the cross, he took some time to watch people putting their gifts into the Temple treasury. He watched many rich men make large donations and said nothing. But when he saw a poor widow put in two very small copper coins, he turned to his disciples and said, "This poor widow has put in more than all the others. All these people gave their gifts out of their wealth; but she out of her poverty put in all she had to live on."[10] For many, it's a familiar story. But I wonder what would happen if the Lord's people actually started giving like the widow.

I believe we should rethink the gift of generosity, because the true measure of generosity isn't how much we give, but how much we keep. I'm happy to hear that several massively wealthy people have vowed that they won't die with anything left because they've pledged to give it all away (and not to their kids). Of course, if they wait to give it all away until just before they die, I don't see how that's much different than keeping it all until after they're gone. How much of a sacrifice is it to keep something until you're forced to leave it all behind anyway?

On Quantifying Life Change

How do we quantify how much someone's life has changed? I believe we can tell by seeing how they spend their money, their talent, and their time. When someone's life changes, they change the way they invest all three.

The reforming of our lives means the reordering of our priorities. When we approach missions properly, our lives are bound to get reordered. In fact, if we do missions and our lives *don't* change, we're doing something wrong. In *On Christian Doctrine*, St. Augustine says we all love things, but we love them in the wrong order. When we reorder our loves, it changes our priorities, leading to a deeply formed life.

> Living a just and holy life requires one to be capable of an objective and impartial evaluation of things: to love things, that is to say, in the right order, so that you do not love what is not to be loved, or fail to love what is to be loved, or have a greater love for what should be loved less, or an equal love for things that should be loved less or

> more, or a lesser or greater love for things that should be loved equally.[11]

When we reorder our use of time, talent, and treasure, it inevitably leads to change all around us. "When the righteous prosper, the city rejoices; when the wicked perish, there are shouts of joy."[12]

Generosity—whether with our time, talent, or treasure—shows life change. We give because Jesus gave it all. And because *he* gave it all, we can dare to give it all. That's how we want to be formed in our discipleship.

I met Jim and Inés Franklin shortly after I came to Mariners Church. They were kind enough to host my bachelor party a few years later, which was not your typical American bachelor party. Men of all ages took turns sharing wisdom or giving me a blessing as I was about to reach a new milestone in my life. This beautiful celebration was filled with deep substance. Since then, Jim and Inés have become my very good friends. We have been a part of the same life group at church for more than a dozen years.

This couple has a unique story that Inés captures in her book *Uncharted: Navigating Your Unique Journey of Faith.*[13] It's a great account of personal transformation.

Inés highlights stories of community that can help us navigate our faith journey. She and Jim have hosted several of our church's Global Residents, including Thilini De Visser from Sri Lanka. Their home has become a home away from home for our entire Global Resident family. The Franklins' lives have been so dramatically changed through these encounters that one time they decided to vacation in Sri Lanka. After spending some time alone, they invited the entire De Visser family to take them to their favorite places on that beautiful island. I never imagined that Jim and Inés would ever go to Sri Lanka for anything other than a missions trip, but because their lives were transformed through the relationships they developed with many of our Global Residents (and their families), they changed even the way they vacation.

Life change is seen in how we spend our time. How are we going to share the Good News with others? It's seen in how we invest our talent. How are we helping the hurting? It's seen in how we spend our treasure. How are we using the money God has given us to help others find a new, full life in Jesus?

The explosion of Christianity after the Day of Pentecost had nothing to do with great sermons, beautiful buildings, or lovely songs. Instead, it had everything to do with recklessly loving people. Let's do what Jesus did, and let's do it tangibly. Let's begin to rethink *life change* as our measure for global missions.

11

STRATEGIC ENGAGEMENT

The American soft drink company Coca-Cola was incorporated in 1892. It is the largest nonalcoholic beverage manufacturer in the world, sold in more than 200 countries under more than 300 brands. To my knowledge, only Cuba and North Korea don't have Coke.

In 2019, CEO James Quincey was paid almost $19 million to make sure Coke is sold everywhere on the planet. Coca-Cola has created many strategic partnerships, built a robust supply chain, and boasts hundreds of local distributors, all to remain on top. Coke was also the first soft drink in outer space.

Coke had humble beginnings as a soda fountain drink served by the glass at a local pharmacy; today, the Coca-Cola Company sells 1.9 billion servings of their products *per day*.[1] As you might guess, the company puts a lot of brain power into marketing, selling, and delivering its beverages. Since 2015 (with the exception of 2020), Coca-Cola has spent an average of $4 *billion* annually on advertising and marketing.[2]

And it's just flavored sugar water with carbonation.

How much more should we strategize to get the gospel out to the world? How much more effort should we put in to spread the Kingdom of God to change the world for good?

In 1983, Apple founder Steve Jobs famously challenged PepsiCo president John Sculley to move from Pepsi to Apple by asking him, "Do you want to spend the rest of your life selling sugared water, or do you want a chance to change the world?"[3] His great pitch worked, and Sculley accepted the job. During Sculley's ten years as CEO at Apple, the company's sales increased tenfold—but has it changed the world in ways that will count for eternity? Hardly.

Still, if our leading corporations can use their brains to develop excellent strategies to advance their corporate interests, how much more should we, who are taking the gospel and the Word of God across the world? In this chapter, I want to introduce four aspects of strategic engagement that anyone in missions—whether individually or as part of a group—should carefully consider before moving out.

1. Intelligent Design and Deep Thinking

We serve a God who created the universe, including us, by the word of his mouth. Creation displays amazing intricacies and complexities. If you were to move our planet off its axis by even a few degrees, for example, or move it out of its orbit either closer to or farther from the sun, life could not exist here. Creation reveals a highly intelligent Creator.

Our creation in God's image means we display the likeness of an astonishingly intelligent being whose work reveals extremely deep thinking. The same creativity he exhibits is built into *us* as well (even if at a far lower level)—and it shows!

Look at the history of innovation in our world. In everything from cooking over fire, metallurgy, and building an ark to the development of the printing press, the automobile, spacecraft, and the World Wide Web, we see in our own work a reflection of God's intelligent design and deep thinking. Today's innovations include Web 3.0 and artificial intelligence—and the sky is still the limit.

As we engage in Christian missions—from our Jerusalem to Judea, Samaria, and the ends of the earth—it is important that we use good strategy. It requires deep thinking and intelligent design work to achieve our goals. Instead of tackling only the immediate and obvious needs, we must strive to understand and address the underlying causes as well. What is at the root of systemic poverty, discrimination, and inequality? How can we effectively enable people to regain the full human glory we lost in the Garden?

We rightly recognize Africa as one of the poorest continents on the planet, and yet we forget—or never learned—that before the Europeans arrived, some of the greatest kingdoms in world history were in Africa. Egypt, certainly, but also Cush, Mali, Songhai, and Aksum, to name just a few. But then, in the late nineteenth century, at the Berlin Conference of 1884–1885, German chancellor Otto von Bismarck and diplomats from thirteen countries in Europe (plus one from the United States) met to decide how to carve up Africa, with its wealth of natural resources, for their own interests. According to the *Encyclopedia of Africa*, "the Berlin Conference did not initiate European colonization of Africa, but it did legitimate and formalize the process. . . . Following the close of the conference, European powers expanded their claims in Africa such that by 1900, European states had claimed nearly 90 percent of African territory."[4]

We continue to reap the consequences of that meeting to this day.

Many people want to "help Africa" without stopping to consider how to *unscramble the scramble*. What deep thinking are we doing about addressing root causes? The missionaries who came to Africa from Europe and America did a great job of evangelizing, but the same boats that brought the missionaries also brought explorers and colonizers. Did the missionaries get on the wrong boat with the right message?

How do we think deeply about this? How do we apply human innovation and creativity to unscramble the negative consequences that have accrued over centuries around the world? In part 4, we will consider some specific, practical ideas about how to undo systemic problems; but for now I want to highlight the necessity of deep strategic thinking and planning as a precursor to effective action.

We can no longer take things at face value; we must examine the issues deeply to avoid merely dealing with symptoms. Let's forthrightly address systemic issues within a genuinely biblical framework, whether regarding evangelism or in demonstration of the gospel. Part of the solution, I believe, is to partner with indigenous leaders, who are the ones with real skin in the game.

2. Long-Term, Collaborative Partnerships

One thing that makes Coca-Cola enormously successful around the world is the company's commitment and ability to create and maintain strategic partnerships, especially with independent distributors. Coke has taken the time to build up local distributors who enjoy a huge amount of autonomy. Consequently, the company has created dozens of localized models wherever it has gone—with significant differences, based on dissimilarities in each locality.

Why can't we do something similar with the gospel, with long-term, sustained relationships and partnerships instead of independent distributors? Such partnerships must be forged over time, and then we must work to keep them active and productive.

Localized partnerships can be powerful and beautiful, but they can also be *messy*. Many Western organizations lack the fortitude or the willingness to engage in messiness, because we prefer things to be clean and orderly. We want things our way, and we don't always understand contextualized differences in how to get things done. But adapting to local differences is something Coca-Cola has mastered.

The difficulty in world missions comes from both directions. In general, people from the Global North are looking for quick, efficient wins, while their counterparts in the Global South have become accustomed to everything being at a standstill—a form of apathy that says, "This is just the way things are. Nothing works here."

With such differences in expectations between them, both sides can get frustrated and end up clashing, without ever really trying to understand the other side's perspective. Instead, we keep lobbing bombs at each other, and never quite come to the table as long-term partners. Effective partnerships require commitment, understanding, and a willingness to adapt. They demand thoughtful, prayerful engagement. If a partnership has any hope of becoming long-term, it must be informed by strategic, future-minded thinking—especially with visionary indigenous leaders. That's imperative.

Let's suppose we want to venture into Africa, and we choose Kenya as our destination. Going in, we know that close to 40 percent of the population lives in abject poverty. And even those whose standard of living has improved in the postcolonial era continue to be adversely affected by "the lasting impacts of colonialism . . . [that] are still embedded within the fabric of Kenyan society. These include economic disparities, political struggles, and cultural changes that continue to shape the nation's identity."[5]

Whom should we approach when looking for a potential long-term partner? I would say it this way: We should look to partner with someone who isn't looking for *us*. We want to partner with indigenous leaders who have a plan, who know what kind of help they need, and who can use whatever good assistance we can offer. We want to partner with people who understand their own context and are able to articulate how an outside partner can catalyze their efforts. We want our work to be mutual and reciprocal, rather than causative or dependent. Long-term partnerships with visionary indigenous leaders are imperative if we want our efforts to be strategic.

3. Sustainability

Sustainability, as I'm using the term here, refers to the process of "meet[ing] the needs of the present without compromising the ability of future generations to meet their own needs."[6]

By "needs," I don't mean only physical and material needs. I'm also thinking of the need to disciple, pastor, and spread the gospel through proclamation. Too often, African communities have relied on outsiders to proclaim the gospel. We need new, contextualized ways and models for proclaiming the gospel locally, without outsiders having to teach and train us in *their* methods and styles. The idea of sustainability is critically important here. Let me explain why.

The first time you give someone a gift, they say, "Thank you."

The second time, you create *anticipation*.

The third time, you create an *expectation*.

By the fourth time, you have created an *entitlement*: "Hey, give me what is mine."

Sustainability avoids the problem of entitlement. The long-term goal is for the community to start doing things for themselves.

Sustainability is a crucial component of long-term partnerships. We must always be asking ourselves, "How can this good thing we've created together continue on after we've left?" Unfortunately, many of the strategies and practices we employ in missions today, whether in proclamation or demonstration, end with our direct involvement. When we leave, so does the project, outreach, or mission.

I recently heard about a church facility constructed in South America by an outside group. They put their name on it. Sometime later, when the building started to fall apart, the indigenous people called the builders and said, "Hey, your church is falling apart. Come fix it."

Instead of creating dependence, how do we foster a sense of ownership, such that when something needs repair, the people say, "Our church is falling apart. Let's fix it"? How do we create enterprises that will continue on after we're gone? Sustainability is a fundamental part of strategic engagement.

One thing that is *certainly* sustainable to the very end is the gospel. As C. S. Lewis once said, "All that is not eternal is eternally out of date."[7] It's useless. If we want to be strategic, we must invest in the most important thing, the eternal gospel. People need to know Jesus and that he cares about their needs. When we take his mission into the world, we must both *share* and *show* his love. That's the kind of work that will reverberate into eternity.

Though we cannot keep for eternity *any* of the valuable things of earth, we can "send ahead" certain treasures by investing in human beings. *That's* where we want to invest our time, effort, and other resources.

Just as a venture capitalist takes a good, hard look at any investment under consideration, we want to look for ways to invest in things that pay eternal dividends. We need to think long and hard about how to make the results of our earthly investments sustainable and long-lasting.

I believe the Holy Spirit is a great model for sustainability. Jesus began his ministry with twelve disciples. Later, he commissioned seventy-two and sent them out. And by the time the Spirit came at Pentecost, some 120 followers of Christ were meeting together, waiting as per the Lord's instructions. The number of committed followers had grown over time, but it needed to grow far more. Our Lord knew that 120 disciples would never be enough to accomplish the mission he had given to his church. So before his crucifixion,

Jesus prepared his disciples for what was to come. He told them, "I'm about to leave, but I won't leave you alone."[8]

What started with Jesus did not die with him on the cross. In fact, it multiplied exponentially. Why? Because the Holy Spirit came to make sure that the work Jesus started with a few others would mushroom around the world after the Lord returned to heaven. The Holy Spirit is all about sustainability.

I've started using Christ's words metaphorically when one of our teams is preparing to return to the US after working with an overseas partner. I tell these partners, "We're leaving, but we're not going to leave you alone. We're going to give you something that will continue on long after we're gone."

Right now, about half the world knows the gospel or about Jesus, because the Holy Spirit is present and active in men and women living in every corner of the globe. That fact alone presents a great case for emphasizing the importance of sustainability.

And yet I've learned through experience that some people push back against sustainability. They say, "If we create sustainability, what will our role be? If we create sustainability, we will no longer have a place here." In my view, such an assertion is both myopic and untrue. Certainly, we will still have a role; but it will differ from what it used to be. And maybe that new role will be much better.

Let's commit ourselves to intelligent design and deep thinking. Let's emphasize and prioritize long-term, reciprocal partnerships, especially with visionary indigenous leaders. And let's strategize for sustainability.

4. Reflection

Through reflection, we can turn a *nice* experience into a *transformative* one. By examining our experiences and learning from them, we can move from simply accumulating information to being intellectually and spiritually formed. As the Greek philosopher Socrates said, "The unexamined life is not worth living."[9]

Too often we come and go into global missions, whether long-term or short-term, without ever taking time to evaluate our experiences. And even if we do, we often don't learn from them. If we are to gain knowledge, insight, perspective, and wisdom, we absolutely *must* examine our missions experiences.

Whenever I lead a missions group, I first orient our team members to where they're about to go and who they'll be engaging with. I work to prepare them for the experience, which I consider an essential part of being strategic.

One of the key ways I try to orient my team members is by focusing their attention on *who they're going to become* rather than on *what they're going to do*. I ask them to think about who they're going to be when they arrive in-country and how they will hear God's voice while they're there.

Ordinarily, when we talk to someone about going on a short-term missions trip, the first question they ask is, "What are we going to do?" I flip that question on its head and say, "Instead of asking what you're going to be doing, ask what *God* is going to do *in you*; and then prepare your heart and attune your ears to hear his voice." If you go in with an attitude of learning and listening, you will hear things and see things you might otherwise miss. You'll see things that *you need*, not just things you can give.

I let that idea sink in before adding, "But if you go in with a gung-ho mentality, thinking, *I'm going to save Africa or Haiti or Latin America*, you'll have a savior mentality that will not put you in a posture of learning."

Adopting a listening-and-learning perspective is a hard thing for most Westerners to swallow. They want to go and do good things for people, especially since they're coming from materially wealthy places. They expect to go to a comparatively poor place and find ways to meet people's needs there. Westerners naturally think they have something to offer, not realizing that—if they will attune their hearts to God—they may find as much to *receive* as to give. But they won't grasp that truth unless their leaders strategically and purposefully prepare them for the experience.

The other half of the equation—and equally as important—is the after-mission debriefing. Effective leaders ask their team members, "How did God speak to you?" "What did you learn?" "How were your heart and your mind changed by the experience?" Some of what God says to them might become a key part of their own spiritual formation. In other words, a key lesson from the mission field might not have any ongoing application to the global world, but what they've learned there might end up deeply affecting how they live in their own community after their return.

Debriefing, therefore, must also be strategic and well thought through. Examining our experiences is not only important, it's absolutely essential.

Shortly before my groups leave an area to return home, I ask my team members to grab a rock that's big enough to write on. Then I ask them to write one word on the rock that marks the moment and characterizes their experience. At some point after our return to the US, we'll regather the group and ask each person to describe how their rock and their chosen word have continued to affect their life.

I pattern this practice after two key moments in the Old Testament when the people of God created "stones of remembrance."

The first instance occurs after Israel has crossed the Jordan River to enter the Promised Land.

> When all the nation had finished passing over the Jordan, the LORD said to Joshua, "Take twelve men from the people, from each tribe a man, and command them, saying, 'Take twelve stones from here out of the midst

of the Jordan, from the very place where the priests' feet stood firmly, and bring them over with you and lay them down in the place where you lodge tonight.'" Then Joshua called the twelve men from the people of Israel, whom he had appointed, a man from each tribe. And Joshua said to them, "Pass on before the ark of the LORD your God into the midst of the Jordan, and take up each of you a stone upon his shoulder, according to the number of the tribes of the people of Israel, that this may be a sign among you. When your children ask in time to come, 'What do those stones mean to you?' then you shall tell them that the waters of the Jordan were cut off before the ark of the covenant of the LORD. When it passed over the Jordan, the waters of the Jordan were cut off. So these stones shall be to the people of Israel a memorial forever."

And the people of Israel did just as Joshua commanded and took up twelve stones out of the midst of the Jordan, according to the number of the tribes of the people of Israel, just as the LORD told Joshua. And they carried them over with them to the place where they lodged and laid them down there. . . .

And those twelve stones, which they took out of the Jordan, Joshua set up at Gilgal. And he said to the people of Israel, "When your children ask their fathers in times to come, 'What do these stones mean?' then you shall let your children know, 'Israel passed over this Jordan on dry ground.' For the LORD your God dried up the waters of the Jordan for you until you passed over, as the LORD your God did to the Red Sea, which he dried up for us until we passed over, so that all the peoples of the earth may know that the hand of the LORD is mighty, that you may fear the LORD your God forever."[10]

Later in the nation's history, after a great victory over the Philistines, the prophet Samuel "took a stone and set it up between Mizpah and Shen. He named it Ebenezer, saying, 'Thus far the LORD has helped us.'"[11]

Both the rocks and the words can be powerful reminders. The words that team members write on their rocks should encapsulate their trip—not just what they *did*, but who they *became*. Their words should remind them of who they are becoming.

The global mission field can be a place where God marks us for life. The experience is for a moment, but the impact can be transformative.

As we examine our experiences, it's imperative that we do some "heart surgery." When we venture into the global world, we may hear and see God in ways we've previously not experienced. Why does it affect us so powerfully? Because we're outside our normal routines, in a new environment where our senses are heightened. Away from home, it's easier to be attentive to everything—the noises, the crowds, the individual people, and other things.

When I take people from Southern California to Africa, they often say, "Man, this place is *loud*. Loud and busy."

I find that amusing. When I first came to America, I said, "This place is a ghost town. Where are all the people? What's happening? How come everybody is hidden? As soon as they drive home, they open the garage door and disappear inside while the door closes behind them. You never even see them."

It felt to me as if I had landed in a zombie apocalypse. It was eerie, too quiet. But I used those moments to examine my heart, to ask God to speak to me in ways that I'd never heard. Sometimes it takes being out of your comfort zone to hear God's voice clearly. You don't have to go overseas, of course. But when you do go away, a certain attunement of your heart often allows you to do the necessary heart surgery.

I learned something beautiful when I came to America. I had a strong desire to be known and to belong, but I always feared that if I were fully known, I wouldn't be fully loved. But when I arrived at Mariners Church, I discovered something very different—which is a credit to Kenton and Laurie Beshore and the church's entire leadership team.

After I had been on staff for a couple of years, I was pretty well known throughout the church. Being from Kenya made me stand out, but what happened next really rocked my world and has shaped me in many ways.

As a single man at the time, I struggled spiritually with some aspects of my faith journey. My failure to deal with some hidden areas in my life led me to a place where I needed to be shepherded and cared for—being fully known for all that I am and not just for my gifts. At that moment, I felt a strong urge to run and hide, just like Adam in the Garden of Eden. I felt embarrassed that I had let my church down, along with the leadership team and especially my boss at the time, Robin Riley. She had been such a big cheerleader for me, seeing in me things I had never seen in myself. She continually called me to lead at a high level. But here I was, a failure who had let everyone down.

The church leaders told me they would remove the spiritual weight of leadership from me for a time so I could be fully known to be fully loved, something I had never before encountered. I felt eager to learn, but as soon as I found out the process included radical candor and even sharing these issues with my Kenyan leaders, Bishop Oscar and Pastor M, and also letting everyone else in my realm of influence know that I had to let go of leadership for a while, I felt totally overwhelmed. Deep inside, I decided to quit.

On hearing how wishy-washy I had become about the process, Kenton called me aside and said in a stern spiritual father's voice, "I don't need you to work at Mariners anymore if you don't want to, but you're not going anywhere before you get some help. You will never change if you don't deal with these challenges head-on. It will be a brutal process, like deep heart surgery, but it is absolutely necessary."

I think that's all I needed to hear. For the first time in my life, I understood someone saying to me, "You have failed, but you are not a failure. We want you to be fully known and fully loved."

After that, I mustered all the courage I could find to face the gravity of my failure, I started sharing it with everyone as required, and I walked around feeling as if the word *failure* was stamped on my forehead. It was brutal, but I wouldn't trade it for anything.

My team focused more on *who I was* and *my identity* than on behavior modification. I realized I had made some very crazy covenants with myself. I had to come to terms with my major need to be needed, to be in the limelight and draw attention to myself. I wish I could say that is all behind me now, but we are all works in progress, and we will never be perfected until we meet the perfect one face-to-face. However, I was able to raise my hand and say, "I need help." And to my surprise, everyone embraced me as a child of God. It was earth shattering for me.

After that experience, I adopted a posture of deep humility. I took Luke 7:47 quite literally: "He who is forgiven little, loves little." I knew I'd been forgiven much, and therefore I wanted to love much more.

That's how I came to feel part and parcel of my new home. It was a place where I had not been born, a place where I had felt so foreign, and yet, it had become family. Why? Because somebody cared enough to do heart surgery on me. The experience was priceless.

Examine your own experience, and let it show you what could grow deeper within you. It's *far* more than a cerebral thing. Unexamined experiences may *feel* nice, but they can turn into life-changing experiences when you carefully analyze them.

I love how ministry partnership advocate Daniel Rickett

encouraged individuals returning from a missions trip to examine their experience by asking themselves, "Was it just an event, or was it a narrative?"[12] There's a big difference.

An event starts and ends, while a narrative is an ongoing story. Is going to Africa (or some other place in the world) an event or a narrative for you? Were you on a trip, or on a journey? Was it purely pragmatic, or was it communion? Did you go just to build a house, or to make friends? Have you created a community? Do you continue to communicate with the people you met?

Do we go for self-interest, or do we go for servanthood? Do we go just to make ourselves feel good, or do we go to become a servant? Ultimately, Rickett asked, is it charity or is it development? Is it going to poor Africans (or poor Latin Americans or poor Asians), or are both sides seeing some development occur?

I think this framework can help us examine our experiences in ways that will lead to spiritual growth and formation. It's heart surgery, going deep within, but because the image of God has been marred in all of us, such examinations can help us restore one another and repair that blemished image.

Engaging with the Global World

Let's be strategic in our outreach to the global world by utilizing intelligent design and thinking deeply. Let's develop long-term, sustained partnerships, especially with visionary indigenous leaders, because those relationships will reverberate into eternity. Let us create sustainability in sharing the most important thing in the world, the gospel. And let's examine our experiences in such a way that it leads to spiritual formation, an important step for engaging effectively with the global world.

Why should Coca-Cola have anything on us? Our strategic engagement can truly change our planet for the better.

PART FOUR

PRACTICE

Now let's focus on the practical expression of a truly people-centered Christian mission. It tries to counteract the widespread assumption that because humans are primarily cognitive beings, the church should emphasize knowledge. Whenever such a faulty premise takes hold, the church tends to degenerate into classes, courses, and curricula, where studying doctrine and thinking about issues takes precedence over loving people. In fact, as image bearers of God we are fundamentally and intrinsically lovers. If you want to really know someone, don't ask them what they think or know; ask them what they love or what they want.

A far better way to understand the human experience is captured in a prayer by an African bishop, St. Augustine of Hippo: "You made us for yourself, and our hearts are restless until they rest in you."[1] We were created *by* God *for* God, and our whole purpose is to joyfully worship God. The locus isn't the head but the heart. If we want to effect change, we must change what we love, and our behavior will inevitably follow. The goal of missions is practical service to others for the sole purpose of showcasing the Kingdom of God in the present, even as we await its eventual consummation.

12

CHURCH DEPLOYMENT

While in Germany recently, I observed how one church handles the benediction at the end of their Sunday services. It blessed my soul so much that I copy it every chance I get. At the end of their time together, they say, "We have come to the end of our celebration, and now as we go out into the service, receive God's Word." And then they recite Numbers 6:24-26:

> The Lord bless you and keep you;
> the Lord make his face shine on you
> and be gracious to you;
> the Lord turn his face toward you
> and give you peace.[1]

Did you notice how they characterize their Sunday gathering? They call it a *celebration*, not a "service." In fact, they reserve the word *service* for what they are about to do as they leave the building: "As we go out *into* the service."

And what is *the service*? It is whatever God has called us and equipped us to do in his work of bringing order out of chaos.

Missions Is for Everyone

The work of missions is not for missions agencies or vocational missionaries alone. God calls *every* Christian into missions work.

Neither is Christian missions limited to specially gifted individuals. No, it is intended for the *entire community* of Jesus followers. As a community of faith, we live out God's original design as he expressed it from the very beginning.

One of the first things I really appreciated about Mariners Church was its insistence that *every believer is a minister with a ministry*. That statement spoke to me of a high view of humans made in the image of God, which means that *everyone* has inherent value and dignity. This truth has huge implications for our deployment into Christian missions and the global mission field. For one thing, it means that *all* our work is God's work and that *every* worker is God's workmanship. The apostle Paul says this explicitly: "We are his workmanship, created in Christ Jesus for good works, which God prepared beforehand, that we should walk in them."[2]

God creates every person and has a specific work for that person. Every work we do is God's work, which means that every Christian is called into missions work of some kind. God intends to involve us in his work of restoring all things to order, including our relationships, whether with God, with each other, with ourselves, or with our environment. This presupposes that every Christian, doing any sort of work, is called to a mission that showcases (by both deed and word) our ultimate relationship with God.

God's original intent in creating the world, including humans, was the harmonious integration of all things. At the very beginning, God brought order out of chaos. He then created Adam and gave him a job, telling him in essence, "Continue to keep chaos at bay by watching over the garden and working it." When Adam and Eve sinned, they brought chaos back into the creation—but God immediately went to work once more to bring order out of chaos. Today, through the Great Collaboration, he invites us into that work.

God, in his grace, beckons us to become participants in restoring what sin utterly shattered. Christ alone can save us, of course, but he calls us, as his ambassadors, to partner with the Holy Spirit in his global restoration project, to recreate the harmonious, interwoven, intertwined, interlocking fabric of goodness he originally created.

Every one of us "in Christ" is called into God's mission. While the Lord clearly prioritizes proclaiming the gospel to those who have never heard it, the life of Jesus (and that of the apostles after him) shows us that he wants us to work with him to bring *all* of life out of chaos and back to order.

What if we deployed the entire church as a community of restorative change agents—a countercultural corporate community? What if we became real-life examples of how the priesthood of all believers is supposed to work in the world throughout the week? Why not leave our celebrations this Sunday with a word from God in our ears, ready to "go out into the service."

Every Believer Has Been Called

Ephesians 4 declares that God gave several outstanding gifts to his church—apostles, prophets, pastors, teachers, evangelists (sometimes referred to as the fivefold ministry)—to equip believers for "the work of ministry."[3] Everyone who is in Christ has been deployed for this work.

As redeemed image bearers, we are all called into ministry. Service in ministry and missions is meant to create an interwoven fabric that restores shalom. The motivation for our deployment and engagement in ministry and in missions comes from God's invitation for us to work with him in restoring all things back to order as he intended them. When we serve, empowered by a vision of a glorious future, it becomes a lifelong passion, regardless of our specific vocation. We understand that God has gifted us to serve others and not ourselves.

I've heard a few vocational missionaries who occasionally make it sound as if they are the tip of the spear and no one else is really living. I've heard some castigate others who do not swim in the same vocational lane, as if there's only one right way to reach the world. I sometimes wonder whether these people realize that some of the global poverty we see is caused by self-aggrandizing multinational corporations that are pillaging resources from places like the Congo without paying fair wages or ensuring safe working conditions. Some very prominent companies produce their goods in sweatshops in the two-thirds majority world, where workers are paid peanuts while the products they manufacture are sold in the West for tons of money. Some of the people in our churches, and supporters of various missions around the world, work in these corporations but they are oblivious to the plight of the people who make their products. Maybe the real "tip of the spear" is in our own backyard.

Every Christian is called to missions and ministry. When it's done well, it will be fully integrated into a gospel-centered community. We don't "do ministry" to improve our sense of self-worth. In missions work, we heed God's call to proclaim Jesus and make him known by making disciples. Ministry and missions should be inextricably linked, with one hinging on the other.

In a very real sense, the equipping described in Ephesians 4 depends on every believer knowing they are created in the image of God. When we know we are made in God's image, we understand that we have inherent dignity and value. And we begin to grasp how and why we can be deployed in the Great Collaboration.

Our first task in missions, then, is to reveal to others what they may have forgotten; namely, that the image of God is in *them*. Once they understand what it means to be made in God's image, the gospel begins to make sense. Once they come to faith in Christ and start the discipleship process, they can be deployed wherever God has them situated, to take on their role in the Great Collaboration.

That deployment might be across the street in their neighborhood, in the office where they work, at the gym, on the playground, or anywhere else God has placed them. It could be across the tracks, to people who are not like them and to people who may not like them. Or it could be across the world.

Jesus says in Acts 1:8, "You will be my witnesses." Witnesses are people who have *seen* something and who can give an accurate account of what they've observed. Whenever someone comes to an understanding of what Jesus did for them on the cross, they can become a witness for him. "Christ has done this for me," they can say, "and he can do it for you, too." A very simple and effective witness.

We're called to witness for Jesus first in Jerusalem—wherever we live, work, and play. We don't necessarily have to go to Africa in order to participate in missions. Opportunities abound right on our doorstep.

We're also called to be witnesses in Judea—to surrounding areas and across the tracks. Additionally, we are called to expand outward to Samaria, to those places that are further distant geographically and culturally. These might be places where we would never venture otherwise.

And, of course, Jesus calls us to be his witnesses "to the ends of the earth." Maybe you're a businessperson whose work often takes you to Japan or South Korea. That's probably your "ends of the earth." Perhaps you vacation in Cancun or have relatives in Norway. Jesus calls us to be his witnesses wherever we find ourselves, even across the ocean.

When Mavuno Church in Nairobi was launched in 2006, Pastor M did not create a missions department. Instead, he said, "Everyone's on mission." That conviction still echoes strongly in the church's motto today: "Turning ordinary people into fearless influencers of society."

Mavuno Church leaders divided their "Jerusalem" culture into six sectors of society: arts and entertainment, business and economics, church and mission, family and education, science and education (or health and environment), and politics and governance. Leadership challenged everyone in the church to identify which sectors they were in, and then to strategize how they could be deployed into those sectors with the gospel, in both proclamation and demonstration.

"Your job is to go out," they said.

The mindset they wanted to create is that *everybody* has been deployed *somewhere.* A stay-at-home mom might be deployed as a change agent in her home, in her neighborhood, in her groups. A businessperson might be deployed at the office, at the coffee shop, or in the business community. Long-haul truckers and diesel mechanics are deployed to truck stops. Missions is for everyone. *Every* Christian is called to missions.

Nairobi Chapel, which helped plant Mavuno Church, has a slightly different take on how to engage various segments of society. They have an outreach ministry that focuses on missions and the Great Invitation (their term for the Great Commission). They also have a social justice ministry that focuses on *demonstrating* the gospel. Different churches take different paths, but the mission and the goal are the same.

My personal view is to have both organic and organized methods of deploying church members. After orienting people to their specific purpose and call, we unleash them into their own sectors of society, where they can have the greatest impact. Churches should develop strategic ways to proclaim and demonstrate the gospel *as a community*. I believe this is where smaller churches have an advantage. They can engage every member, starting with the following two exercises:

1. *Create an asset map of your church members.* Get to know your members' gifts and which sectors of society they are called to.
2. *Find partners in your Jerusalem, Judea, Samaria, and the ends of the earth.* Collaborate with indigenous leaders far and wide, based on a mutual and reciprocal view of missions and ministry. Globalization has opened the door, but let's also not miss the opportunities that are right down the street, because the world has come to our backyard.

Two Pitfalls to Avoid

When we talk about starting in Jerusalem and then going on to Judea, Samaria, and the ends of the earth, some people think of it as a sequential process.

It might be tempting to say, "We can't go to Africa, because we haven't finished evangelizing our own city yet," but that would miss the point of God's fourfold vision for reaching the world with the gospel. If it helps, think of Acts 1:8 as more of a recurring divine pattern than as a strictly historical trajectory. Or look at it as a complex, interwoven network of contacts, and your Jerusalem, Judea, Samaria, and ends of the earth are somewhere in the midst of it all. It all depends on where you start, and we all start somewhere.

It's true that the spread of the gospel began in the city of Jerusalem, and then went out through Judea to Samaria and across the known world. We can easily trace that historical expansion in the book of Acts. But the process is ongoing, ever-changing, and constantly being renewed. As individuals, we're to go wherever God has called us or placed us; and the church as a whole should have the entire picture in view.

The book of Acts showcases how we can be engaged in various spheres and sectors of society. In Acts 8 we see the gospel reaching an Ethiopian eunuch, who happened to be the "secretary of finance" for his country. In Acts 9 we see the gospel reach a religious leader named Saul (later called Paul), who previously had been an enemy of the church. In Acts 10 we see the gospel go out to a Gentile named Cornelius, a military leader and government official. I believe God shows us a variety of people in various occupations and locations to prove that no one is beyond the reach of the gospel, and therefore we should deploy people anywhere and everywhere. The point of the fourfold vision, I believe, is that we're to blanket the earth with the gospel, and we're not to overlook someplace as being too close, too foreign, or too far.

Jesus did not invite only the Jerusalem church, or the North American church, or the European church into the Great Collaboration. He invited everyone who counts him as their Lord. If you're a Christian, you're *invited*.

If we're engaging globally, we help each other accomplish our mutual mission, whatever that might look like for us. That's why getting more connected is so crucial. When we understand God's design for community and connection, the gospel spreads in ways that are not strictly sequential and reaches people everywhere.

The second pitfall to avoid is thinking that the work has been completed and therefore we don't have to go. As long as people are being born into the world, and as long as the enemy is opposing our efforts, there will always be a mission field before us—until Christ returns in glory.

First Steps for Deploying Your Church

We are called to create communities that bring order out of chaos. This will eventually lead to a restoration of all things—shalom with God, with ourselves, with each other, and with the environment.

Consider a few practical ways to mobilize and deploy your church.

1. *Assess your community.* Who are your people, where are they already deployed, and what giftings do they have? Start with what you *have* instead of with what the world needs. Look inward and evaluate the assets in your community. And don't overlook the janitor.
2. *Identify your Jerusalem, Judea, and Samaria.* Look especially for opportunities to collaborate with a partner to deploy the assets and giftings in your church. When gifts and opportunities align, it blurs the line between missions and ministry and your service becomes more integrated.
3. *Create a discipleship pathway for your people.* Disband your specialized missions committees and encourage everyone in the church to engage in their neighborhoods, cities, counties, across the tracks, and globally via partnerships across the seas. Create a robust avenue to raise awareness among your church community about where the church is involved. Missions and ministry should never be things that are talked about only once a year; rather, they should be part of the fabric of your disciple-making process.

At Mariners, we adapted the Mavuno transformational loop and made it our own. Everything is interconnected and intertwined.

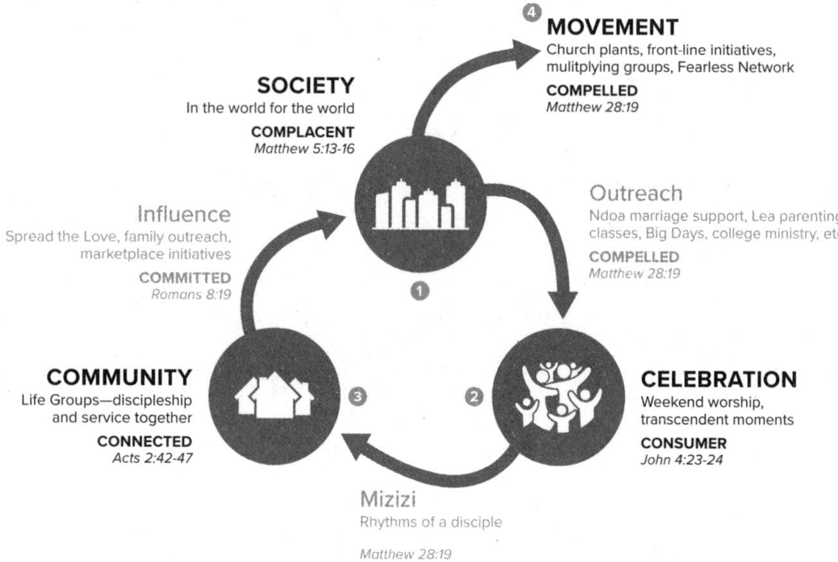

The first step in the journey of lifelong discipleship at Mariners is an intentional experience called Rooted, which I mentioned earlier. During the ten-week experience, we create the impetus for people to connect with God, with their community, and with their purpose. That combination thrusts disciples into the lifeblood of the church. This transformational loop leads to a lifestyle of missions and ministry.

Next, we built a pipeline of deployment that encourages disciples to engage with missions and ministry. Mariners has core teams whose main purpose is to equip and deploy as many church members as possible by inviting them to use their time, their talent, and their treasure to partner with the Holy Spirit to restore everything in accordance with God's original intent for shalom. That's part of the discipleship mandate.

Kenton had established one of the church's main values: "Every believer is a minister with a ministry." I resonated with this value. No one was looking to me as a leader in the church to *do* ministry;

instead, they were asking me to *mobilize the church* so we could do ministry *together*. This guiding principle has been instilled in me since my boyhood years, so I ate it up. Everything is better when shared in community.

I have never really met a stranger. I can talk to anyone, anywhere, at any time. But it was exciting for me to not have to be the expert; I just had to invite people and engage them.

Unfortunately, far too many churches have relegated ministry to the "experts," to pastors or other astute leaders. They may be gifted, but that doesn't mean they should be carrying the full load while the rest of the congregation stands by. What a false view of ministry! We all have inherent value, and God calls us all to *something*. The journey of discovering our purpose and why we exist is such a beautiful thing.

Robin Riley, my first boss at Mariners, taught me not only how to tell people what they wanted to hear, but even things they *never* wanted to hear. Kenton also encouraged me not to be a conformist, but to openly share alternative perspectives, based on my own gifting, experience, and background. That freed me up tremendously as a leader, and with that freedom, I wanted to set others free to do the same.

This ethos is deeply entrenched in the DNA of Mariners, and it's still one of my favorites. When our new senior pastor, Eric Geiger, came on staff, he doubled down on this value. He had already written a book on how to develop and deploy teams, titled *Designed to Lead*, a seminal work in this area. What Kenton emphasized for years has now reached a new high point at Mariners.

The work of the pastor is to "equip the saints for the work of ministry, for building up the body of Christ,"[4] not to do all the work alone. As a church, we are called to be thermostats, not thermometers. A thermostat activates while a thermometer only reacts. One sets a standard and the other responds. The church is a called-out people waiting to be activated for missions, with every person bearing a unique aspect of God's image. The work of the church is exponentially propelled when it is done as a community or a team. We should measure our churches by their *sending* capacity, not their seating capacity.

Does It Work?

Someone might rightly ask, "Yes, but does it work?" Let me give you a few examples from both Mavuno and Mariners.

Daisy Waimiri was a stay-at-home mom who joined Mavuno Church. The church's emphasis on transforming sectors of society prompted her to start a community-based microloan program, loaning small amounts of money to fledgling small-business owners in Nairobi's Kibera settlement. With catalytic help from some members of Mariners Church, including elder Bob Drobish, a tech company CEO, by 2015 she was able to expand her efforts to reach more than one thousand businesspeople, with loans totaling $100,000.[5]

Anne Nzilani was a marketer who decided to use her gift to live for others rather than for herself. She decided to open markets for struggling Kenyan artisans. Bawa Hope is now serving thousands of artisans through fair trade, and providing dignity to marginalized communities through the gospel.

Brian Murimi was a high school student who found himself challenged to feed individuals experiencing homelessness. Today, Brian is on the path of creating savings and loan banks for this demographic in Kenya, through a company known as Cerren International.

These individuals are not only making an impact in Kenya, but through their stories and by meeting some of our Mariners members on short-term missions trips they have inspired many of our people to change how they use their time, talent, and treasure. And all of this happened through just *one* of Mariners' current eleven global partners.

There is enough room for *every* church member to be deployed.

On the local front, we have seen many people from Mariners deploy with after-school programs in marginalized communities. They have engaged with the foster care system, serving more than 2,800 foster kids in Orange County alone. They have engaged with military families at nearby Camp Pendleton. They have served in centers for the elderly and with rehabilitation organizations in our county. The opportunities are endless.

Do you remember the partnership we formed with Pastor Sam in Haiti to help him build a school (see chapter 3)? That wasn't the end of the story. A lawyer who is a member at Mariners watched the whole process unfold, from reinforcement to reform. He was on the core team that helped serve Pastor Sam as a volunteer. He felt so moved by his experience that he said to Pastor Sam, "Because you've done so well with one school, I want to fund another one." He gave Pastor Sam $2 million to build a second school.

And even that isn't the end of the story. (Good partnerships are like that; they continue to bear fruit.) Some of our high school kids also went to Haiti, and Pastor Sam told them, "Hey, we're going door-knocking and talking to people about coming to church. We want you to come with us."

Those kids went along, but they had a hard time. The language was different. The culture was different. It was tough sledding. But when they came back to Mariners, it was with a brand-new sense of boldness. One of the kids said, "Man, these guys go door-to-door, inviting people to church. They preach to people and evangelize them. I can't do that . . . *yet* . . . but I want to learn."

So does it work? *Yes!* The experience changes them.

Deploying the Entire Church

Again, the *entire* church must be deployed. It must be everybody, using whatever gifts and abilities God has given them. If everybody did what God is asking them to do, don't you think we'd see major changes in the global mission field? It would no longer be about sending experts, but rather *everybody* realizing they have something to offer.

It all begins with rethinking our missions approach and reimagining the deployment of our people. Let's not leave missions to the professionals, and let us not be satisfied with merely giving money. If you are a believer in Jesus, *you* are called to ministry *and* to missions. There's a place for everyone to play a role, and it begins by revealing the image of God in people.

James writes, "Someone will say, 'You have faith and I have works.' Show me your faith apart from your works, and I will show you my faith by my works."[6] Our good works point to who God is; and as we engage in this way, people will see the essence of who we are and see the beauty behind it, the glorious and majestic God who invites them to live with him forever.

It's time to mobilize the full priesthood of believers. *Everyone* has been called to engage in our interconnected world.

Finding Solutions That Work

As I've said, it's possible to try to solve difficult problems with solutions that ultimately don't work. In deploying the church into God's work around the world, we need to go back, if necessary, and equip people to do things on their own.

When the AIDS epidemic began to sweep through sub-Saharan Africa in the 1980s, gaining strength in the 1990s, it wiped out a productive generation of people in their thirties, forties, and fifties, leaving behind young kids and old people. In response, well-meaning Western relief agencies came in and built a proliferation of orphanages throughout Africa to meet the perceived need.

In some ways this was helpful, but it was also debilitating because it undermined the very essence of the African care system, which is based on *family ties*. Before the early 1980s, nothing like an orphan existed in traditional African society. If someone lost their parents, they were taken in by an extended family member, and that's how we handled it.

This idea is so embedded in our culture that even our language supports the way we take care of kids. For example, in my native Kikuyu language, there's no word for *uncle*. The words we use instead mean "older father" or "younger father." If my father had died when I was young, I would have immediately been assimilated into my older father's family or my younger father's family.

When the relief agencies came in with their Western solutions, they looked at all these displaced children and said, "These kids are orphans," and they put them in an institution rather than placing them with families.

Some kids ended up kind of liking it, because the new orphanages had TVs and other modern conveniences. Some kids wanted to move to an orphanage even if they still had living parents. But though an orphanage can be a good temporary place of rescue, it is not the best way to raise a generation of children.

Milele was still active during this time, and my bandmates and I thought it would be far better to reintegrate kids with their own families or adopt them into new families. In Kenya alone in 2005, there were two million orphans. So we decided to embark on a journey to find two million families to adopt them. Our goal was to close down every orphanage in Kenya.

Of course, we were young and naive and thinking idealistically, but we did help at least one orphanage close down, and we helped sixteen kids get into families.

First, we investigated whether the children had any family members in the area. If so, we paid psychology professionals to interview the families. Could these families take on a child? If so, we would build two houses for them: one for them to live in and the other to rent out. The families used the income from the second home to take care of their adopted kids.

Over time, our strategy evolved. We discovered that a group of Kenyan parents had a strong desire to adopt kids, but they simply didn't have the means to do it because an adoption cost about two thousand dollars. So we moved to a cheaper way of finding available families, and then helped them acquire the legal fees necessary to take in these kids.

Eventually, the burden became too heavy, and we had to curtail our efforts. But we had succeeded, if only on a small scale, to address the problem of AIDS orphans with a solution that fit well with our traditional culture. To find better solutions, we must deploy the entire church. We need everyone to be engaged. Solutions are rarely one-size-fits-all; but what kinds of ideas can we come up with as we deploy everybody?

Different situations will call for different strategies, but we need to get into the practice of thinking deeply about the problems we want to address before we spring into action. Let's strive to meet every need, but let's also make sure that future generations know how to meet their own needs and are equipped to do so. This, too, will mean deploying the entire church, the priesthood of all believers, as we engage in the work God has given us to do.

13

DIASPORA ENGAGEMENT

I have a Rwandan friend named Flora—a single mom with two daughters—who lives in the United States. She works in health care with individuals nearing the end of life, and most of her clients are from Iran, China, or other parts of Asia. Flora says she has never had one person die in her care who did not first come to faith in Jesus. Not one. Every patient who has died on her watch has died knowing the Savior.

Though Flora has long been involved in a local American church, they have yet to recognize that she is at the tip of the spear of Christian missions—with a significant cross-cultural reach. Why? Probably because she works with hospice care patients and is not a "traditional missionary." But I believe Flora may have personally led more people to faith than many pastors.

What if the church were to recognize the opportunity Flora has and could bolster her and encourage her as an image bearer who spends a ton of time with other image bearers who are about to transition from this life? It's a rare opportunity, not only to engage with these dying souls, but also to help people from the global world reach many with the gospel.

And Flora isn't the only one. I've observed that the Filipino community in America is involved in much of our health care, with many working as nurses. We have seen a trend emerging of Filipino nurses leading people to Christ like never before. Why? They are taking care of individuals at the end of life. They reach them in ways that most of us never could.

Dispersed Around the World

Flora is part of the global diaspora that has been gaining steam in recent years. A *diaspora* is a scattering of people groups from their original homelands who relocate to another place where they form new communities. Engaging globally means we *must* engage with the diaspora.

As we discussed in chapter 4, about polycentric missions, there is now someone from somewhere *everywhere*. It may help to recall a few diaspora trends.

- 56 million people have immigrated into the US since 1990, but only about 400,000 have been challenged to join the church.
- During the 2023 school year, there were more than one million international students in the US, making up 5.6 percent of the US higher education population.[1]
- An estimated 75 percent of those students will never be invited into an American home.[2]

If we're practicing global engagement, we must pay special attention to diaspora trends. The diaspora community is huge—not just in America, but throughout the world.

I say these same things to my countrymen in Kenya. Today, the Chinese are building roads throughout the African continent, from Egypt all the way down to South Africa. Many of the UN's African operations have headquarters in Kenya, and therefore expatriates from many countries have clustered there.

This phenomenon means that a Kenyan church with its eyes set on the Great Collaboration can now reach people from around the globe just by looking for them within the borders of Kenya. This proliferation of people from everywhere to everywhere is a global trend, not limited to only a few nations.

As of May 2024, about 120 million people have been displaced due to persecution, conflict, violence, and human rights violations.[3] More than 68 million are internally displaced, and another 43 million are scattered around the world.[4] Some 57 percent of current refugees originate from Syria, Afghanistan, Venezuela, and Ukraine.[5] Of the asylum seekers, 5.8 million need international protection.[6]

Where have they all gone? Iran and Turkey have taken in 3.8 million and 3.1 million refugees respectively.[7] Colombia has taken in 2.8 million refugees, Germany has taken in 2.7 million, and Uganda has taken 1.7 million.[8] That means refugees are going to the Middle East, Europe, Asia, and Latin America. The trend is *everywhere.*

This also means that we have an unprecedented opportunity to reach refugees and international students for Christ through discipleship. They're coming into our neighborhoods, so reaching out to them in discipleship is simply welcoming the stranger.

Who Are They?

Almost anywhere you go in the world today, you will find the same reality.

If you go to London, you'll find people from everywhere.

If you go to Nairobi, you'll find people from everywhere.

If you go to Reykjavík, you'll find people from everywhere.

If you go to Shanghai, you'll find people from everywhere.

When Sandy Lu, an international student from China, came to UC Irvine, Mariners Church welcomed her, discipled her, and baptized her before she returned home to work in a high-level business position. Before she went back to China, she told her story to the entire church, on screen, in Mandarin Chinese. We didn't have to reach out very far to welcome her; UC Irvine is basically right across the street.

The church in the US has a real opportunity to engage with the more than one million international students on American college campuses today.[9] How sad to realize that three-quarters of those students will never be invited into an American home. What if we showed them biblical hospitality and made friends out of strangers? What if we allowed our witness to be strong and loud, whether in deed or in word?

We also have international artists, professors, and businesspeople in our midst. I know of one church in Nigeria that has begun planting churches *in America*, using professional businesspeople who have moved to America to work for one of the Big Four accounting firms. As they work their day-to-day jobs, they also start house churches here. They're professionals, working and interacting with other professionals.

We have a phenomenal opportunity to engage with foreign nationals in our own backyard. Let's try to engage them in ways we've never attempted before.

Sometimes we fear the immigrants and other foreigners among us, but despite all the stories about terrorists and criminals entering our country illegally, the overwhelming majority of immigrants are people looking for a better life than they had where they came from.

Years ago, a Mariners staff member helped us get connected to a local mosque, and we developed a friendship with several of its leaders, including the imam. The relationship grew to the point that we started visiting each other. At one point, we asked the Muslims to explain to us what they believe. As you might guess, they were very happy to do so. We held four forums in which we listened intently about their beliefs. After the four weeks, some of the Muslims at the mosque said to the imam, "We got to share what we believe; isn't it time for us to hear from *them*?" Sadly, no one in our group felt prepared to reciprocate, myself included. But a door had clearly been opened, and an important lesson had been learned. As Peter says, we must "always be prepared to give an answer to everyone who asks you to give the reason for the hope that you have. But do this with gentleness and respect."[10]

One time, the chair of the mosque got a chance to visit Israel with a group of real estate agents from Orange County. While he was there, a most remarkable experience occurred in the Grotto of the Nativity in Bethlehem, when he felt deeply moved by a Lutheran pastor named Mitri Raheb and declared him a powerfully influential man. This Muslim man not only introduced me to Mitri, but he also arranged for Mitri and a team from Palestine to come and speak about their Christian faith journey, especially about ministering at a church in the cave where, according to tradition, Jesus was born. From strangers of different faiths to introducing us to fellow Christians in another country. We soon discovered that Mitri is a highly respected theologian in the region.

We don't need to fear the strangers among us. After all, the church itself began as a group of expatriates.

The Church Began in Dispersion

In one sense, the early church began as a refugee organization. In its earliest days, it was essentially a Jews-only club. Most believers at the time didn't know whether non-Jews could even qualify. So they all stuck around Jerusalem, meeting regularly in homes and at the Temple until the martyrdom of Stephen.

Stephen's death changed everything.

Luke tells us, "On that day a great persecution broke out against the church in Jerusalem, and all except the apostles were scattered throughout Judea and Samaria."[11] "Scattered" sounds like a description of refugees, doesn't it? It's a diaspora. "Those who had been scattered," Luke continues, "preached the word wherever they went."[12]

Philip, one of the church's original deacons, traveled to "a city in Samaria," where an evangelistic crusade broke out, along with healings, deliverances, and "great joy" citywide.[13] God soon sent Philip to witness to a traveling African dignitary, who quickly came to faith and joyfully returned to Ethiopia as a believer in Jesus.

Things happened quickly after that. Saul of Tarsus was converted in Damascus; Peter preached in Lydda and people in both Sharon and Lydda put their faith in Jesus; and then a Roman centurion in Caesarea (along with some Gentile friends and family members) came to Christ. The latter incident prompted some astonished Jewish believers to mutter, "So then, even to Gentiles God has granted repentance that leads to life."[14] It seemed impossible to them.

Luke tells us that "those who had been scattered by the persecution that broke out when Stephen was killed traveled as far as Phoenicia, Cyprus and Antioch."[15] Most of these believers spoke the Good News only to fellow Jews, but some "men from Cyprus and Cyrene, went to Antioch and began to speak to Greeks also, telling them the good news about the Lord Jesus. The Lord's hand was with them, and a great number of people believed and turned to the Lord."[16] It's worth noting that the believers were first known as Christians in Antioch, not Jerusalem.[17]

When the apostles heard what happened, they sent a disciple named Barnabas to confirm the reports and to encourage the new believers in Antioch. Barnabas witnessed the amazing scene and immediately left to find Saul. He brought him to Antioch, and for a whole year the two men "taught great numbers of people."

What we know and recognize as the church today didn't really begin in Jerusalem. The church that combined both Jews and Gentiles did not exist until a great persecution broke out, prompting a diaspora. Only after believers were dispersed did the church in Jerusalem become integrated. It might help us to remember that.

Being a Good Neighbor

I love the book by Matthew Soerens titled *Welcoming the Stranger*. Soerens, the vice president of advocacy and policy at World Relief, writes, "Through immigration, God is bringing citizens of many closed and unreached countries into contact with American Christians. We therefore welcome the opportunity to share our faith with people who might otherwise have no opportunity to hear the good news."[18]

Many of the strangers we are to welcome have come from what we used to call the 10/40 Window. But the 10/40 Window has been blown wide open. We now see refugees fleeing from Syria, Iraq, Iran, Ukraine, Sudan, Myanmar, Venezuela, Afghanistan, and South Sudan, among other places. What an amazing opportunity for us to disciple the people of today's diasporas, who are now everywhere.

But how can we meet the challenge? Fortunately, there are organizations that we can either partner with or work through to create engagement with a refugee community. We can even partner with churches that have formed in those communities.

Some time ago, I ran across a church known as the Assyrian Church of Nineveh. It meets in Panorama City, about sixty miles from Mariners. The pastor, William Nissan, is from Iraq. He ministers to people from Iraq, the location of ancient Nineveh, where

God sent the prophet Jonah. At this very moment, people from Nineveh are living in Los Angeles County. Pastor Nissan's church has around sixty or seventy members. They once visited our church, and we did a prayer gathering with them. I still vividly recall them praying in their native tongue. It was spellbinding.

We have also worked with an Iranian congregation led by Pastor Jonathan Nazanin, who is bi-vocational. He leads two congregations, both predominantly Persian, even as he works for Apple. Most dispersed Persians are nominal Muslims, perhaps a little jaded with religion, and therefore very open to the gospel.

In addition, we've worked with several Kenyan congregations, including three that meet within twenty miles of Mariners.

An Arabic congregation led by Pastor Nabil Abraham also has been a partner. Pastor Nabil coincidentally hails from our partner church in Egypt.

Every time we've worked with one or more of these congregations, we've had a foretaste of heaven on earth. We've taken a sip from the blessed cup shared by people of various tongues, kingdoms, and nations.

I believe it's imperative that majority-culture congregations in America, such as Mariners, learn how to partner with the diaspora Christian churches all around them—even if it's just having a prayer or a worship time together. These moments give us practical ways of engaging with the diaspora community, allowing us to learn from them. They may also open a door to reach people in the global world, because many of these refugees and expatriates maintain contact with friends and loved ones back in their home countries.

A Persian woman named Faye at our church somehow heard about the construction of a school for internally displaced people in Kenya. Nairobi Chapel, one of our two partner churches in Kenya, had launched the project. Faye felt deeply moved by hearing the stories of these very resilient people who had left their homes to escape the post-election violence that erupted in Kenya after a contested 2008 election. Faye loved it that the Kenyan church wasn't standing idly by but was actively engaged in caring for and supporting these internally displaced people who were then living in a camp they dubbed *Jikaze*, which in Kiswahili means "stay strong" or "persevere." Nairobi Chapel decided to create a school for these people who had moved away from home, hoping to find a new home elsewhere.

Mariners Church Vacation Bible School helped raise $25,000 for the school, and Faye was able to match that amount. As a side note, the school's initial costs were more than $150,000. Mariners gave about a third of the total, and Nairobi Chapel raised the bulk of the rest—another example of how mutuality and reciprocity matter in working partnerships.

The shocking thing about Faye's gift was that the money came from her son, Ali, who is not a Christian. But he felt moved by the story and decided to contribute to this Christian school built by a Nairobi church in partnership with an American congregation. What an example of the opportunities we have to reach and engage with others through the proliferation of diverse diaspora communities across the globe.

Your church might not be able to financially underwrite an entire school, but could you teach language skills to immigrants? In the US, you could teach English as a second language (ESL). In Brazil, you could teach Portuguese. In Ukraine, it might be USL. You get the idea.

Might there be opportunities near you to help international students with life skills they need, such as how to drive a car or how to shop in an unfamiliar country?

Could you translate your church's Sunday messages into the language of a predominant diaspora constituency in your community?

None of these are *big* options, but they could well open the door to bigger things. People dispersed across the globe are a resource that many times gets overlooked, and yet these individuals represent "fields . . . white for harvest"[19] in sharing the gospel.

For us to embrace this opportunity, however, we may have to recalibrate our view of refugees and immigrants. They may appear different from us, at least on the surface; but when we look beyond face value to see the image of God in each and every one, we begin to understand that under our *skin* we are *kin*.

Mariners Church has had a long-standing relationship with Christian Arabic Church in Anaheim. We have done medical clinics together for Arab-speaking diaspora constituents. We also have done various activities with Voice of Refugees, which at one time had its offices in the same building as Christian Arabic Church. When we show up to partner with them, we relinquish our Mariners name and take on the identity of Christian Arabic Church and Voice of Refugees. We want *them* to be the tip of the spear.

One of my favorite experiences took place when Christian Arabic Church reached out to Mariners for help after years of working together. The church had been raising money to buy its own building for more than twenty years. (Patience and tenacity are hallmarks of diaspora congregations.) By God's grace, an opportunity came for them to purchase a former Islamic school building in Anaheim. To their dismay, they found they were $150,000 short of being able to complete the purchase. At the rate they were saving, it would take several more years to reach that milestone.

Because of their long-standing relationship with Mariners, however, they asked if we could help them get the ball over the goal line. Our leadership team agreed to help them get the funding they needed to finance the rest of the building.

I see this as a perfect example of a majority-culture church linking arms with a diaspora church to acquire a tool to reach constituents that would be very difficult for the majority-culture church to even contact. This is what can happen when we embrace the diaspora communities around the world.

The Benefits of Diaspora

Maybe one of the top benefits we have reaped from working with diaspora communities is that we've learned tremendous lessons from the persecuted church. Many of those coming to America are persecuted Christians. We can learn a great deal from them.

The US enjoys several economic advantages by bringing in refugees. Many end up owning homes, starting businesses, and enrolling in higher education. It takes an eighteen-month screening process to get a refugee into the country legally, a fact that should debunk many of the myths about refugees.

Moreover, the one million–plus international students who go to school in the US inject $38 billion into our economy and create 335,000 jobs.[20] And these students are often the crème de la crème from their countries.

Not only can individuals from the diaspora be exposed to the gospel here, but some can even help us with foreign policy and national security concerns. I'm not joking.

Not long ago, I saw a video of police harassing a tall man with dark skin. It was very embarrassing, especially when I discovered the man was from a tribe in Sudan known as the Dinka.

"Look," the police said, "this guy's a tall Dinka," as if he were a suspect.

"I'm not guilty, I promise you," he said, but they continued harassing him. The man remained calm, but at one point he got agitated.

"I may look like a suspect," he said, "but you don't even have a warrant. You don't have anything."

They slapped handcuffs on him anyway. At that point he said to them, "Would you please look in my back pocket?"

When they did, they found his Federal Bureau of Investigation ID. They had arrested an FBI agent of Sudanese descent.

If even the FBI knows how to engage with people from the diaspora, how much more should the church—we who have the ultimate mission?

Yes, There Are Challenges

Most benefits in life also come with challenges. That's certainly true in considering the diaspora as a viable missions target. Consider just a few.

- *Psychological and emotional strain.* The stress of migration, potential trauma from incidents occurring in their home countries, and the challenges of adjusting to a new environment can all affect an individual's ability to engage fully and effectively in work of any sort, including gospel work.
- *Perception and stereotyping.* Diaspora missionaries may be stereotyped or viewed with suspicion by both their own community and the host society.
- *Intergenerational gaps.* First-generation immigrants tend to be less adaptable to a new society than younger persons.
- *Language and cultural adaptation.* It isn't easy to learn English as a second language. And cultural differences can be challenging.
- *Limited resources.* A lack of funds and other material resources can make ministry difficult.

- *Syncretism.* Differences in theological and cultural backgrounds can lead to the fusing of incompatible spiritual concepts.

In addition, diaspora communities usually come together, at least in part, because individuals like to maintain a connection with their home culture. This makes these communities very homogenous, which can make it difficult for people from the majority culture to engage with them, let alone help them integrate.

Nevertheless, it is biblically incumbent upon us to take the time to build and cultivate relationships with diaspora communities. Typically, this is better achieved as a group—a church rather than an individual, for example. It takes a tenacious majority culture to break through the diaspora identity and create a sense of belonging, which leads to integration.

Fair warning: It will take patience and persistence to break through the immediate rejection you may face in trying to reach a diaspora community. But I encourage you to create an environment that encourages some form of engagement and integration. In my own experience as a foreigner in the US, I have seen well-meaning churches offer separate worship services for diaspora groups and yet do very little to create mutual worship and fellowship experiences. I see this as myopic. Heaven will not have a Korean or Kenyan or Kuwaiti or Kazakh section. It will be one big family. So then, how do we live *today* in anticipation of that future glory of every nation, tribe, and tongue?

Three Suggestions

We have an unprecedented opportunity to engage individuals from the diaspora. Let me suggest three simple things we can all do to make these engagements more successful.

First, let's check our assumptions that foreigners have come here to do bad things. The overwhelming majority have not.

Second, let's create places and spaces where people can study God's Word, where we can serve as a refuge for the refugees. Let's show hospitality to strangers, and who knows? Maybe we'll entertain angels unawares![21]

Third, let's offer biblical hospitality. The Greek word translated "hospitality" is the term *philoxenia* (from *philos* = friend + *xenos* = stranger), which means to make a friend out of a stranger. An even deeper aspect of hospitality is *receiving* hospitality from a stranger. Biblical hospitality means we're not only hospitable, but we also welcome the opportunity to receive hospitality.

Refugees from the Middle East tend to be very hospitable. What if we went and shared a meal with them or allowed them to welcome us with biblical hospitality?

Today we have a wide-open opportunity to engage globally for Jesus' sake, without going long distances. We already have among us a very large group of artists, business professionals, musicians, diplomats, international students, refugees, and other immigrants. The world has moved into our neighborhoods—and yet too often we overlook them while still sending missionaries out to the global world. We can do both, of course, but let's not fail to recognize that the global world has come to our doorstep.

We can reach many hard-to-reach people *right now* if we will start engaging in practical ways with the diaspora all around us.

Other Ways to Be Intentional

Members of the diaspora community can help us in our missions efforts, both locally and globally, by identifying the key systemic issues in their countries of origin. Not only can they suggest helpful strategies, but they can also help us become bridge builders for both proclamation and demonstration of the gospel.

Immigrant communities can also help us contextualize theological principles to help us engage effectively with people like them. And they can become part of leadership development and training for missions.

In addition, these communities can provide great ground for resource mobilization that goes beyond finances. We could harness various vocations in these communities for missions. For example, in Orange County we now see an influx of the Indian diaspora. Many of these individuals work in the engineering world. Local churches can engage them to be a part of developing long-term solutions for age-old challenges, both globally and locally.

The key, again, is to engage them as a *community* rather than as individuals. Ultimately, diaspora communities have a wealth of cultural, linguistic, social, and worldview perspectives. We miss out on all these things by not engaging the communities.

It Only Takes One

If you want to reach Kenyans, all you have to do is get to know one—and you'll soon find out where the others are.

It only takes one.

I found my fellow friends from Milele because someone told me a group of Kenyans were meeting in Pomona. When I went, I found there were *two hundred* Kenyans in the group. And from those two hundred Kenyans, the community of people I've met has become a big network.

I live more than twenty miles from Anaheim. Today, the city is known as Little Arabia because it has the second largest Arabic community in the US, behind only Dearborn, Michigan. In Southern

California, you don't have to look hard to find a Little Tokyo, a Little Saigon, a Little China, and a Little Korea. Everywhere you go, there's a little town of people from a different country, many of whom need to hear the gospel. You might reach them initially simply by being a good neighbor. Many come from other faiths and have never encountered and do not understand the Christian God or the Christian worldview. Because you're already in close proximity, it's a wonderful opportunity to get to know them.

And it only takes *one* to get the ball rolling.

Give Us the Nations

For years at Mariners, we have prayed the prayer of Psalm 2:8: "Ask me, and I will make the nations your inheritance, the ends of the earth your possession."[22] I can say unequivocally that this prayer has been answered with the scattering of the nations across the world.

Maybe, just maybe, we should open our eyes and move from praying to seeing, and then from seeing to engaging with the people from all these nations—whether they are from Africa, Europe, Asia, Australia, the Americas, or elsewhere. The world has made its home in our backyard. Let's lift up our eyes and see these precious image bearers who are ready to be reached. And let's partner together to reach even more people around the world.

14

GLOBAL MOVEMENTS

I read a fascinating book many years ago titled *The Starfish and the Spider: The Unstoppable Power of Leaderless Organizations.*[1] The book uses the metaphor of spiders and starfish to show how decentralized movements or organizations are much more resilient and adaptable than highly centralized ones, which positions them to create out-of-this-world innovation.

A spider relies on a centralized nervous system; if you cut off any of its body parts, it dies. A starfish, on the other hand, has a decentralized nervous system; so even if it loses some parts, it can regenerate them. The book is really about the power of movements.

As an example from the world of human innovation, the authors point to Wikipedia, which lacks a centralized management system. People from anywhere can contribute articles and edits to Wikipedia, enabling it to offer more than 61 million pages of information.[2] Alcoholics Anonymous is another good example. AA has a core set of values and principles, but anyone, anywhere in the world, can start an AA group just by following the organization's Twelve Steps. Nobody has to sign up to join a group, and every participant takes turns facilitating, which has created a resilient and powerful movement.

The Starfish and the Spider also describes how the Native American Apache tribe was difficult to defeat in battle because it was so decentralized. The book's authors profile contemporary disrupters such as eBay, Napster, and Linux, as well. All these examples illustrate a robust way of thinking that helps to generate unstoppable open-source movements.

The best example in the book, however, is the early church. I have no reason to believe that the authors, both entrepreneurs from Stanford, are Christians. But they make the case that because the early church was decentralized, it enjoyed rapid growth, primarily due to its ability to innovate quickly. (Of course, there's also the empowerment of the Holy Spirit to consider!)

I believe the starfish model could help us create a global movement for the gospel that doesn't rely on a single, individual base but utilizes the shared wisdom, knowledge, and dignity inherent in every human being. Could we tap those resources to create movements that reverberate into eternity? A high view of the image of God in every person leads us to recognize the staggering power of collective ideas. And it is that wealth of ideas, experience, and perspectives that create unstoppable movements.

Two Examples

It only recently dawned on me that we could follow such a prescription to create powerful movements in evangelism as well as in justice and compassion. Consider evangelism first.

Global media outreach now happens at the intersection of technology and decentralization. Did you know we now have online missionaries? I didn't until recently, but I have since interacted with a few of them. When individuals have theological questions, they often go online to look for answers. When they do, a missionary chats with them online about their faith. When the conversation ends, the missionary connects the individual to a local church. This approach has created a global movement with leadership from tech people working all over the planet. Together, they've created an evangelism movement based on the idea of collective knowledge, taking advantage of the cumulative wisdom of a large group.

For similar reasons, I believe YouVersion is a big deal. YouVersion is an online mobile Bible platform that makes the Bible available for free to anyone in the world. As of this writing, it has been downloaded on more than 725 million devices and offers 3,100 Bible versions in two thousand languages.[3] Users can read the Scripture text or listen to it being read aloud. It has bookmarking, highlighting, and note-taking features. Users can find live church events in their area and can share Bible passages on social media. YouVersion has created a global tech movement that has made the Word of God more accessible to millions.

As I think of the success enjoyed by movements like these, I ask myself, "Why not create global movements accessible around the world beyond evangelism?" Consider an issue such as justice and compassion.

I have a friend named Justin Dillon who lives in Silicon Valley. He started a supply chain transparency company called FRDM (pronounced *freedom*), which has attracted huge corporate clients. His firm thoroughly investigates a company's supply chain and tells them how many slaves are working for them—that is, people around the world who are forced to work under slave conditions. FRDM creates accountability in the supply chain so that companies can say, when they take their products to market, "These products come from people who pay fair wages and take good care of their employees."

FRDM has found a way to address principles of justice we find in the Bible, such as making sure that God's people treat foreigners the same way they would treat the native born.[4] The Bible insists on fair wages and condemns unjust employment practices. It demands fair market prices and forbids cheating. God tells us, "Do not hoard goods."[5]

Justin does his part by helping to clean up dirty supply chains. He and I have been talking about trying to create a movement among evangelical churches to come together and take an example from FRDM's corporate clients. What if churches found out how many slaves are working for them in their supply chains? We may not know where our paper comes from and how it is produced, for example, but what if we created a movement of churches that intentionally cleansed their supply chains? Maybe we could stop human trafficking at a very high level. I envision a movement of churches that co-labor on this issue, working together because they realize that every human being has inherent value and dignity.

Since we're talking about the tech world here, did you know that many of the best coders on the planet come from Central Asia, from countries like Uzbekistan and Ukraine? We would like to get them engaged in some aspects of these movements I'm proposing. Why not create movements that consider people from every tribe, every nation, every tongue, whether it's in evangelism or in works of justice and compassion? Let's move toward global engagement in a big way.

The Thumb Effect

I'm focused right now on leadership development, working to raise up the next generation of globally minded leaders. But it didn't start out as a movement. When I first came to Mariners Church, we brought together our then-lead pastor, Kenton Beshore, and

Bishop Oscar Muriu of Kenya. The American church is perfectly suited for catalyzing global movements, Bishop Oscar told us.

"The American church has incredible gifts," he challenged Kenton. "One of those gifts is what we call the thumb effect."

What is the thumb effect? Because the thumb is opposable to the fingers, it gives us tremendous dexterity, making our hands far more versatile and effective than, say, our feet.

As it pertains to the American church, the thumb effect has two main components. First, Americans can easily use their US passports to go to Asia, Latin America, Africa, and Polynesia. Americans can choose to travel almost *anywhere* without restriction. Second, many Americans have the financial resources to go where others can't. We have by far the world's largest economy. China's economy, the second largest in the world, doesn't even come close to America's GDP.[6]

The primary role that I envision for the American church is that of *connector*. Though many Americans know Asians, Africans, Latin Americans, and other people from around the world, the truth is that Asians and Latin Americans don't often connect with each other. Africans and Polynesians don't often connect with one another. The American church could spark movements by bringing other people to the table as equals, without insisting that Americans sit at the head of the table. Instead, we come to a round table where we embrace the collective wisdom gathered there, the shared knowledge from *every* person in the room.

That's what we did at Mariners in 2007 and 2008. We brought together a roundtable of leaders from Egypt, Sri Lanka, Peru, Mexico, Kenya, and the US, and we asked, "How can we create a time of learning together, growing together, and serving together?"

The challenge for the American church was to step down from the head of the table. So after those initial meetings in California, we said, "Let's move our meetings overseas. The church in America can still be a catalyst, helping to gather people together, and perhaps covering a large portion of the bill, but let's meet in Kenya." So we met in Kenya from 2011 to 2014.

When 2015 rolled around, the question became, "What can we do *together* that we can't possibly do apart?" That's how Global Convene got started, which I'll come back to at the end of the chapter.

This is just an example of what the American church can do because of the thumb effect. The gift of passport access and finances, combined with multiple existing relationships worldwide, creates a unique leverage. But, again, the goal is to be a *catalyst*, to allow vision, innovation, initiative, and action to be developed in the other churches and cultures at the table.

The Global Residency Program

After I'd worked at Mariners for about five years, I looked around and realized that two things had happened.

First, I had learned a ton from Mariners through its leaders, things I never would have learned without being there. I had learned vital information about its systems, organization, structures, expediencies, and efficiencies.

But the second thing surprised me. I recognized how much Mariners had learned from *me*, whether it was in bringing *Rooted* to this country or allowing us to rethink how the church approached global missions—by engaging with global partners instead of just sending money and missionaries. I had seen my impact at the church grow to such a degree that Mariners had started changing the way it did things.

We had been a menu-driven church, for example. In fact, we had so many menus and so many doors and on-ramps for people to join the ministry of the church that whatever someone wanted to do, they did. But then we shifted to a single menu and a single on-ramp, which was *Rooted.* Now we had just one "front door" for individuals to get involved with our church, which streamlined and standardized our approach to spiritual formation.

As I watched Mariners change, I saw reciprocity begin to flourish. The church was changing me, and I was changing the church. That was so beautiful to me that I wanted other Africans and others from around the world to experience the same thing. So I went to my boss and said, "Robin, would you allow me to start a global residency program?"

I chose my words carefully. I said a global *residency* program, not an *internship*, because an intern denotes a novice, a newbie who's still learning, but the term *resident* comes from the medical world and refers to a full-fledged doctor who is given time to practice medicine in an environment with other physicians. Residents work alongside other, more seasoned doctors and practice their profession in community for a few years before going out on their own. An intern and a resident are *very* different animals. At the time, I wasn't aware of any other global residency program, and I admitted as much.

Unfortunately, we didn't have the budget for it.

"That's okay," I said, "I have two full-time employee (FTE) slots. How about if I take those FTEs and use the money earmarked for them to start a residency program?"

"That's your call," Robin said. "You're the head of that."

So in 2013, I recruited five residents: two from Kenya, two from Mexico, and one from Sri Lanka.

During that year, they got to experience what I had been experiencing. They learned from Mariners, but they also brought unique insights from their own experience. I still remember one pastoral staff meeting when Kenton came in and gave a great leadership lesson. He had just returned from a sabbatical and said he needed to apologize about what had happened during his time away.

"I told myself I was never going to take a sabbatical again," he said, "because it felt like the church dwindled when I was gone. But then I came to realize that I was being arrogant. God was actually raising up new leaders. So I apologize."

One of the residents sitting in on that meeting put his hand up.

"You know, Kenton," he said, "in my country, when someone apologizes, they need to hear the people say, 'You're forgiven.' They don't just brush over it. When you say, 'I'm sorry,' people need to tell you, 'I forgive you.' I have never seen a leader apologize. But it's beautiful to see a leader of your status apologize. Now, can we hear people say, 'I forgive you'?"

Kenton thought for a moment and said, "Okay, let's use my example. Anybody want to say anything?"

One by one, every pastor in the room said, "I forgive you."

"I forgive you."

"I forgive you."

Hearing every "I forgive you" broke Kenton's heart, because only then did he grasp the magnitude of the pain he had caused. At that moment, he could not continue the staff meeting. He closed it down and said, "We're done for today."

It was a pivotal lesson, to have somebody from the global world help the staff realize that we should never gloss over a mistake by apologizing without hearing "I forgive you" in response. That was a big change within our church and our staff, because we learned something uniquely powerful from one of our global residents.

If I had time and space, I could give you example after example of what our other residents have brought to the table.

A Growing Movement

The residency program helped us create a movement that continues to grow. Leaders come from various parts of the world and help us see things in different ways. During the ten years of the Global Residency Program, we have had more than forty leaders from thirteen countries come to Mariners. Most have returned to their own nations, and some have hosted program residents there, based on their yearlong experience at Mariners.

We've hosted individuals from Germany, Mongolia, Kenya, Uganda, Egypt, and other nations. They've all come through our church and then returned home with what they learned. But they also left behind at Mariners some great things that they brought with them. Through the Global Residency Program, we are helping to create a movement of global leaders.

We plan to host a ten-year anniversary reunion in 2025. All the individuals who've participated in the Global Residency Program from around the world will return, and we'll get to engage with them once more. The program has quite literally brought the world to Mariners—and it has changed us for the better.

Because of our Kenyan residents, the people of our church have grown to love Kenya. They came to love Germany because of Christian Boguslawski. They came to love Sri Lanka because of Thilini De Visser.

This is what global missions can look like. It makes strangers into family.

That's the call for every Christian living on mission. A deeper dive into hospitality involves *receiving* friendship and hospitality from strangers. Think of Jesus in John 4, when he went into Samaria, met the woman at the well, and stayed for two days. What "missions work" did he accomplish there? How can we emulate our Savior?

Adrian De Visser, Thilini's father, is the pastor of Kithu Sevana Church in Sri Lanka and also a renowned missiologist in the South and Southeast Asia region. Representatives of Mariners Church met him after the catastrophic 2004 tsunami. Pastor Adrian has worked in a tough and contentious context, yet the ministry there has thrived due to its well-integrated mission of justice and compassion. Pastor Adrian contends that reframing identity and worldview is at the heart of change in the region.

Kithu Sevana Church's efforts to serve its community and country earned it a reputation for a heart of compassion, which allowed the church to make the gospel attractive. Pastor Adrian has often said that the way to find compassion in a place where persecution exists is chiefly through prayer. That's where the battle is won, he insists; evangelism is basically gathering the fruit.

Due to the efforts of Pastor Adrian and others from A3, a global leadership development group, the gospel has been introduced in Mongolia. We have had the opportunity to get to know Baolerhu Ligden, a church father in Mongolia who is barely forty years old. He runs an incredibly redemptive entrepreneurship venture called the Asian Leadership Development Network. Baolerhu was one of the first two hundred Christians in Mongolia. He affirms the work and ministry of Pastor Adrian as the foundation for the gospel in the region. Pastor Adrian and others have sparked a movement of Christians in Mongolia by engaging with young leaders who are now becoming movement forces for the gospel within the region and beyond.

I'm more connected to Mongolia today because we've had two individuals from there on our staff. Enkhee and Badralt are both mentees of Baolerhu. I didn't know much about Mongolia before they arrived; I had no connection to it. But through these young men, I came to love Mongolia and am now starting to learn about Genghis Khan, the Kazakhs, Ulaanbaatar, and so many other things.

I've also learned a lot from James Kasirivu of Uganda and from Kilang Zulu from Nagaland, India (who works on the border of Myanmar and Thailand). And on and on it goes. These individuals have friends in places I've never visited, and we've learned so much from them, as well. I recently received a message from Kilang in which he said he had just accepted a job as the lead pastor of a church in Bangkok. He told me that lessons he learned at Mariners have helped him a great deal.

This program has helped our people at Mariners understand how powerful globalization really is. Our international residents have helped our people connect to the world in ways they had never experienced or imagined.

We're creating a leadership development track, a global movement of leaders around the world all connected by the same ethos. Remember the starfish and the spider? These leaders don't have a leader. I'm not their leader; I simply facilitate when they come together. Then they return to their home countries and continue to function as they have. Some no longer work in a church but have taken some of the principles they have learned and are creating unique movements around the world.

The residency program became so compelling that some of our global partners have said to us, "How come *you* get to be the ones to benefit from this? We want to do the same thing." So in 2019, we launched a global residency program in Kenya. Somebody came from Congo, somebody from Uganda, somebody from the US, and they all went to Kenya for a year.

Last year, our Egyptian partners hosted residents for six months; afterward, our Ugandan partners hosted them for another six months. That cohort was one of the most amazing we've ever had, because they spent no time at all in America. We had somebody from Tunisia, somebody from Iraq, somebody from Egypt, somebody from Kenya, somebody from Rwanda, and somebody from Germany, all spending six months together in Egypt and then six months together in Uganda. That cohort really connected, and all of them have become great friends, even though they had no contact and no connection with one another before the program.

At one point I was with them and watched them all sharing a single hamburger. *That's something that would never happen in the US*, I said to myself. Here were six people from six different countries literally biting into the same food. And I thought, *They're like brothers and sisters.* This is the future of our world, a movement of global leaders who are comfortable enough with each other to eat from the same hamburger. These are people who probably never would have met, but now they deeply love and care for each other.

The Global Residency Program has become for me a great example of a worldwide movement . . . and it's just one example of what the American church can do. What if other churches did something similar?

Global Convene

For me, the most salient example of a global movement is the worldwide family we're creating through Global Convene. Global Convene is a movement of multicultural, multigenerational global leaders who are pursuing unity in diversity for the sake of the gospel around the world.

I would love to spend time with each Global Convene leader around the world, hearing how intergenerational, multiethnic, multicultural, multi-sectoral elements of society share their perspective as an example of what it means to put into practice the principles laid out in this book. If I could distill *People Are the Wealth* down to one objective, it would be this: creating a global family.

From the question we asked ourselves in 2015, "What can we do together that we cannot possibly do apart?," we realized that the answer is *nothing*—well, except for one thing. Every church can do evangelism. Every church can do leadership development. Every church can do discipleship. If you have the resources, you can do all these things by yourself. The one thing that *no* church can do alone, however, is become a global family. No single church can foreshadow heaven here on earth.

Heaven will include people from every nation, tribe, and tongue. Global Convene is an exercise in trying to understand what it means to have believers from around the world working, praying, and worshiping together as a foreshadow of heaven on earth.

At our last Global Convene meeting, held in 2023 in Berlin, Pastor Muriithi Wanjau of Kenya shared a fascinating presentation on what he called "movement churches," which are growing like wildfire. I don't have the space to recreate his superb talk in full, but let me pass along a few of his findings that especially resonated with me:

- Movement churches emphasize creating a *culture* over developing a *strategy:* "Culture eats strategy for breakfast."
- A "holy dissatisfaction" exists among these churches that drives them to multiply.
- Movement churches emphasize creating "great members" rather than "great missionaries."
- These churches teach for "impartation," not only for "instruction." Impartation is about speaking life into someone and conveying God's Word and call to them, versus just good teaching, which may increase knowledge but doesn't necessarily help people know what exactly to do with that knowledge.

Now, there's a small difference between Pastor M's movement churches and the movement I've been describing. Pastor M's concept is a very centralized, very hierarchical movement, whereas I have in mind a decentralized movement. But both can be effective.

The truth is, the need is so great and the opportunities so abundant that we should be trying all sorts of approaches, all around the world. I think here of the apostle Paul's approach when he said, "I have become all things to all people so that by all possible means I might save some."[7]

So, too, with Global Convene and movement churches of various kinds. What a joy and a privilege it is to become all things to all people so that by all possible means we might save some.

APPENDIX

Keys for Identifying a Ministry Partner

Shortly before I turned in the manuscript for this book to my publisher, I jotted down nineteen things I've learned about finding a ministry partner. A lot more could be said about each of these, but in the interest of time and space, I'll give you just a brief outline here.

1. Look for a partner who isn't looking for you. What I mean is this: Too often in missions, we find ourselves responding to a perceived need rather than a real opportunity. People call and say, "Hey! Come over and do this; we need your help!" and off we go to build a building, start a school, or dig a well, along with sharing the gospel. All good things, perhaps, but nothing that will set us on the path from *relief* to *reinforcement* and *reform*. A better approach is to go and spend some time, looking to see what God is already doing there and who he is moving through.

   Here's a real-time example: I'm currently working on developing partners in Brazil. The way I started was by asking our global partners, "Who do you know who is doing some great work in Brazil?" As people started giving me names, one name came up over and over again. "You need to talk to Paulo Mazoni in Belo Horizonte." So I went to Paulo and asked him, "Who are other people like you in Brazil?" And he said, "Oh, let me tell you about this pastor from such-and-such church." So now we're listening to the local leaders and voices and looking for partnering opportunities. If you ever go to a place and somebody's name comes up two or three times, go see that person. The people on the ground know what's working, what's good, and who's doing it right.

2. The premise of all partnerships is *relationship*. Before you *do* anything, take the time to sit and learn—I call it "the slow incarnation"—and partner only with people with whom you have built and established a relationship. Start with people, not projects.

3. The success of your partnership largely depends on your local partner. Therefore, look for partners who don't really need you, or who have a vision and a strategy to achieve their goal even without you. When you engage with such partners, your role as a *catalyst* can help them go further and get to their goal faster.

4. The best partnerships are formed with visionary indigenous leaders. "People of peace" live in every region, and the locals can identify the honest and true leaders in their community. Unfortunately, you may find only a handful. Most partners have learned what Westerners "need," and hence they create an attractional model geared to drawing Western funds. Look for someone with an audacious, bold vision that can radically change a community, country, and continent.

5. Avoid being the hero in the partner's community; always deflect attention to the local church or local partner. Let the

people being served see and know more about the local partner than about your outside organization or visiting church.

6. Make sure every project has a timetable and an exit plan. Though good relationships are everlasting, any project that requires a continuous flow of outside funding will most likely create dependency, so begin projects with the end in mind. Think beyond relief to reinforcement and reform.
7. Hit the ground listening. Be slow to speak and quick to listen.[1] Debrief what you learn with a diverse team, not only with people who think like you. Lead with questions. If you immediately start giving answers, you will disempower the local leaders, as Westerners will likely be perceived as correct.
8. Gather a team to help you discern and determine a partner; do not do it alone. Get some buy-in. There is safety in wise counsel.[2]
9. Dream with your partner about what you can do together that you cannot possibly do apart.
10. Envision and establish what *reciprocity* and *mutuality* will look like. Find ways for your partner to advance the Kingdom in your congregation.
11. Have a memorandum of understanding for projects, and consider drafting a covenant for your partnerships.
12. The most formidable partnerships develop when there is a shared vision—for discipleship, transformation, reinforcement, and reform.
13. Always determine how sustainability will emerge in two key areas: *finances* and *human resources*. Anything that continues to depend on outsiders for manpower and funding will most

likely not last beyond the initiators of the project. Think in terms of *legacy*.

14. Determine what accountability looks like. If your partner is not already accountable, you're not likely to change them. Avoid lone rangers who have no accountability structure—especially for their character and finances.

15. Relationships within a partnership are best engaged at multiple levels. Avoid having one person from your church or organization as the only relationship holder. Try to develop deep relational connections, including various departments. Some of the deepest connections occur when the children of the partners become friends.

16. Be willing to live in each other's contexts for a long time. Explore exchange of staff, volunteers, and other resources.

17. Never treat the poor poorly. Look for the image of God in every person in every place, and work to reinforce their inherent dignity and worth.

18. Find local expressions of global vision. This may be as simple as finding people from partner countries who live near you. Leverage the diaspora, engage with people, and draw them in.

19. Spend significant time with your partners in situations where you're not doing a project but simply relaxing, having fun, meeting each other's family, and getting to know them.

Notes

FOREWORD

1. Galatians 3:13, CSB.
2. John Stott, *Basic Christianity* (Downers Grove, IL: IVP, 2006), 103.
3. CSB.
4. Revelation 5:9, CSB.
5. Matthew 28:19.

INTRODUCTION: SHIFTING THE FOCUS OF GLOBAL MISSIONS

1. Mitchell Landsberg, "Claremont Seminary Reaches Beyond Christianity," *Los Angeles Times*, June 9, 2010, https://www.latimes.com/archives/la-xpm-2010-jun-09-la-me-claremont-20100609-story.html.
2. Claremont School of Theology website, https://cst.edu/.
3. Jim Hinch, "A New African Revival Comes to Orange County," *Boom California*, December 23, 2015, https://boomcalifornia.org/2015/12/23/a-new-african-revival-comes-to-orange-county/.
4. Wikipedia, "Ugly American (pejorative)," last modified September 9, 2024, 07:57 (UTC), https://en.wikipedia.org/wiki/Ugly_American_(pejorative).
5. Laurie Beshore, *Love Without Walls: Learning to Be a Church in the World for the World* (Grand Rapids, MI: Zondervan, 2012), 137.
6. "Oscar Muriu—Urbana 06," December 28, 2006, evening, copyright © 2006 InterVarsity Christian Fellowship/USA, Vimeo, 32:09 (quote starts at 29:22), https://vimeo.com/69504380.
7. "Muriu—Urbana 06," quotes start at 31:30. Italics added.
8. "Muriu—Urbana 06," quote starts at 30:27.
9. "Muriu—Urbana 06," quote starts at 22:12. Italics added.
10. "Muriu—Urbana 06," quote starts at 20:34. Italics added.
11. Romans 12:2.
12. Matthew 25:34-40.

CHAPTER 1: CONNECTION BEFORE CONTENT

1. Romans 10:17, NKJV.
2. Genesis 1:26-27. Italics added.
3. Acts 1:8, NLT.
4. Gregory Boyle, *Barking to the Choir: The Power of Radical Kinship* (New York: Simon and Schuster, 2017), 77.
5. Matthew 5:14.
6. See Romans 12:2.
7. Mark 2:27.
8. Genesis 1:10, 12, 18, 21, 25. See also Genesis 1:4.
9. Genesis 2:2.
10. 1 Corinthians 12:21-22.
11. Oscar Muriu at Urbana 2006 conference, December 28, 2006, evening, copyright © 2006 InterVarsity Christian Fellowship/USA, Vimeo, 32:09 (quote starts at 14:40), https://vimeo.com/69504380.
12. John 17:21. Italics added.
13. John 17:23. Italics added.
14. Revelation 7:10.
15. Revelation 7:12.
16. C. S. Lewis, *The Weight of Glory and Other Addresses* (New York: Macmillan, 1949), 14–15.

CHAPTER 2: THE GREAT COLLABORATION

1. "About Us: The Jesuits," https://www.jesuits.org/about-us/the-jesuits.
2. "What's So Great about the Great Commission?," World Mission Prayer League, accessed October 23, 2024, https://wmpl.org/whats-so-great-great-commission.
3. Colossians 1:15-16.
4. Colossians 1:17.
5. Matthew 28:18.
6. Philippians 2:5-8.
7. Mark 16:15.
8. Laurie Beshore, *Love Without Walls: Learning to Be a Church in the World for the World* (Grand Rapids, MI: Zondervan, 2012), 138–139.
9. *The Confessions of St. Augustine*, modern English version, trans. Hal M. Helms (Brewster, MA: Paraclete Press, 1986), 1.
10. See James 1:19.
11. Genesis 11:4.
12. Genesis 11:6, NIV.
13. Acts 2:1, 4.
14. Acts 2:5, NIV.
15. Acts 2:11.
16. "The Great Commission: Big & Important!," Missio Nexus, September 20, 2014, https://missionexus.org/the-great-commission-big-important.

17. John 17:11.
18. Philippians 2:2, NIV.
19. Samuel Deressa, "The Shift of Christianity to the Global South and the Need for Discipleship and Church Health," *Word & World* 40, no. 4 (Fall 2020): 364.
20. See Romans 1:3-4; 1 Corinthians 15:42-43.
21. James 4:8.
22. John 15:5.
23. Ephesians 6:4.

CHAPTER 3: JUSTICE AND COMPASSION

1. NIV.
2. NIV.
3. Leviticus 19:15.
4. Acts 10:34.
5. Deuteronomy 24:17; Job 31:16-22; Psalm 41:1, 146:7-9; Isaiah 58:6-8.
6. NIV.
7. Nicholas Wolterstorff, *Justice: Rights and Wrongs* (Princeton, NJ: Princeton University Press, 2008), 75-80.
8. Zechariah 7:9-10, NIV.
9. NIV.
10. Isaiah 58:1, NIV. Italics added.
11. Isaiah 58:10-11.
12. Compare Isaiah 58 and Matthew 25:31-46.
13. Exodus 17:8-13.
14. Job 29:16-17.
15. Elizabeth Heath, "Berlin Conference of 1884–1885," in *Encyclopedia of Africa* (Oxford University Press, 2010), accessed October 28, 2024, https://www.oxfordreference.com/view/10.1093/acref/9780195337709.001.0001/acref-9780195337709-e-0467.
16. Psalm 146:6-9, NIV.
17. Deuteronomy 10:17-19, NIV.
18. 2 Corinthians 8:9.
19. Luke 4:17-19, NIV.
20. Luke 4:21, NIV.
21. Galatians 4:19.
22. Ephesians 4:24.
23. Colossians 3:10.
24. Romans 8:29.
25. 2 Corinthians 3:18.
26. Matthew 14:14.
27. Matthew 15:32.
28. Luke 7:13.

29. Luke 10:30-37.
30. Colossians 3:12.
31. 1 Peter 5:5.
32. Acts 6:7.
33. Lillian Kwon, "Kay Warren Questions Christianity of Persons Who Neglect Orphans," Christian Post, April 24, 2010, https://www.christianpost.com/news/kay-warren-questions-christianity-of-persons-who-neglect-orphans.html.

CHAPTER 4: POLYCENTRIC MISSIONS

1. World Christian Database, www.worldchristiandatabase.org. Subscription required. See also Philip Jenkins, *The Next Christendom: The Coming of Global Christianity*, 3rd ed., (New York: Oxford University Press, 2011), 3.
2. Philip Jenkins, *Next Christendom*, 1–2. Italics in original.
3. World Christian Database.
4. Viktor E. Frankl, *Man's Search for Meaning*, trans. Ilse Lasch (Boston: Beacon Press, 1959).
5. Benson P. Fraser, *Hide and Seek: The Sacred Art of Indirect Communication* (Eugene, OR: Cascade Books, 2020).
6. Henry T. Blackaby, Richard Blackaby, and Claude V. King, *Experiencing God (2021 Edition): Knowing and Doing the Will of God* (Nashville: B&H Publishing, 2021), ch. 9.
7. Jude 1:3.

CHAPTER 5: GLOBAL TRENDS

1. Jason J. Mulikita, "Young People's Potential, the Key to Africa's Sustainable Development," United Nations Office of the High Representative for the Least Developed Countries, Landlocked Developing Countries and Small Island Developing States," accessed November 14, 2024, https://www.un.org/ldc5/tags/youth.
2. International Monetary Fund, "Globalization: Threat or Opportunity?," IMF staff, updated January 2002, https://www.imf.org/external/np/exr/ib/2000/041200to.htm#1.
3. J. D. Payne, *Pressure Points: Twelve Global Issues Shaping the Face of the Church* (Nashville: Thomas Nelson, 2013), 69.
4. Todd M. Johnson, cited in Abby Stocker, "The Craziest Statistic You'll Read about North American Missions," *Christianity Today*, August 19, 2013, https://www.christianitytoday.com/2013/08/non-christians-who-dont-know-christians/.
5. "2023 Fast Facts," Open Doors, https://opendoorsdata.org/wp-content/uploads/2023/11/Open-Doors-2023_Fast-Facts.pdf.
6. Matthew Soerens, " Mission on Our Doorsteps: Thinking Biblically About Refugees and Immigration," PowerPoint presentation, MOVE Conference 2022.

7. Cited in Bob Smietana, "Churches Are Twice as Likely to Fear Refugees as to Help Them," *Christianity Today*, February 29, 2016, https://www.christianitytoday.com/2016/02/churches-fear-refugees-lifeway-survey-world-relief-vision/. Results are from a 2016 phone survey of 1,000 Protestant pastors by LifeWay Research.
8. Smietana, "Churches Are Twice as Likely."
9. Smietana, "Churches Are Twice as Likely."
10. Aaron Earls, "More Evangelicals See Immigrants as a Threat and Economic Drain," *Christianity Today*, February 28, 2024, https://www.christianitytoday.com/2024/02/evangelical-immigration-reform-lifeway-safety-threat-econom/.
11. "New American Fortune 500 in 2023: The Largest American Companies and Their Immigrant Roots," American Immigration Council Special Report, August 29, 2023, https://www.americanimmigrationcouncil.org/research/new-american-fortune-500-2023.
12. Patrick Gibbons, "Economic Benefits of Admitting Refugees Outweigh Costs," *Notre Dame News*, June 14, 2017, https://news.nd.edu/news/economic-benefits-of-admitting-refugees-outweigh-costs/.
13. Tim Annett, "Illegal Immigrants and the Economy," *Wall Street Journal*, April 13, 2006, https://www.wsj.com/articles/SB114477669441223067.
14. Abby Stocker, "The Craziest Statistic You'll Read."
15. "How Many Christians Are There in Saudi Arabia?," Open Doors website, accessed November 12, 2024, https://www.opendoorsuk.org/countries-watch/saudi-arabia.
16. Ephesians 2:11-13.
17. John 4:1-42.
18. John 4:40.
19. Acts 8:26.
20. Acts 8:29.
21. Acts 8:30
22. Acts 8:31.
23. Acts 8:39-40.
24. Matthew 28:19, author's paraphrase.
25. World Population Review website, accessed October 30, 2024, https://worldpopulationreview.com/country-rankings/most-christian-countries.

CHAPTER 6: INDIGENOUS LEADERSHIP

1. Ephesians 2:14, NIV.
2. Ephesians 2:15.
3. Juli McGowan Boit, "A Glimpse into My Journey," embedded video, 2:23–2:33, accessed October 30, 2024, https://julimcgowanboit.com/about/.
4. Juli Boit, *Brave Love: A Nurse's Story of Courage and Compassion in a Kenyan Hospice* (audiobook self-published through Hope Books, 2024);

Juli Boit, *From Beyond the Skies: An Invitation into the Wonder of Love* (New York: Morgan James Publishing, 2022).
5. John 1:14.
6. Philippians 4:15, NIV. Italics added.

CHAPTER 7: BIBLICAL POVERTY

1. Psalm 51:5, NKJV.
2. Revelation 22:2.
3. Author unknown. This quote has been attributed to everyone from Bob Marley to Jack Kerouac to radio personality Patrick Meagher. The line appears in songs by Alicia Keys and Oliver Tree and probably elsewhere. That's why I've opted for "Somebody once said."
4. Galatians 4:19.
5. Luke 19:10, NKJV.
6. Matthew 27:46.
7. Mark 14:36.

CHAPTER 8: RELATIONSHIP-BASED MINISTRY

1. Romans 12:3; Philippians 2:3.
2. James 2:5.
3. After a manner of speaking. See 2 Samuel 6:14-22.
4. See John 13:4.
5. William S. Plumer, *Studies in the Book of Psalms* (Philadelphia: J. B. Lippincott, 1872), 640.
6. James 2:1.
7. John 1:14, MSG.
8. "Serve Experience" in week 6 of *Rooted: Connect with God, the Church, Your Purpose*, copyright © 2011 Mariners Church, 130.
9. 2 Corinthians 3:3.
10. Daniel 9:3-19.

CHAPTER 9: SERVANT LEADERSHIP

1. Robert K. Greenleaf, *Servant Leadership: A Journey into the Nature of Legitimate Power and Greatness*, 25th anniv. ed. (New York/Mahwah, NJ: Paulist Press, 1977), 21. Italics in the original.
2. Stephen R. Covey, *The 7 Habits of Highly Effective People: Powerful Lessons in Personal Change*, 2004 ed. (New York: Free Press, 1989), 235–260.
3. John 10:10.
4. Philippians 2:7.
5. John 17:5, NIV.
6. Luke 9:32.
7. John 1:14, NIV.
8. 2 Peter 1:16.

9. Hebrews 1:3, NIV.
10. Philippians 2:1-4.
11. See *Strong's Lexicon*, under "kenódoxos," (2755), accessed January 8, 2025, https://biblehub.com/greek/2755.htm.
12. Matthew 1:18-25; Luke 2:1-7.
13. Hebrews 2:17.
14. Luke 2:52, NIV.
15. Luke 3:23, NIV.
16. Luke 2:52, NIV.
17. Hebrews 5:8.
18. See Matthew 13:24-30. Author's paraphrase of verse 30.
19. Luke 8:22-25, NLT.
20. Matthew 24:1-51.
21. See, for example, Mark 9:33-36; 10:35-45; Luke 9:46-47.
22. John 13:34-35, NIV.
23. Matthew 4:19.
24. John 14:12-21, 25-26.
25. See John 8:21; 14:28; 16:17.
26. John 14:12.
27. Mark 9:34-35.
28. Hebrews 11:35-38.
29. 2 Corinthians 11:23.
30. 2 Corinthians 11:24-27, 30.
31. 2 Timothy 1:15.
32. 2 Timothy 3:11.
33. 2 Timothy 4:6.
34. 2 Timothy 4:9-11.
35. 2 Timothy 4:14-16.
36. 2 Timothy 4:18.
37. John Bisagno, *Pastor's Handbook* (Nashville, TN: B&H Publishing Group, 2011), 453.

CHAPTER 10: LIFE CHANGE

1. Genesis 5:24, NIV.
2. Genesis 5:23.
3. 1 Corinthians 4:7, NLT.
4. 2 Kings 4:1-7, NIV.
5. Philippians 4:15-16, NIV.
6. Alex and Pearl Ganta, "India Community Thrives Off 'A Handful of Rice,'" *Sinlung*, July 16, 2012, http://www.sinlung.com/2012/07/india-community-thrives-off-handful-of.html.
7. Acts 3:6.
8. Acts 3:7, NIV. Italics added.

9. Acts 4:32-34.
10. Luke 21:2-4, NIV.
11. St. Augustine of Hippo, *On Christian Doctrine*, book 1, section 27, in *Teaching Christianity*, ed. John E. Rotelle, trans. Edmund Hill (Hyde Park, NY: New City Press, 1996), 118.
12. Proverbs 11:10, NIV.
13. Inés Franklin, *Uncharted: Navigating Your Unique Journey of Faith* (Austin, TX: Fedd Books, 2023).

CHAPTER 11: STRATEGIC ENGAGEMENT

1. FAQ, Coca-Cola Company website, accessed November 1, 2024, https://www.coca-cola.com/ng/en/about-us/faq/how-many-drinks-does-the-coca-cola-company-sell-worldwide-each-d.
2. "A Look at Coca-Cola's Advertising Expenses," Investopedia, February 3, 2023, https://www.investopedia.com/articles/markets/081315/look-cocacolas-advertising-expenses.asp.
3. Walter Isaacson, *Steve Jobs* (New York: Simon & Schuster, 2011), 154.
4. Elizabeth Heath, "Berlin Conference of 1884–1885," *Encyclopedia of Africa*, online version, Oxford University Press, 2010, https://www.oxfordreference.com/display/10.1093/acref/9780195337709.001.0001/acref-9780195337709-e-0467.
5. Shaan Roy, "Colonial Legacy in Kenya: Impacts on Society and Culture," Afro Discovery, March 14, 2024, https://www.afrodiscovery.com/country/kenya/kenya-history/colonial-legacy-in-kenya-impacts-on-society-and-culture/.
6. Adapted from *Report of the World Commission on Environment and Development: Our Common Future*, United Nations Brundtland Commission, 1987, 16, http://www.un-documents.net/our-common-future.pdf.
7. C. S. Lewis, *The Four Loves* (New York: Harcourt Brace, 1960), 188.
8. John 16:7, author's paraphrase.
9. Socrates, quoted in Plato, *Apology*, 38a, in *Plato in Twelve Volumes*, vol. 1, trans. Harold North Fowler (Cambridge, MA: Harvard University Press, 1966). Accessed online at https://www.perseus.tufts.edu/hopper/text?doc=Perseus%3Atext%3A1999.01.0170%3Atext%3DApol.%3Asection%3D38a.
10. Joshua 4:1-8, 20-24.
11. 1 Samuel 7:12, NIV.
12. Ideas attributed to Daniel Rickett here are from notes I took during a talk he gave at Perimeter Church in the Atlanta area in 2010.

PART FOUR: PRACTICE

1. *The Confessions of St. Augustine*, modern English version, trans. Hal M. Helms (Brewster, MA: Paraclete Press, 1986), 1.

CHAPTER 12: CHURCH DEPLOYMENT

1. NIV.
2. Ephesians 2:10.
3. Ephesians 4:11-12.
4. Ephesians 4:12.
5. Jim Hinch, "A New African Revival Comes to Orange County," *Boom California*, December 23, 2015, https://boomcalifornia.org/2015/12/23/a-new-african-revival-comes-to-orange-county/.
6. James 2:18.

CHAPTER 13: DIASPORA ENGAGEMENT

1. "2023 Fast Facts," Open Doors International, https://opendoorsdata.org/wp-content/uploads/2023/11/Open-Doors-2023_Fast-Facts.pdf.
2. Craig Thompson, "International Students, Hospitality, and Squishy Statistics," August 18, 2019, *Clearing Customs* (blog), https://clearingcustoms.net/2019/08/18/international-students-hospitality-and-squishy-statistics.
3. "Worldwide Levels of Forced Displacement Hit New High: UNHCR," UN News, June 12, 2024, https://news.un.org/en/story/2024/06/1150981.
4. "Figures at a Glance," UNHCR (The UN Refugee Agency), June 2023, https://www.unhcr.org/us/about-unhcr/who-we-are/figures-glance.
5. "Global Trends Report 2023," UNHCR, https://www.unhcr.org/global-trends-report-2023.
6. "Global Trends."
7. Refugee Data Finder, UNHCR (The UN Refugee Agency), last updated October 8, 2024, https://www.unhcr.org/refugee-statistics.
8. Refugee Data Finder, UNHCR.
9. "United States Hosts over 1 Million International Students, Fastest Enrollment Growth Rate in More than 40 Years," Institute of International Education (IIE), accessed November 4, 2024, https://www.iie.org/news/us-hosts-over-1-million-fastest-growth-for-40-years.
10. 1 Peter 3:15, NIV.
11. Acts 8:1, NIV.
12. Acts 8:4, NIV.
13. Acts 8:5, 8, NIV.
14. Acts 11:18, NIV.
15. Acts 11:19, NIV.
16. Acts 11:20-21, NIV.
17. Acts 11:26, NIV
18. Matthew Soerens and Jenny Hwang, *Welcoming the Stranger: Justice, Compassion, and Truth in the Immigration Debate* (Downers Grove IL: IVP Books, 2009), 194–195.
19. John 4:35.

20. "United States Announced as Leading Destination for International Students, Annual Impact to US Economy Is $38 Billion and 335,000 Jobs," US Department of State media note, November 13, 2023, https://www.state.gov/united-states-announced-as-leading-destination-for-international-students-annual-impact-to-u-s-economy-is-38-billion-and-335000-jobs.
21. See Hebrews 13:2.
22. NIV.

CHAPTER 14: GLOBAL MOVEMENTS

1. Ori Brafman and Rod A. Beckstrom, *The Starfish and the Spider: The Unstoppable Power of Leaderless Organizations* (New York: Penguin, 2006).
2. Wikipedia, "Wikipedia: Size of Wikipedia," last edited November 5, 2024, 03:44 (UTC), https://en.wikipedia.org/wiki/Wikipedia:Size_of_Wikipedia.
3. "YouVersion Bible App," YouVersion website, accessed November 5, 2024, https://www.youversion.com/the-bible-app.
4. Leviticus 19:34; 24:22; Numbers 9:14; 15:29.
5. See, for example, Matthew 6:19-21; 19:21.
6. Caleb Silver, "The Top 25 Economies in the World," Investopedia, updated October 4, 2024, https://www.investopedia.com/insights/worlds-top-economies/#toc-1-united-states.
7. 1 Corinthians 9:22, NIV.

APPENDIX: KEYS FOR IDENTIFYING A MINISTRY PARTNER

1. See James 1:19.
2. See Proverbs 11:14.

About the Author

CHRISTIAN MUNGAI is a native Kenyan who has answered God's call to be a missionary to the United States. He serves as the global movement pastor at Mariners Church in Irvine, California, where he has been on staff since 2007. Christian is passionate about deploying the global church into what God is doing around the world. He is currently leading a global next-generation discipleship movement that is galvanizing the engagement of multicultural, multiethnic, multisectoral, and intergenerational church leaders via an initiative dubbed Global Convene (globalconvene.org).

Christian was previously a member of Milele, an urban Afro-fusion and humanitarian singing group that began as a celebration of God through music and eventually became a vehicle through which to carry out Kingdom work.

Christian graduated from BAMU University in India with a bachelor's degree in social legislation and later attended Claremont School of Theology to work toward a master's of divinity. He is married to Delta, and they have a daughter named Kabi.